# 180° Degrees in 180 Days

# 180° Degrees in 180 Days

*Fear is No Longer a Forecast*

WAYNE MEADS JR.

ARCHWAY
PUBLISHING

Archway Publishing books may be ordered through booksellers or by contacting:

Archway Publishing
1663 Liberty Drive
Bloomington, IN 47403
www.archwaypublishing.com
844-669-3957

ISBN: 978-1-6657-3791-3 (sc)
ISBN: 978-1-6657-3790-6 (e)

Library of Congress Control Number: 2023901637

Print information available on the last page.

Archway Publishing rev. date: 01/27/2023

# Contents

# From the Author

The purpose of this devotional is for others to have a tool to assist them on their 180-day journey. The topics, verses, quotes, and insights are from my personal experience as a Christian in recovery, and they continue to aid me today. My only hope for this book is that what has successfully worked for me in recovery has the power to work for you, if applied daily.

This book contains lots of quotes and phrases from individuals that date back centuries. If you feel I have used a quote, phrase, or slogan that may be yours without proper citation, please inform me, and if your claim is factual, I will be happy to give credit.

The Twelve Steps of Alcoholics Anonymous are mentioned and printed with permission of Alcoholics Anonymous World Services, Inc. ("AAWS"). While AA is a spiritual program, the use of the twelve steps of Alcoholics Anonymous in this book does not declare they are affiliated or allied with any sect, denomination, or specific religious group or belief.

Lastly, I understand people experience and overcome addictions in many different ways. This book is not intended to replace or substitute any medical advice given by a doctor or trained professional. Those professionals familiar with your condition should continue to be sought as it pertains to your circumstances.

# Dedication

First and foremost, this book is dedicated to our Lord and
Savior Jesus Christ, from whom all things are possible.

To my entire family, who stood by me with their prayers
of confidence in our Savior's power and love.

To the men and women who are currently struggling and are
desperately seeking answers, I pray this book gives you the assurance
you need to realize God has a purpose for you, and through
Him, your life will begin to take on a whole new meaning.

For through the law I died to the law so that I might live for
God. I have been crucified with Christ and I no longer live, but
Christ lives in me. The life I now live in the body, I live by faith
in the Son of God, who loved me and gave himself for me. I
do not set aside the grace of God, for if righteousness could be
gained through the law, Christ died for nothing!

Galatians 2:19–21 (NIV)

# Introduction

There have been a million books with millions of different ideas and suggestions on how to overcome addiction and spiritual strongholds. This book merely lays down the idea of what I have found to work as a result of complete surrender. To allow myself to incorporate all the facets of suggestion by others, along with the sovereign guidance and biblical direction from our heavenly Father.

I embraced this new method of recovery in 2012 when I was at my lowest point in life. I was out of ideas, and worst of all, I was chronically relapsing and tried every suggestion known to man except one, a personal relationship with God. Living this new way of life has redefined my knowledge and understanding of recovery and has moved me to share with you the tools that changed my life and can change your life forever.

The goal for this devotional is for you to have a tool that enlightens and redirects some of your thoughts and actions in a more productive and successful direction. Remember, this is a marathon and not a sprint. Start with Day 1 and begin to reflect. Try to take the current day's scripture verse and messages to discover what it is saying to you. You and only you.

Whether you desire to discover your freedom from active addiction or merely redefine your perception of what is needed to live a complete and fulfilling life, then this book is for you. For the next 180 days, commit yourself to fifteen minutes a day to read and incorporate the suggestions inside these pages.

Most importantly, begin to construct a plan of purpose on this journey. Start by being still and recognizing that life begins when we put God first so we have clarity. Clarity received from each daily devotional will spark the flame needed to generate new life within you. Remember, the drugs and alcohol are gone, and you must replace those substances that have left a void within you. Fill that void with the presence of God, and experience His redemptive grace immediately.

God's purpose for you, along with a plan of action, such as the 12 steps of AA, will forever direct you away from the strongholds of this world and into the arms of Jesus. Embrace your new life, and become a beacon of light and hope for others to follow. You can do it. God bless.

# Day 1: Everything's Anew

He will wipe away all tears from their eyes. There will be no more death, no more grief or crying or pain. The old things have disappeared.

—Revelation 21:4

Never let it be said that God doesn't hear prayers of desperation. Our heavenly Father knows when we are sincere and when we are simply looking for an easier, softer way. Not necessarily because of what we say from our mouths but because the Holy Spirit recognizes the desperation in our hearts.

Desperation is an excellent tool for those who have come to the end of the road. When obstacles in our lives become so unbearable, and the only decision we have is to go left or right, that's when God knows we are sincere. When we no longer give the Lord ultimatums, and we no longer try to bargain with Him, that's when He picks us up from the valleys where we have fallen.

The apostle John affirms for us in Revelation that all "can and will" be forgiven and that the living death we once took part in has been substituted by a new life. On Day 1 of the rest of your life, how will you honor your heavenly Father as well as yourself for the answered prayers of desperation? The doors to a new life have been opened; we now have food on the table and a new place to pray and to lay our heads. How will you give thanks? May the prayers of desperation be the guiding force for a new life with your heavenly Father.

Prayer for the day: Heavenly Father, I give thanks for the answered prayers that I recognize are from You today. To finally be able to see a shimmer of hope and the possibilities of a wonderful tomorrow, I say thank You. When all was lost and my best thinking continued to destroy me, You were there, faithfully protecting me every day. May I begin to recognize the possibilities that come only from You, and may I turn my will and my life over to You so Your will may be done. In Jesus's name, amen.

# Day 2: So Many Questions

I permitted Myself to be sought by those who did not ask for Me; I permitted Myself to be found by those who did not seek Me I said, "Here am I, here am I," To a nation which did not call on My name.

—Isaiah 65:1

There is an inner voice that is demanding answers to questions that sound something like this: "Where am I?" "Just exactly how did I get here?" And most importantly, "Do I even belong?" God speaks to us all in so many different ways and aligns us to go into so many different directions. Nothing is recognizable. Everyone is unfamiliar, and there is an inner voice saying, "I should just leave now."

God has desired to find you and bring you home. He does not wish for us to wrestle with punishment nor try to gauge our self-worth. Moreover, our heavenly Father is simply saying, "Surrender to me, and let the wonderful journey I have planned for you begin."

At this moment in time, we are strangers in a strange land. The same as the Gentiles who were referred to in Isaiah 65:1. God loves us so much that all He is saying today is that in your new walk, may you make the decision to seek His Word. The beautiful message of God is easily found by simply opening the Bible and reading. He is so glad that you are home, and on this day, when the whole world seems to be somewhat of a blur, all He says is, "Seek, and ye shall find" (Matthew 7:7).

Prayer for the day: Lord, I come to You today with an open heart and an open mind to display a willingness of change. I thank You for the love You continue to show me and the grace I have received once again. Lord, help me to realize the old is gone and there is a new life ahead. Please help me to become unchained by my never-ending worries and shame so I may hold my head up high and praise Your name. In Jesus's name, amen.

# Day 3: One Hundred Different Directions

> Jesus saw the huge crowd as he stepped from the boat, and he
> had compassion on them because they were like sheep without
> a shepherd. So he began teaching them many things.
>
> —Mark 6:34

In this fresh and new life that you have begun, there is a tendency to feel like we have the world at our fingertips. Such joyous statements as, "I have the world in my hands," "I'm ready to take anything that life throws at me," and "Whatever it is that brought me here has been completely erased" will surely give us the feeling of invincibility. Many of our peers will refer to these statements as being on a pink cloud. Once we have decided to turn our lives over to God, there is truly joyous freedom when we say, "Lord, I am feeling a thousand different emotions, and I don't know which one is real."

We must always remember that regardless of what we feel, God is in control. The ability to see the importance of patience early on is pivotal in an intimate relationship with God. This new Father-to-child relationship is the development of small baby steps. Let us be mindful that there is a force still working against us that must be addressed, and sometimes that debilitating force shows up as undeserved success.

If early on in this new journey, you feel like a sheep wandering around in a pasture with no sense of direction, don't worry. Mark 6:34 assures us Jesus will guide us in the right direction if we let Him.

Prayer for the day: Heavenly Father, today, I pray for wisdom to recognize the danger of being overly assured of my situation based on my thoughts. I pray You may continue to guide me and lead me, direct me and strengthen me, and always reveal to me those things You want me to see and experience. Today, I choose to find joy in the simple fact You are guiding and leading me. I will take joy in knowing we will walk hand in hand safely by avoiding those things that will take me away from You. In Your heavenly name, I do pray. Amen.

# Day 4: I'm a Busy Bee

For the Spirit God gave us does not make us timid, but gives us power, love, and self-discipline.

—2 Timothy 1:7

One morning, we wake up, see a plan that God has for us, and instantly, we are baffled and overwhelmed. It is safe to relate this new inner feeling to the feeling Noah must've had when he was given his instructions in preparation for the Flood. The same is true for Abraham when God gave instructions to go and encounter and inhabit new land. Or better yet, the feeling Moses must've had when God said to lead His people out of Egypt.

The one common denominator between them and yourself is that God continues to give instructions to those who are willing and able. Our way of thinking tells us that what we are about to embark on is impossible. But as we see throughout the Old and New Testament, God faithfully stands by those who accept His guidance and instructions.

Did Noah reach dry land? Did Abraham become the father of many nations? Did Moses successfully lead God's people out of the grips of Pharaoh? You know the answers. The answer to God is always yes. With His arms safely around us, we can tackle those things that seem unnecessary and impossible. Your job is a requirement in your relationship with God.

Prayer for the day: Heavenly Father, I pray today the tasks and work that lies before me glorify Your love. I pray to have an attitude that displays my love for You and that assures others my labor and achievements are for Your Kingdom. Please guide me and direct me on those things that seem impossible and sometimes unnecessary. In Your heavenly name, I pray. Amen.

# Day 5: Steered by Grace

Now when these things begin to take place, straighten up and
raise your heads, because your redemption is drawing near.
—Luke 21:28

A good friend of mine once told me, "Be thankful that you are unsure of where
you are going because that is proof that you are not doing the steering." Slowly but
surely, we are starting to see God's omniscient power at work. A beacon of light
comes on in our heads, and we identify small things in our lives that were once
lost. The greatest clarity is that we feel and see a sense of direction.

Luke tells us that when we recognize these pivotal moments in our lives, it is
our sovereign Lord faithfully at work. We are to stand tall and prepare ourselves
for what He has planned. The wonderful thing about redemption is that it is
being steered by grace, God's grace. Because of our commitment and faithfulness
to Him, we're on a path of restoration, which includes restoring so many things
of the past that we lost.

Two of those gifts He has restored are our clarity and our direction. To have
a clear head and a direct path is priceless. To be able to begin to properly use the
gift of self-will instead of being "willed by self" is enormous. Clarity of God's will
means it's going to be a good day.

Prayer for the day: Heavenly Father, as I begin to take notice of the redemption in
my life, I straighten my head and give thanks. For those things You are trusting
in me so I may become a good steward, I give You thanks. I pray I always remain
in a position so Your work may be fulfilled in my life. Most of all, I pray to be a
good disciple of this newly redeemed life. In Your heavenly name, I pray. Amen.

# Day 6: I Recognize Him

Though you have not seen him, you love him; and even though
you do not see him now, you believe in him and are filled with
an inexpressible and glorious joy.

—1 Peter 1:8

The Holy Spirit has an amazing way of being able to communicate to others just
exactly what we feel. I am always amazed when somebody looks at my face and
says, "What is it about you that has changed? You seem to have an amazing glow
about you. What is different about you?"

The work of the Father cannot always be put into words. As we read the verses
of 1 Peter, we recognize it is difficult to describe what it is we have not seen or
touched. But be assured God has touched you. Be assured He sees the commitment
and the determination that comes with the desire for change.

Internally, we can recognize and feel God is there. We take notice things
are happening in our life that are not by our doing. Our thoughts and words, as
well as actions, are taking on a different nature and have a comfortable feel, like
a brand-new pair of shoes. Hold onto it because although you may not be able to
see Him, rest assured your feelings have been justified.

Prayer for the day: Heavenly Father, what a wonderful day it is for me when I can
recognize through the comforts of my soul that You are there. It is so glorious to
feel a thousand pounds lighter with an awesome assurance You are guiding me.
May I remain determined to see You from the inside rather than focus so hard on
the things from the outside. In Your heavenly name, I pray. Amen.

# Day 7: Power Restored

So that Christ may dwell in your hearts through faith. And I pray that you, being rooted and established in love, may have power, together with all the Lord's holy people, to grasp how wide and long and high and deep is the love of Christ.

—Ephesians 3:17–19

Acquiring a stronger physical body or manipulating how we feel by the foods we eat is achieved by our own conscious decision. Through these actions, we can become physically stronger and mentally sharper. But what about our spiritual strength? What would we gain if God was the master of our heart?

We are so limited when it comes to our ability to maintain our spiritual development. Without God being the chief officer in our heart, we surely set ourselves up on a pathway of failure. The hope that Paul has for the Ephesians in chapter 3 is that the love God displays in their heart bleeds over into love for others.

Regardless of your current condition or present state of mind, it is never too late to show love to a stranger. If you don't have money, don't worry. It will cost you nothing. If you do not feel you have the words that can assist, don't worry. Sometimes people need someone to listen. When we allow God to rule in our heart, He will automatically display a gift that can be applied in service to others. Have you allowed God to encompass your heart and display your gifts to help others? If God is truly present in your life, then you will embrace the fact that you lack for nothing, and God's children need your services. Do not let your current condition dictate your willingness to help others.

Prayer for the day: Heavenly Father, it is so apparent You are so active and alive in my life. There is nothing You would want more than for me to take comfort from the assurance of Your guidance. I pray today I realize I lack for nothing and You wish nothing more of me than to be of service to others. May I take this new assurance and display it radiantly so others may see all things are possible with You in their heart. In Your heavenly name, I pray. Amen.

# Day 8: Worth the Wait

Wait for the LORD; be strong and take heart and wait for the
LORD.

—Psalm 27:14

If we have come to understand and believe God knows us better than anyone, would it not make sense to wait patiently for when He is ready to advise us? In God's glorious and infinite wisdom, even He knows that for His plan to take hold in your life, it is going to take time.

Satan loves to sit by and tease us with grandiose and lustful ideas that easily distract us from the purpose God has in store for us. When, out of the blue, some so-called brilliant idea pops into your mind, stop and ask yourself, "Is this truly God's will for me?"

Being able to wait patiently is a tool our Lord and Savior wants us to acquire. The ability to wait on Him strengthens our knowledge of who He is, faith in what He wants us to be, and a better understanding of the direction we are on. When David wrote, "Wait for the Lord" in Psalm 27:14, he did so out of experience. David knew precisely that jumping the gun and acting too fast would lead to devastating consequences.

Ask yourself today, "Am I waiting patiently for God's plans to transpire in my life, or have I taken the wheel and tried to be the captain of my journey?" If you have begun attending AA or NA, ask your sponsor or other members if you are acting in haste or displaying patience. God assures us that His plan is greater than any plan we may have thought up and that He wants nothing more than for you to watch His blessings in your new life unfold right before your eyes. It is truly worth the wait.

Prayer for the day: Heavenly Father, I pray today I come to a better understanding of what it means to be patient. I pray I may be so grounded in faith, I wait for nothing more than Your perfect direction in my life. I pray my thoughts be centered on You, my heart filled with Your Word, and whenever life throws me a curve, I will take assurance when I say, "I will wait patiently for the Lord." In Your heavenly name, I pray. Amen.

# Day 9: Sound Suffering

Who shall separate us from the love of Christ? Shall trouble or hardship or persecution or famine or nakedness or danger or sword?

—Romans 8:35

Take a moment to reflect on all the painful moments that have occurred in your life, all the physical, spiritual, and emotional pain, and ask yourself, "Am I still suffering? What is the very root of my suffering? Am I suffering because of the answers I seek? Why does my suffering leave me with so many questions? Am I suffering today because I choose to follow Christ and His teachings?"

A lot of times, we recognize our suffering as a result of our self-induced punishment. We looked for other ways and means to be able to feel better about our current status and yet remained incomplete, with even greater troubles than in previous times.

Ask anybody, especially in the rooms of recovery, and they will say, "Happiness comes at a price." Today, we begin to understand what Paul meant when he wrote in Romans 8:35 that no matter your current situation or whatever problems you may be facing, nothing this world throws at you will separate you from the love of God. In our feeble efforts to make our lives secure, we have begun to realize that true happiness lies in God's hands, and if we trust Him, our current problems are only a learning tool He uses to guide us. Hallelujah.

Prayer for the day: Heavenly Father, as I wake up to face the day, I pray I take assurance in knowing whatever situation I am faced with, You are always in control. May I remember the problems I face today may be the groundwork for me to be closer to You. May I remember nothing this world offers will separate me from Your love, and today, I cling to that love as my assurance and understanding all is well. In Your heavenly name, I pray. Amen.

# Day 10: Be Still My Heart

Take delight in the Lord, and he will give you the desires of
your heart.

—Psalm 37:4 (NIV)

All of us can remember a time and a place when we had our hearts set on a certain material item. We vigilantly saved our money until we could afford what we wanted, or we begged and pleaded with our family to have it as a gift or a surprise. We would do all that was necessary to speed up the process of receiving this gift until, finally, it was ours. Inevitably, this certain gift did not bring about the satisfaction and enjoyment we longed for, and after a week or two (or less), the excitement and joy had all but dissipated.

We always seem to tell ourselves we have a better and brighter idea for our future. We begin our mornings on our knees, proclaiming to do God's will, but as soon as we stand, our ideas and grandiose wishes flood our minds with a vengeance. Our heavenly Father knows the desires of our heart, and He promises to deliver those desires that are in line with His will (Psalm 37:4).

The problem for us lies in the fact that we cannot wait patiently for the Lord. The desires of the heart are not brought to us by a mere magic trick, where our Lord snaps His fingers, and your wishes are granted. Our Lord knows the value that comes with struggles. He knows the value of patiently waiting and having faith in Him. He knows that ultimately, when the desires of the heart are acquired, and you become assured it was God's plan that just transpired, your intimate relationship with Him will be stronger than ever before. If your desire today is to live out the plans God has in store for you, then ask yourself, "Isn't it worth the wait?"

Prayer for the day: Heavenly Father: I humbly come before You today patiently waiting on Your perfect timing. Give me the strength and the wisdom to know that with Your infinite wisdom, You know what's best for me. I pray I go forth today with the assurance and the knowledge that all the desires of my heart are being taken care of. Most importantly, I pray to be a shining example of the desires that have already come true and to proclaim those gifts in Your heavenly name. Amen.

# Day 11: Table Talk

For the grace of God has appeared that offers salvation to all people. It teaches us to say "No" to ungodliness and worldly passions, and to live self-controlled, upright and godly lives in this present age.

—Titus 2:11–12

Some of us may be old enough to remember a popular slogan from First Lady Nancy Reagan, who stated, "Just say No." All over the world, people were able to grasp hold of this idea, and saying no quickly spread. So what does this have to do with table talk?

Many of the brightest and best of ideas and intentions began at the table. You need to look no further than the Passover meal with the disciples to realize that much can be accomplished at a meal. With our stomachs full and our minds at ease, our relaxed tongues and subdued hearts can easily be led to contrite actions. Instead of designing plans to be uplifting to others and praising God for the blessings we have received, we may find ourselves presenting our emotions and feelings of the day in a way that is harmful to others. Bitter complaints and idle gossip are the catalysts for igniting Satan's plan.

In the second chapter of Titus, we quickly see that saying no keeps us from falling into the ideas or notions that can be brought about from complaints. The problems we face and the situations we find to be difficult can only be rectified by one-on-one prayer with your heavenly Father. When we sit around with friends and become boisterous of our likes and dislikes, we immediately open the door for Satan to instigate his cunning plans. Whether doing this type of complaining at a twelve-step meeting or in a gathering of friends, let's remember the newcomer and recall that we should always strive be a positive and uplifting blessing to them and others with our words.

Prayer for the day: Heavenly Father, in our new journey with You, Lord, may we always remember You ask us to bring our troubles and our heartaches to You. May we remember when we are amongst others, it is Your desire for us to be a shining beacon of light of Your living Word. May we always remember to think before we speak and continue with our inner desire to be good stewards to others. Even at the table. Amen.

# Day 12: Community Connection

I appeal to you, brothers and sisters, in the name of our Lord
Jesus Christ, that all of you agree with one another in what you
say and that there be no divisions among you, but that you be
perfectly united in mind and thought.

—1 Corinthians 1:10

When I was a child, I was elected to be the group leader in a school assignment.
You can only imagine my brain as a young boy, as it was flooded with ideas
on how to bring these wonderful plans to life. With my sensational thoughts
all jotted down, I quickly presented these tidbits of grandiose ideas to my
classmates, but to my amazement, as well as disappointment, they were quickly
rejected.

Although I was elected leader, it became evident very fast that my cohorts
would rather inject their thoughts and plans into their recipe for success, rather
than the following direction from someone else. The problem wasn't that I had
really bad ideas; the problem was, in the scheme of things, feeling divided and left
out because my excitement and joy left me feeling crushed and deflated.

So many times, we want everybody else to get on board with the great
ideas and plans we have for ourselves. We tend to believe instant confirmation
from others is our recipe for success, which in turn gives us an immediate sense
of achievement. But what about God and His plans? In our awareness, are we
completely aware of God's presence and His work in our lives? Better yet, have you
let any of God's plans mold and shape the plans you now have for yourself? Who
is responsible for this brand-new direction you are going on?

In today's verse, Paul is telling the leaders of the church of Corinth to be in
tune with God's plans and to make sure they are not being led by their grandiose
ideas. When we all as a community come together and take time to understand
God's Word and direction, we quickly see how our community begins to strengthen
and grow. This type of connected community is not only in the church, but it is in
the workplace, schoolyards, institutions, hospitals, and government. Let us always
remember that our best ideas are guaranteed success when they are in place with
God's will.

Prayer for the day: Heavenly Father, I have become aware my best plans and intentions have somehow led me to the position I am in today. I pray I always institute a policy of following Your Word so Your plans for my life come to fruition. I pray for a community that is strengthened by the success of Your will in all our lives, as we rely on the words from Matthew 6:9: Thy will be done on earth as it is in heaven. Amen.

◆

# Day 13: Just a Little Extra

Ask God to bless those who persecute you—yes, ask him to bless, not to curse.

—Romans 12:14

We all have people in our lives who seem to create roadblocks and barriers. We are bound and determined to start our day on a good note, leaving all the problems of yesterday behind, and yet there is always that one.

The one who is the last one you want to see, the last one you want to hear from, and the only one you would rather not be around. Let's just cut to the chase and realize that sometimes, there are people around us where a little extra grace is required.

Let's consider what Paul is writing to the Romans. To sum it up, he is asking them to realize their shortcomings and to be able to comprehend the grace that was bestowed upon them. It is this type of grace we need to recognize in our own lives and be willing to share with others. Sometimes people with extra grace required are deliberately put into our lives to work on an area that God wants us to focus on. Maybe God wants us to learn how to

- not be offended,
- refuse to gossip,
- look at your behavior before reacting to theirs, and
- better learn how to love others.

Sometimes being closer to Christ forces us to do things out of the ordinary and do something extraordinary. Maybe God is ready for you to go above and beyond your normal range of reacting. Let's always remember that Christ never ignored anyone but always gave them the extra grace required.

Prayer for the day: Heavenly Father, regardless of who I come in contact with today, may I always remember to extend the same grace to others that was extended to me. May I have the mindset that through others, You are working Your sovereign plan for me. May the words of Your scripture sink so deeply into my heart that it continues to flow into my actions. Amen.

# Day 14: Getting Connected

It is the Father, living in me, who is doing his work.

—John 14:10 (NIV)

What a marvelous statement to try to grasp as you read John 14:10. When we learn something like this, one of the first questions that arises is, "Am I worthy of anyone living in me much less the God of my understanding?" We tend to believe that only Jesus Christ Himself could be a worthy vessel for God to be found. Only a better man than I could there be the very presence of God.

These thoughts challenge us to raise our standard of living to a higher level. It is presumptuous to think we would make a worthy vessel for God to reside. Let's not forget that Paul himself made such a bold statement in Galatians 2:20 when he declared he had been crucified with Christ and that he no longer lived, as well as all the other verses where Paul says that Christ lives within him. For example, Romans 6:6–7 says, "For we know that our old self was crucified with him so that the body ruled by sin might be done away with, that we should no longer be slaves to sin—because anyone who has died has been set free from sin."

You see, what Paul did was the one thing we need to begin doing today. We need to come to a point where we realize we need to raise our standard of living and become a worthy vessel. When we begin to live out God's message outwardly in the presence of others, we begin to have an inner craving for more of what the Lord has in store for us. We start to see Christlike behavior stems from a Christlike conscience, which craves a Christlike connection. The first thing we have to do is to begin to raise our standard of living to the highest of levels, allowing us to start to believe we are worthy of God living in us.

Never has a verse been made from the living Word of the Bible that declares you're not worthy of God's grace. God's Word says openly of His desire to be one with you. What does that mean for you? It means you are worthy. Now go and raise your standards to the highest level, and start believing it.

Prayer for the day: Heavenly Father, so many times I have declared out loud I am not worthy. I give thanks today for the understanding and belief You desire a relationship with me and I desire a relationship with You. I pray today I will raise my standard of living to the expectations You have of me, therefore, allowing my body to be a vessel for You. Amen.

# Day 15: Mission Minded

Therefore, my dear brothers and sisters, stand firm. Let nothing move you. Always give yourselves fully to the work of the Lord, because you know that your labor in the Lord is not in vain.
—1 Corinthians 15:58 (NIV)

What is mission-minded, or better yet, what is it not? If you woke up this morning and your first thought was the work you were going to perform today or an agenda list you have been trying to conquer, then the odds are you're not mission-minded.

I used to wake up every morning, thinking an essential part of my day would be prioritizing those things that needed to be accomplished. How can I best utilize my time, thereby maximizing my achievements? I find it amazing when I look back on my accomplishments, it is so apparent I have not accomplished that much at all. I have worked so hard and fallen so short. What a disappointing and crushing feeling.

In today's verse, Paul makes it so clear when we give ourselves entirely to God's work, none of our time, efforts, accomplishments, or even our failures would be in vain. The problem arises when we become sidetracked, lose focus, and lose our ability to stay mission minded. What are we to do? How do we stay focused?

We can find the answer in Luke 9:62: "Jesus replied, 'No one who puts a hand to the plow and looks back is fit for service in the kingdom of God.'" Jesus gives the answer by stating if you trust Him, you will never look in the past for your answers nor will you jump ahead of Him to sweeten your current circumstances. Being mission-minded means your thoughts, your actions, your prayers are firmly planted in His message. So when you wake up tomorrow, determined to be mission-minded; let the message of Jesus Christ sink deeply into your soul, and you can be assured your mind will be in the right place.

Prayer for the day: Heavenly Father, I realized today how short I fall due to my way of thinking. Lord, I pray today I will remain mission-minded and focused on Your words only. The plans You have for my life are for the best. The plans You have for me allow me to stand firm and to know, with assurance, all will be well. Help me to remain focused on those things that allow me to do Your will. Amen.

# Day 16: It's So Crowded

When Jesus had again crossed over by boat to the other side of the lake, a large crowd gathered around him while he was by the lake.

—Mark 5:21

I am so grateful that God is so comfortable in crowds. Why? Think about it for a moment. We live in a crowded world, with crowded thoughts, with packed information, and with crowded living spaces. This type of crowded lifestyle has bombarded our way of living and affected how we handle and process situations in our life. We have become self-destructive, and no matter how hard we seem to work, we are more unproductive than ever.

There is a massive problem with this type of lifestyle. We continue to accept the fact that it's okay to be so busy and we will somehow incorporate God and His will into our crowded and active lifestyle. We are saying, "God, I have a lot of things on my calendar to take care of today, and I will get to you when I get it organized." How's that working out for you? How many problems have been solved? How many opportunities that you were trying to gain did you end up losing?

Isn't it wonderful to know even amongst our crowded lifestyle, God wants to come to you? He would love nothing more than to be able to take the bits and pieces you and I and the rest of society have so much trouble with and organize it in a way that is compatible to a healthy relationship with Him. There is a natural attraction to our Lord and Savior. There is a reason why it says in Mark 5:21 that when Jesus stepped off the boat, a large crowd immediately gathered around Him. Maybe the group was a lot like you. Some are lost, some are desperate, some have nowhere else to go but to Jesus.

Jesus understands the problems with a full life; He knows there are times when it is impossible to put some of those things aside. The one thing He asks us to do, regardless of the size of the crowd, is to take Him with us. Take Him on your job, with its never-ending problems. Ask Him to assist in planning next month's calendar of events. If need be, ask Him to get you away from the crowds so you can have time with Him.

Prayer for the day: Heavenly Father, there are so many times when I can't get away from my full life. I become so consumed with all the things that happen during the day, I have left You behind. Lord, today, I pray You may come into my full life and help me to be crowded with Your love. Take control of my entire life, and make me whole. Amen.

◆

# Day 17: Sacred Plans

"For I know the plans I have for you," declares the Lord, "plans
to prosper you and not to harm you, plans to give you hope and
a future. Then you will call on me and come and pray to me,
and I will listen to you."

—Jeremiah 29:11–12

Many times when we read verses, such as the one above, we can become our own
worst enemy. After reading this verse, we tend to believe we can sit back and do
nothing, and we somehow are letting God's will prevail in our lives, and all is well.
This is somehow an overinflated security blanket. Boy, do we get confused when
we misinterpret scripture and what it truly means.

Here's what was happening. The Israelites were in exile, a punishment
from God as a result of their disobedience. God does indeed have a good plan
for the Israelites, and it is a plan that will give them hope and a prospering
future. Sounds good, right? The thing is, God tells them there are a few things
they have to accomplish first to fulfill His glorious plans. You see, God does
indeed know the plans He has for us, but that doesn't mean we are exempt
from the efforts that are needed from us for His ideas to come to fruition.
God's plans for you are only as good as the desire you have to completely obey
all His directions.

What demanding situations are you going through? What problems do you
have that are so overwhelming you need God's intercession? Whatever you're
going through, go ahead and cling to the promises of Jeremiah 29:11, but stick
to it for the right reason. Not with the false hope that God will take away your
suffering, but in the pure, Gospel confidence that He will give you hope amid
your suffering. Then you will realize the strength you have in the Lord begins
with your efforts. Your solution to your situation starts with your power. Be
strong, and accept what God wants you to go through as the learning tool to
strengthen you and prosper you and give you life and hope. Jeremiah was so
correct.

Prayer for the day: Heavenly Father, I pray I may never assume living a Christian
lifestyle is meant to be a cakewalk. Lord, I want to learn from the situations I'm

currently in and how best to come out of it for my relationship with You to be stronger. You know the plans you have for me. May I accept today all this verse entails. May I never misread or misquote what it is You're trying to say to me. Amen.

◆

# Day 18: My Curse Is My Cure

> Therefore, just as sin entered the world through one man, and death through sin, and in this way death came to all people, because all sinned.
>
> —Romans 5:12

Just a little over two weeks in this new way of life, and you may begin to experience an overwhelming clarity of where you are and your current conditions. For some of us, there may be some underlying issues or problems we are beginning to experience and want to rectify. Here are some examples of some thoughts you may be experiencing:

- How will I ever get out of this mess?
- Shouldn't I start thinking about where I'm going to live after this?
- I cannot believe I was doing the things I did.
- I am not even sure God will forgive me for what I've done.
- Will I be able to find a job when this is over?
- My troubles and issues with the law are just too significant.

There is nothing difficult or complicated about focusing on past behaviors or current problems. With that being said, there is also nothing complicated about trying to become a problem solver and fixing all the things of the past. The problematic issue is, we never have our solution for overcoming our guilt, nor do we have our answer for rectifying our mistakes. None of our plans or solutions are working.

If we look at the fifth chapter of Romans, Paul gives a direct contrast between Adam and Jesus. Adam was directly responsible for the sin that was brought into the world, no matter how great or how small, and Jesus was the direct answer and cure for the problem. Where sin prevailed, grace inevitably triumphed.

Society itself has made our wrongdoing so apparent that it bears a heavy weight on us, a burden society cannot fix. It may hold us accountable, but it doesn't present a solution. Paul is telling us whatever you're faced with or going through, Jesus paid it all so you may call yourself righteous before God. Never convince yourself that society can make the wrongs of the past right again. This is a job for someone higher.

Your Lord and Savior does not want you to muddle in the past or walk through life in shame. He is crying out to you to give Him the one thing that kept you from Him: the lies, the cheating, the drugs, the manipulation, and so on. Only God can take the one thing that was your curse and transform it into your cure, making you aware of His awesome love for you and confirming that the answer to all your questions lies in Him. Don't be overwhelmed with the past. Jesus already paid the price.

Prayer for the day: Heavenly Father, I pray today I recognize my decisions and actions of the past were a direct result of my choosing to be distant from You. I thank You for paying the price for me and making my life with You a possibility. I have nothing to offer You except the one thing that was keeping me from You. Only You can take this curse and turn it around for it to be used to do something good. I give this to You today. Amen.

◆

# Day 19: The Past and Procrastination

Another of the disciples said to Him, "Lord, permit me first to
go and bury my father." But Jesus said to him, "Follow Me, and
allow the dead to bury their own dead."

—Matthew 8:21–22

Staying in the here and now can be as challenging as learning how to forgive
yourself from the past. Our walk with Jesus along with our twelve-step journey
can take on a couple of different personas, and we are confused as to how to
direct our focus. The verse you just read is a perfect example of an individual
who wants to tie up all his loose ends to be entirely focused on what he is
about to embark on. How many times have you said, "Let me do these things
first, and I will be better equipped to handle my situation afterward"? Sound
familiar?

How hard would it be to convince you that your problems in the past
will never be rectified without making Jesus your future? By making Jesus the
sole focus in our life, we are declaring openly, by faith, that He will assist us
in making the problems of the past right. So often we are in a battle with the
guilt and shame of past behaviors, and it is our guilt that tries to convince us
we need to solve past problems. Isn't that what a good Christian response is all
about, taking responsibility for our actions? Remember, when we first came into
recovery, we were only good at causing problems, not solving them, so let's not
be fooled by the idea that we are in a perfect position to rectify the issues from
the past. The question you may be asking is, "Do I have the strength to focus
on the now?" In Philippians 4:13, Paul says, "I can do all this through him who
gives me strength."

What kind of Savior would we be serving if He were to ask us to dwell on the
old while He promised to make us new? Jesus is saying that your first choice in
every situation should be to follow Him and realize that in time, along with His
guidance, we will have the opportunity to take care of those things in the past.
It is a biblical promise as well as a twelve-step promise. Self-destruction is at the
center of your solutions. Decide today to continue following Christ.

Prayer for the day: Heavenly Father, I realize my desperate need to take responsibility for my actions of the past is something I must learn to take care of in due time. Today, I realize it took a long time to get to where I'm at, and it is going to take a while to return to a good standing with those I may have hurt. Help me today, Lord, to stay focused on Your guidance and where You want me to be. May I always remember with You by my side, I truly can do all things. Amen.

———————————————— ◆ ————————————————

# Day 20: Learning to Listen

> To those who listen to my teaching, more understanding will be given, and they will have an abundance of knowledge. But for those who are not listening, even what little understanding they have will be taken away from them.
>
> —Matthew 13:12

I am impressed by people who take a lot of their time memorizing bible verses. I am also concerned that so many people feel they are closer to God because of this practice. Let me explain.

A father tells his son, who is sitting in the kitchen, "Go to your room and do your homework and then clean your room."

An hour later, the father comes back to find his son still sitting in the kitchen. The father says, "Didn't you hear what I told you to do?"

The son replies, "Yes, and I remember what you told me, word for word."

The father responded by saying, "What good does it do only to remember what I told you to do?"

In the above verse, Matthew is telling us it is not enough to recognize what the Bible is saying. So often, people are under the impression that by memorizing a few scriptures or even listening to KLove on the radio, they are adhering to the principles and teachings Jesus gave us. To live a life pleasing to our Lord and Savior, we need to listen intently to what the verses are saying and, most importantly, begin to apply it in every facet of our lives.

Listening to what is being taught in your churches, Bible study groups, and twelve-step meetings gives a clear and better understanding of those verses you so intently memorized. For those who aren't listening and acting accordingly, the verses you have learned will slowly fade away.

Hold the verses you've memorized firmly to your heart, and by all means, continue to learn more, but let your actions demonstrate you truly understand what the living Word of God means and you comprehend what you've memorized.

Prayer for the day: Heavenly Father, I pray today I may never look for shortcuts when it comes to being a Christian. May I always remember the substance of what I've learned needs to be a direct reflection of how I act. Faith without works is truly dead. Amen.

# Day 21: The Final Minutes

However, as it is written: "What no eye has seen, what no ear has heard, and what no human mind has conceived"—the things God has prepared for those who love him.

—1 Corinthians 2:9

If you're a football fan like I am, you will probably have vivid memories of Super Bowl 51. To watch Tom Brady rally back from a 21–3 deficit against the Atlanta Falcons would have been incredible to see, had I not turned the television off at halftime with the assurance that the Falcons were going to win. There was no doubt in my mind that the New England Patriots could not bounce back the way they did. When I woke up the next morning, I was shocked and amazed to see the final score. New England had won in the greatest comeback in Super Bowl history, and once again, I missed it.

Isn't that typical behavior to give up so soon? To quit before the finish, feeling sure you know what the outcome is going to be before the end of the race. On this twenty-first day of this new way of living, we may already be facing difficulties that are forcing us to believe there is no hope in sight. Please understand that the most exceptional outcomes in your life are going to be recognized at the end of the race. Not the beginning, not the middle, but in the end.

So many times, we give up on the things God is doing for us in the same way. We can't understand or recognize what He is doing; therefore, we think it is futile and pointless, and turn in the towel. What would our lives be like today if we had never given up in the past? The verse above assures us we will never honestly know what God has planned for us until the day He calls us home.

This is the race I want to finish. I am never more aware of God in my life than when I live out the problems I am facing and not giving up. It's okay today to say, "I am not in control." It's okay to realize you are unsure of what the future may hold for you. Just imagine yourself with the same courage and determination the apostle Paul had when he wrote to Timothy in this verse, "I have fought the good fight, I have finished the race, I have kept the faith. Now there is in store for me the crown of righteousness, which the Lord, the righteous Judge, will award to me on that day—and not only to me, but also to all who have longed for his appearing" (2 Timothy 4:7–8 NIV).

Prayer for the day: Heavenly Father, I pray today whatever path You may have me on, I stay on course and finish the journey. I openly admit today You know what is best for me in my life and the direction You're taking me. May I not let the things of this day keep me from the things You want me to experience tomorrow. I promise today to finish the race, follow Your commandments, and rest assured all will be well. Amen.

---

# Day 22: Do You Trust Him?

> Now he who supplies seed to the sower and bread for food will also supply and increase your store of seed and will enlarge the harvest of your righteousness. You will be enriched in every way so that you can be generous on every occasion, and through us your generosity will result in thanksgiving to God.
>
> —2 Corinthians 9:10–11

If you have ever been in a state of crisis, where you have lost almost everything, then you know what it means to hold on to the little bit you may still have. We begin to cling onto and find hope in these little things, feeling as if it may be of use someday. Holding onto such items may indicate we are not willing to give up everything and rely entirely on God. A lot of times, we display this behavior in giving of our tithes and offerings. We are so financially devastated when we first come into recovery that we are very apprehensive when it comes to giving 10 percent of anything or letting go of those material items we try to find comfort in.

If you ever wonder why God isn't supplying your desires of the heart, it may be because you don't fully trust Him 100 percent yet. In the verse above, Paul is assuring the church that God faithfully blesses those who believe in Him completely. God wants to demonstrate to you that even with your last penny, He not only could take care of the needs of others, but He witnesses the faith you display in Him. It is this type of faith God rewards. The act of sacrificing all you have for others is one of the greatest gifts you can ever display. God honors this type of sacrifice, and in return, you will receive the desires of the heart (Mark 11:24).

Has God ever seen you sacrifice all you have? Do you trust Him enough to give Him your last dollar or release those material items that keep you in bondage? You know what I'm talking about, those things that give you a false assurance that if all else fails, you can rely on them. You can't out-give God, and He wants to demonstrate this to you by you expressing your complete faith in Him. How far will you trust Him? Are you willing to see the words from 2 Corinthians 9:10–11 come true in your life? Start learning today how much you truly have when you give in faith.

Prayer for the day: Heavenly Father, today I recognize there are so many things I am holding onto to find comfort. Today, I want to trust in You genuinely and realize all my needs and all the desires of my heart will be met when I display true faith in You. I release those things I am holding onto so you can work entirely in my life. I thank You for all the things You have done for me, and I am grateful for all the things You're going to do. Today, I give You all I have, physically and spiritually. Amen.

# Day 23: Awesome Awareness

No temptation has overtaken you except what is common to mankind. And God is faithful; he will not let you be tempted beyond what you can bear. But when you are tempted, he will also provide a way out so that you can endure it.

—1 Corinthians 10:13 (NIV)

There are lots of guarantees in life. For example, it's a guarantee that you can't avoid paying taxes, a guarantee that you are going to die one day and meet your heavenly Father, and it's also a guarantee that the same demon that caused the most havoc in your life will rear its ugly head and tempt you again. It begins with simple little urges that trigger thoughts that seem pleasant, and ultimately, you are fighting with yourself not to act out on these false pleasantries.

Cravings and urges are not subjected only to people in recovery but affect everyone, and everyone seems to handle their temptations differently. For me, I have come to accept these temptations as my life challenges. Each urge, craving, and life temptation I recognize as potentially devastating to my Christian faith can strengthen my walk with God instead of destroying it. In other words, instead of being overwhelmed and discouraged by my temptations, I accept them for what they are and realize that by overcoming those feelings, my relationship with God is stronger and takes on a whole new meaning.

In today's verse, we read the apostle Paul informing the church of Corinth our God is a loving God, and the things you will be tempted with will never be more than you can handle. If we think about it, Paul is saying God did not promise to make life easy, but the things in our life that have destroyed us can ultimately make us better. What a remarkable awareness it is to realize it is only God Who can take the one thing that has destroyed your life and have it work to your benefit.

Prayer for the day: Heavenly Father, today, I will not let the fear of my past break me. I will not be devastated by my simple, meaningless temptations. I am reliable, and I have found the strength in You, Lord. Lord, today, I pray the things of the past that have destroyed me can now be a weapon in my stronghold, so I may be of service to others. Whatever I face today, assure me that it can be overcome through You. Amen.

# Day 24: Passing the Test

"Bring the whole tithe into the storehouse, that there may be food in my house. Test me in this," says the LORD Almighty, "and see if I will not throw open the floodgates of heaven and pour out so much blessing that there will not be room enough to store it."

—Malachi 3:10 (NIV)

In the 1980s and '90s, nobody played the game of basketball better than the great Michael Jordan. He was so good, a common slogan came out that had everybody saying, "I want to be like Mike." Kids would go out and buy Michael Jordan shoes and jerseys, and watch all the highlight reels to look the part of the great one. But when it came down to doing the one thing that was necessary to be like Mike, the majority of kids fell short. They never understood the part about sacrifice.

Understandably, everybody would like to be able to succeed and be the best at something, without having to work hard for it. But is that realistic? Is it truly realistic to think you can do absolutely nothing and gain the rewards from those actions? How would you ever measure your level of success if everything you wanted was just handed to you? Ask the same question as it pertains to your relationship with God. What kind of Father-to-child relationship would you have with Him if all God did was hand down the things you wanted, without applying any effort or sacrifice?

In today's verse, God wants to see how much you're willing to sacrifice and do without to attain the blessings and riches He has prepared for you. Are you going to be like Ananias and Sapphira, and hold onto some of those things you believe are going to make your life easier and happier, or are you going to relinquish and sacrifice everything to God, fully knowing your efforts will be recognized? In fact, how can you be so sure of receiving God's blessings? He is permitting you to test Him. Read the second line of verse 10.

Ask yourself, "Am I willing to sacrifice everything to be great in the eyes of God? Am I willing to trust and obey God's Word and do what is required?" We sacrifice for God because we genuinely believe that the plans He has for us are more significant than us trying to emulate Michael Jordan (or whoever else your heroes may be). God has an incredible and beautiful plan for you, and only you, a program that cannot be copied by anybody else and a project you can be assured will never let you down. Let your new slogan be, "I want to be like Christ." Today, your recovery depends upon His plan.

Prayer for the day: Heavenly Father, today, I want to be the best You would have me be. Today, I wish to set aside all my grandiose ideas that ultimately have nothing to do with Your plan and embrace Your methods for me. Today, I will sacrifice all, whether that be money, time, efforts, and allow You to work entirely in my life. I will meet the struggles of today head-on and embrace those difficulties that will make me stronger and will enable me to be a living witness not only to You but to others. Amen.

◆

# Day 25: What's the Real Price?

However, if you suffer as a Christian, do not be ashamed, but praise God that you bear that name.

—1 Peter 4:16 (NIV)

Have you ever heard the old saying, "If you are a Christian, you are meant to suffer"? The majority of the time, it will be a Christian who makes this statement. Who else is better to give such witness to suffering than the apostle Peter himself? Read the Bible carefully as it pertains to the life of Peter, especially after Jesus is crucified, and take note of the amount of turmoil he goes through, which we would consider suffering. But if you read even closer, you will realize Peter accepts suffering for Christ as a badge of honor, not as something to avoid.

Like a lot of things, suffering can be relative and take on different meanings depending on the character of the person. The idea we have to remember is that suffering for a purpose is well worth its reward. The one thing you have to ask yourself today is, "Does my suffering have a purpose?" A lot of this can be answered based on your relationship with God.

You will never grow a close relationship with God by merely showing up to church once a week or having a daily devotional time. A relationship with God develops when we carefully exchange our feelings, thoughts, and ideas with God and allow Him to intercede during times of suffering or even joy. By doing this, we begin to acquire a level of confidence that almost welcomes pain because of our assurance of God's presence in our life.

Can you avoid suffering? Of course not, but the way you approach difficult situations is contingent on your assurance that God is now and forevermore in control. Always remember, you can do all things through Christ Who gives you strength (Philippians 4:13).

Prayer for the day: Heavenly Father, today, I recognize the problems I face cannot be fixed by my own doing. Today, I lift my situations and my suffering to You, with the assurance that all is well. Today, I will start a new relationship in which I will walk and talk and share all my feelings with You, to live life today to its fullest. Amen.

# Day 26: Guilty of Guilt

Turn from evil and do good; seek peace and pursue it.
—Psalm 34:14 (NIV)

Old habits indeed are hard to break. One of the things we recognize early in recovery is that it doesn't take long for old behaviors to come back into play. Out of nowhere, we acknowledge our train of thought has somehow been corrupted with horrible ideas, and we may even notice our conversations now leaning toward less-than-popular topics. Don't be discouraged. Let me be the first one to tell you that for the rest of your recovery, you will be plagued with inappropriate thoughts as well as the occasional inappropriate verbal outbursts. Don't be discouraged. Welcome to normal behavior.

There's a reason why the verse above tells us to not only seek peace but to pursue it. Pursuing a relationship with Christ is not a one-time event that is perfected as a result of hitting your knees and asking for forgiveness. God wants you to be able to feel and understand your own human characteristics and realize that first and foremost, we bring glory to the Lord by worshiping Him. What displeases God is when we beat ourselves up for recognizing we are human and still have sinful characteristics. What would happen if you realized your shortcomings and instead of beating yourself up, you turned them over to God, not only because you want to please Him but because you know that without Him, those sinful instincts will eventually take over? Relieve yourself of guilt.

When you are at your fork in the road, will you fulfill your purpose and bring glory to God, or will you shrink back and live a comfortable, self-centered life? The most beautiful thing about guilt is that it is optional and can only truly ruin your recovery when you allow yourself to be separated from Christ. It's okay to feel the guilt, but it's even better when you know how to let go.

Prayer for the day: Heavenly Father, in a time when I am so desperate to do what is right, I continue to be overwhelmed with my own shortcomings. May I accept today my life with You alleviates the need to act upon old thoughts and old behaviors. I continue to surrender my life to You, Lord, and ask You to take these burdens away from me. Relieve me of my guilt, and deliver me to a life of freedom with You. Amen.

# Day 27: Faithfully Forward

Trust in the LORD with all your heart and lean not on your own understanding; in all your ways submit to him, and he will make your paths straight.

—Proverbs 3:5–6

One day, you wake up, and you realize you have a sincere longing to belong amongst a group of individuals who have the same sincerity as yourself as it pertains to this new way of life. You want to belong to a group that is fleeing their old ways to make the best of this new one.

There is something uniquely different about men and women who are in recovery. Because of the things we had to do in the past to obtain those things we wanted, we acquired the ability to see people for who they are, just by their actions. To hustle and round up more money or to receive things that would give us access to our drug of choice, we often had to play the chameleon and pretend to be something we were not. Playing these different characters qualifies us to recognize those individuals around us who may still be acting the part of that old way of life. Choose your new friends wisely.

Sometimes, it is difficult to move forward with Christ when we have relied faithfully on old behaviors, behaviors that provided food regardless of how we obtained it and acquired money irrespective of how we earned it. In other words, our past actions continue to give us a false sense of security and will inevitably fail us.

In today's verse, Solomon tells us that to make wise decisions, we must first let go of our old decision-making. Why is it so important? The answer is simple. Even at twenty-seven days clean and sober, we have not completely broken the old habits of the past. This verse tells us that to line up straight on God's path, we must follow His direction. Being comfortable for the first time in your life and relying on someone else's leadership other than your own is a pivotal point in your recovery. Let go of any plans you currently may have, and evaluate if you are genuinely on God's path. Once you are assured you're following God's direction, then it is possible for you to move faithfully forward.

Prayer for the day: Heavenly Father, today, I recognize I have so many inhibitions and old ideas. I continue to evaluate my life from the past and realize I don't have a clue as to what direction I should take. Lord, today, I pray for the direction, guidance, and level of faith that assures me I am moving forward by Your direction. May I free myself today of past scenarios and ideas, and rely solely on Your guidance and Your promises. Amen.

◆

# Day 28: D + Anger = Danger

Do not be quickly provoked in your spirit, for anger resides in the lap of fools.

—Ecclesiastes 7:9

When I was an adolescent, I would deliberately try to provoke an argument with my sister to have a justifiable reason not to get along with her or to make her feel bad. I think my reason for doing this was because I wanted to separate myself from her and make it appear it was her fault. I wanted the pain I was going to cause her to be supported by any viable excuse or act. In other words, I was looking for a reason to be mad with her.

Recovery can be the same way. Subconsciously, we may not recognize we may be looking for a justifiable reason or feel as if we have an excuse to lash out and revert to old ways, which includes relapsing. We begin to take little things people say and blow them out of proportion or exaggerate some of their actions to justify being mad at them. When we start to feel uncomfortable or angry, any excuse will do to take us back down the road of destruction.

We learn quickly in our walk with Christ and from our twelve-step meetings that being mad or angry is optional. If you look at when Christ was provoked by others, you immediately recognize that His frame of mind never changed anything in His actions or speech. He remained faithful to God regardless of how He was approached by others. To sum it up, there is never a good excuse to let anger interrupt our walk with Christ.

If today you feel like the world is against you, or others are trying to provoke you, stop and realize the devastating result of anger. It can undo everything God has done in your life so far. Ask yourself today, am I truly determined to walk with God, or am I reverting to danger? D + Anger = DANGER.

Prayer for the day: Heavenly Father, the most significant confession I can make today is, I am unsure of my feelings and emotions. Help me today to see where my anger and emotions may be destroying this new life You have given me. May I be slow to anger and quick to respond faithfully to Your commands. Amen.

# Day 29: Remaining Ruthless

> I urge you, brothers and sisters, to watch out for those who cause divisions and put obstacles in your way that are contrary to the teaching you have learned. Keep away from them. For such people are not serving our Lord Christ, but their own appetites. By smooth talk and flattery, they deceive the minds of naive people.
>
> —Romans 16:17–18

After winning their divisional championship, Carolina Panthers head coach Ron Rivera was asked, "What won the game for you, your offense or defense?" Coach Rivera quickly answered, "It was both offense and defense." The combination of both sides took them forward to a Super Bowl appearance against the Denver Broncos. Since I am a Panthers fan, I will not disclose who won. It took efforts from a smart offense as well as a strong defense to prevail in what they were trying to accomplish.

The same is true in recovery. A lot of times, it seems as if we are always on the offensive, trying to come up with a game plan and a schedule that is conducive to sober living. But if we are still coming up with a plan that moves us forward, what are we doing to protect ourselves from the things that could force us backward?

In today's verse, Paul is urging believers to hold tightly to the teachings Christ has given them and watch out for those who want to twist and manipulate what God is instructing us to do. Ask yourself, have you ever tried to proof-text the message of the Bible? What I mean is, have you ever tried to take a verse in the Bible and twist it so it gives you a justifiable reason to do something you know you shouldn't? People try to justify their sins and their actions by only applying one verse instead of utilizing the whole passage.

The whole point of today's message is to remember to be on the defensive side of recovery. Do not be so quick to grasp at misleading thoughts or ideas of others who are looking for an easier way to make life comfortable for themselves. I strongly urge anyone early in recovery to stay away from the internet and all the harebrained ideas that deliver a false message of hope for recovery; they ultimately lead to failure. There is only one way to recover, and that way is Jesus Christ. Be quick to pray and patient to rely on His answer. Boyfriends and girlfriends won't cure you. Fancy jobs that pay well are not the answer to your prayers, and your friends and family can only take you so far. Remember that your answer lies in your Bible. Follow it carefully and remain ruthless with a godly offense and defense.

Prayer for the day: Heavenly Father, today, I pray for strength and guidance in being able to recognize those things that allow me to have a healthy game plan for my recovery. I pray Your Holy Spirit intercedes on my behalf to guide me and direct me to those people who are living a life worthy of Your living words from scripture. I accept the road to recovery is full of twists and turns and even mountains. I will remain determined not to look for the easiest way out of a difficult situation but to learn how my circumstances bring me closer to You. Amen.

# Day 30: Making of a Milestone

Do not be misled: Bad company corrupts good character.
—1 Corinthians 15:33 (NIV)

There's nothing more rewarding for my recovery than going to a twelve-step meeting and seeing someone pick up their thirty-day chip. For a lot of people, this seems like nothing, but for some of us, it is the making of a milestone. Then I see people go on to pick up red chips, green chips, blue chips, signifying one year of recovery. Now don't get me wrong; I genuinely believe it is essential for those who are new in recovery to recognize, with simple symbols such as chips, that recovery is possible. What I don't believe in is when we get to a level of recovery where we feel we should be rewarded and made to feel on a different level than others.

Let me give an example. A gentleman had reached 365 days of sobriety and wanted to treat himself to something extraordinary for others to recognize his achievement. He asked me how I would feel if he bought a 14-karat gold medallion to hang around his neck, signifying his twelve-month achievement. I simply asked him one question: "Why do you feel you need to be rewarded and recognized for something you should have never done to begin with, which was getting high?"

After a long pause, he recognized the point I was trying to make. Humility is a pivotal point in our recovery. Practicing humility will attract humble people. The lack of humility will attract people of the same character, and ultimately, you'll find yourself behaving as they do. After thirty days, you have reached a point in your recovery where people can begin to see if they want what you have or if you have something they don't want. The way you act, talk, speak, and treat others is a good indicator of the type of people you are hanging around with, which includes your sponsor. (By now, I pray you have one.)

Paul is telling the church of Corinth their good character can be disrupted by other bad behavior. We must remember the teachings of Jesus Christ, especially what He said in Luke 6:31. If you don't know it, now's a good time to crack open your Bible and be reminded. Being clean and sober for thirty days gets us excited about new friends and new people, but let's not be naïve. One of our old character defects is, we sometimes don't stop and listen to see if God approves of the people we are associating with.

The people in my life who have had the most significant influence are the ones I ran into by accident. They are the ones who showed up without me having to look for them. I truly believe those are the ones God sent directly to me. I still have unrealistic ideas of who my friends should or shouldn't be and if they are or are not suitable for me. Today, more than ever, I focus on my friendship with Christ. With Him, I can never go wrong. Congratulations on your first thirty days.

Prayer for the day: Heavenly Father, I realize after reading today's passage I sometimes act too quickly regarding who surrounds me. May I remember my past was an example of a life I never want to return to, nor should I ever be rewarded with bright medallions. Today, I pray for Your guidance to surround me with the ones who speak of Your words and act in a way that helps others. Thank you for my first thirty days, and may I never forget Who got me here. You, oh, Lord, are my one true friend. Amen.

---

# Day 31: Time of Reflection

After every thirty days, it is good to evaluate where you were and where you now are. Take this day to list five recognizable changes that have occurred in your life during these past thirty days. You may be surprised at what you find.

1.
2.
3.
4.
5.

Prayer for the day: Heavenly Father, today, I see all the changes that have occurred, and I quickly realize and see your work in my life. All the praise and glory are Yours as we continue on this new journey. I pray I continue to have a heart filled with the desire to continue to do Your will, and may I be an instrument of hope to others. Amen.

# Day 32: Don't Be Fooled

> For the message of the cross is foolishness to those who are
> perishing, but to us who are being saved it is the power of God.
> For it is written: "I will destroy the wisdom of the wise; the
> intelligence of the intelligent I will frustrate."
>
> —1 Corinthians 1:18–19

Have you ever wondered what people see in symbols or trinkets, and why they don them around their necks and on their bodies? Take, for example, Flavor Flav of the 1980s rap group Public Enemy. If you recall, he wore a giant clock around his neck. Others may wear items such as car emblems or clothing logos to present a message. What is the message? I don't have a clue. For me, wearing such items does not represent accurately what I believe or who I am. It doesn't bother me that people choose to wear these items, nor do I oppose it; I simply don't understand it, and for me, it would be foolish to present myself with such things.

Now take, for example, today's message and what it means. "For the message of the cross is foolishness to those who are perishing, but to us who are being saved it is the power of God." Many people choose to wear symbols such as a cross around the neck. For some, this might make no sense at all, for they only see it as an instrument of death and not for its real significance. It would be similar to someone having an emblem of an electric chair because to them, the cross is only viewed as a killing device.

So what is Paul saying? To us who are being saved, the cross is a symbol of the power of God. Though it can be a strange message, and regarded as foolish by the perishing, to those who trust in it, the message of the cross becomes real and is the actual power of God.

Those early in recovery will have a lot of questions as it pertains to our faith in the cross and what it represents. There are some aspects of your new walk with God that may be hard to understand or believe, but don't be fooled by wise words or unrealistic ideas of others. Your salvation and the grace God has bestowed upon you is real. The cross and what it represents in your walk with God confirms its place in your life. For those people who try to rely on their intelligence to explain their recovery, God has a place for them. Just look at verse 19: "I will destroy the wisdom of the wise; the intelligence of the intelligent I will frustrate." Ask yourself today what the cross truly means to you and the significance it plays in your life.

Prayer for the day: Heavenly Father, it is so easy to be misguided by the wise words of unbelievers and their symbols and foolish words. Your Son paid the ultimate price on a real cross for my salvation and the chance to spend eternity with You. I pray today I will state what the cross represents in my life and profess it boldly to others, for today, this is what I believe. Amen.

◆

# Day 33: Hold on Tight

Watch and pray so that you will not fall into temptation. The spirit is willing, but the flesh is weak.

—Matthew 26:41 (NIV)

Jesus had a simple request for His disciples while He was praying in the Garden of Gethsemane, and that was to watch and pray. But as fate would have it, they could not adhere to simple instructions, and they fell asleep anyway.

Why is it we have a hard time following simple instructions? Do we become so confident in early recovery that we immediately feel comfortable with our choices and the direction we're taking? We tell ourselves over and over again how badly we want to have a new way of life, but we are quick to ignore even the simplest of instructions, such as, "Watch and pray."

When Jesus gives us direct instructions about our agenda, it is because it is of significant importance. Take temptation, for example. Are you trying to quit smoking at this point, but the first thought you have after a meal is smoking? How many of us are trying to divert our eyes from those things that are improper on the internet, knowing we have a problem with pornography, but we are quick to be teased with dating sites? How many of us know we have a ravenous addictive behavior, but we make an exception for taking over-the-counter medicine more than is prescribed? Time and time again, your inner spirit has the desire for a new way of life, but the flesh is in combat with those desires.

Can we overcome temptation? Of course we can, with Christ. Even Jesus knows that the Father-to-son relationship grows stronger when we display faith and overcome the attractions that are before us. We all have an inner voice that tells us the difference between right and wrong. Learn how to say no to the temptations of the flesh, and watch a relationship between you and your heavenly Father become solid. God has a plan for you, but He will not make those plans known to you unless you are willing to follow simple instructions. Although the spirit is willing, there has to be an intentional effort on your part to ensure God's will is prevailing in your life.

Prayer for the day: Heavenly Father, you can ask me a thousand times if I have the desire to do Your will, and a thousand times, I will tell You yes, but it's just so hard to follow through. Help me today, Lord, to ensure that my physical efforts are matching my spiritual desires. May the temptations that come before me today be a sign of the areas I need to grow in, and may I be quick to respond by looking up and asking for help. Amen.

◆

# Day 34: Seeking with Persistence

> But I have spared you for a purpose—to show you my power
> and to spread my name throughout the earth.
>
> —Exodus 9:16 (NIV)

One of the things I love so much about recovery is the deliberate persistence that accompanies a genuine desire to live differently. One example is when we are determined to combine a spiritual relationship with God, along with the twelve steps of recovery to reinforce this new way of life. With that being said, most of you have probably completed step 1 with ease. It's not always challenging to look at the past, or evaluate the present, and realize we have a problem. So, if we understand that our lives are unmanageable, it is safe to say around Day 33, we're moving toward the second step.

Being restored to sanity is precisely what it says it is. It is restoration. So many times, people have a difficult time believing in God because life seems overtly unfair. Nobody asks to be born to a dysfunctional family, nor did we choose our addictive predisposition toward addiction. Nonetheless, we are accountable for all those things we have no control over. These reasons may make it hard to initially turn to God to restore us to sanity. Never toy with the idea that you can somehow restore yourself. It will never work.

There are no secure solutions or recipes for this restoration process. Don't be fooled by a quick fix. It will only happen for those who are willing to work through the pain and the unfairness of life but still seek God's accompaniment. Those who deliberately seek God will find Him, and those who find Him and remain with Him will definitely be restored: a new way of thinking, a new life to live for, blessings beyond your belief, and a heart filled with joy knowing you're not destroying yourself any longer. They say the definition of insanity is doing the same thing over and over again and expecting different results, so let's be smart today and do something different. As it says in our verse above, "He has spared you for a purpose," so let's trust in His power, which is definitely much greater than yourself.

Prayer for the day: Heavenly Father, it is incredible having this weight lifted off my shoulders because I have begun to trust in You. I no longer need to seek the advice of myself, which in turn alleviates me from the old results I'm always faced with. Today, I make the rational decision to turn my life over to You and embrace the road that lies ahead. I believe Your power can restore my life, and I will be persistent in being restored. Amen.

♦

# Day 35: True Greatness

You, dear children, are from God and have overcome them, because the one who is in you is greater than the one who is in the world.

—1 John 4:4 (NIV)

If there is one thing I am a firm believer in, it's the deliberate focus on where you have been and where you are going. A lot of people may say you should never focus or dwell on the past, which is partly true, but I also believe that if you don't remember where you came from, you will never truly understand how far you have come.

For so many of us, we have done and said things and acted in ways most people would never dream of doing or saying. We had to learn how to adapt and go without because we lost everything or sold what we owned, or there wasn't anyone who wanted to be associated with us any longer. It is incredible to be able to account for those times when we were utterly lost and without hope. We would often tell ourselves, "There is no way anyone is going to be able to get me out of this situation I've put myself in." But here we are, and yes, you can now say with a firm conviction, "My God is greater than he who is in the world."

A good indicator you are full of gratitude is how amazed and appreciative you are at where you are today, and you openly recognize God has brought you here. You acknowledge you alone could never overcome the evil one or his power, but with God's help, you stand ready to continue walking this new way of life. Never forget what God can do for you, and if He can bring you out of the very depths of hell you were in, imagine what He is going to do if you remain in Him. In your eyes, your problems may seem overwhelming, but in His hands, they are defeated. If you genuinely believe this, then you can begin to understand what it truly means to be redeemed." Welcome to this new way of life.

Prayer for the day: Heavenly Father, today I recognize there is nothing You can't help me to overcome. Today, I see the error of my ways and acknowledge it is You Who has brought me to where I am now. For all the things I now have, I give thanks. For relieving me of my horrible past, I give thanks. For helping me understand Your love and redemptive powers, I give thanks. For all You do, all You have done, and all You are going to do, I give thanks. I can do all things through Christ, Who gives me strength (Philippians 4:13). Amen.

---

◆

---

# Day 36: Put It to the Test

Do not conform to the pattern of this world but be transformed by the renewing of your mind. Then you will be able to test and approve what God's will is—his good, pleasing and perfect will.
—Romans 12:2 (NIV)

I have heard today's verse debated in many different forums regarding what it truly means. So many instances, people want to revert back to when Jesus was in the wilderness, and He told Satan, "It is also written: 'Do not put the Lord your God to the test'" (Matthew 4:7 NIV). Today, you should stop and ask yourself, "What does Paul mean by testing and approving what God's will is?"

So many times, God will reveal Himself to us, but only when we deliberately set forth an effort to change our old lifestyles. God pleads with us to conform and act in a way that He teaches us. It's not because our Savior is trying to be difficult; quite the opposite, but He can only present Himself to us and bless us with the things He wants us to have when we offer ourselves in a manner that is pleasing to Him. God wants us to honestly believe and have faith when we change our way of thinking and acting, He will give us greater things than we ever expected. God cannot approve and bless the old you, but He can work wonders with the new you.

You might ask, "Where is another verse in which God wants us to test Him?" Well, take this verse, for example: "'Bring the whole tithe into the storehouse, that there may be food in my house. Test me in this,' says the Lord Almighty, 'and see if I will not throw open the floodgates of heaven and pour out so much blessing that there will not be room enough to store it'" (Malachi 3:10 NIV).

If you are like me, you begin to realize our heavenly Father would love nothing more than for us to follow His commands and instructions so we can witness and live this new life He has planned for us. If you want to see how God will bless you because you are faithful in tithing what little you may have, then try it and test Him. If you're going to see where God truly wants you to go and what He has in store for your future, then test Him by being obedient and see where He takes you. Putting your Father to the test means following Good Orderly Direction.

Prayer for the day: Heavenly Father, I can see in so many areas of my life where You have passed the test. This new freedom, new vision, new excitement are all the things You have blessed me with by me deciding to follow You. I continue to surrender all to You, Lord, knowing Your words are true and the blessings I have been given are a demonstration of Your love and Your desire for me to have a new life, a life I never experienced before and honestly never expected. May I continue to follow good orderly direction in all I do. Amen.

◆

# Day 37: Priceless Wisdom

> The beginning of wisdom is this: Get wisdom. Though it cost
> all you have, get understanding.
> —Proverbs 4:7 (NIV)

If you want to see something truly amazing, go onto YouTube and look at the late great Walter Payton's off-season workouts. It's truly incredible the lengths he would go to in order to be the best he could be. It dawned on me that this man truly wanted to be the best. He was willing to study all the highlight reels, do all the physical workouts required, and listen to the guidance and instruction of others to be the best he could be. He genuinely wanted to be the best, but wanting to be the best and doing what it takes to be the best are two completely different arenas.

Take today's verse, for example, written by the wisest of them all, King Solomon; the first wise decision a person must make is to get wisdom. Although this may sound trivial and insignificant, it is so true. We are naturally prone to making poor decisions, and so many times, the lessons we end up learning are due to so many wrong choices we made. We need to achieve gaining wisdom the same way Walter Payton went after being the greatest. We wake up every morning, beginning our time of devotion that starts in the book of Proverbs. I say this because I have come to learn there is a wise solution for every scenario life throws at us, especially in recovery.

I urge everyone to go after wisdom as if their life depended on it because, to be honest, it does. For the alcoholic and addict, one wrong choice or unwise decision could be the difference between life and death. Take these scenarios, for example:

1. How do you react when faced with controversy?
2. What decision should you make in a situation that seems to need an answer right now?
3. How do you successfully love the unlovable?
4. How do you make a difference in someone else's life without destroying your own?
5. What does who, what, when, and where mean in your life?

These are real-life scenarios that can only be answered with wisdom and knowledge. What lengths are you willing to go to maintain your serenity, as well as your sobriety? What role does wisdom play in your life, and can you see where you continue to fall short of making wise choices? Through wisdom we get understanding. From understanding, we get success, and success means a relationship with Christ.

Prayer for the day: Heavenly Father, the wisest thing I can proclaim today is how little wisdom I genuinely have. May I seek Your wisdom and Your guidance with a vengeance, oh, Lord. May I go after those things that are pleasing to You. May I do this today with guidance from Your living, breathing applicable words in the Bible. I realize I continue to make choices that are based on my own decisions, which continue to lead me further from You. May I devote my time and energy in gaining the wisdom that makes me an instrument You can use to be of service to others. Amen.

# Day 38: What You Know and Think You Know

Do you not know? Have you not heard? The LORD is the
everlasting God, the Creator of the ends of the earth. He will not
grow tired or weary, and his understanding no one can fathom.

—Isaiah 40:28 (NIV)

I can't tell you how many days I would wake up in disappointment because of
who I was or what I had done. The people from the city I grew up in knew my
name as a reference for disappointment, frustration, and distrust. You see, for
many people, your name represents who you are. If I were to say Larry Bird, you
would say basketball. If I were to say Benjamin Franklin, most people would say
hundred-dollar bill. If you were to say my name, most people would say addict,
thief, dropout, liar, and so on.

For me, my affliction was my personal identification to others. Society
today has a tendency to qualify people based on their setbacks or achievements,
never taking into account who they truly are. The point being made is that your
circumstances, either past or present, do not dictate who you are. Your identity
lies in the hands of God.

Today's verse tells us God understands your dilemmas and your setbacks,
and He will never qualify you based on your past behaviors but by the current
condition of your heart. God understands the sincerity of who you want to become;
He knows that once you put aside your old responses, your true identity begins to
blossom and is demonstrated in your new actions.

I would love to say nobody in this world is going to judge you on the things
you've done in the past. To be honest, nobody is concerned about where you're
going. They just want to know where you've been. Your heavenly Father will not
grow tired or weary in His quest for a relationship with you. We will never begin
to understand or fathom the love God has for each of us. Jeremiah makes it clear
that God knows you because He created you, and He knows the plans He has
for you, plans to help you and not to harm you, plans to give you hope and an
everlasting future (Jeremiah 29:11).

Remember when I said in the beginning that I couldn't tell you how many
days I would wake up in disappointment because of who I was or what I had done?
Today, I tell you it is an incredible and redeeming feeling to wake up knowing
you're being cradled in God's arms, to have a clear vision of where you are going,

and to have people in your life who want to be part of it. It can only come from God and can only begin by trusting in Him. It's a good day to be clean.

Prayer for the day: Heavenly Father, I thank you for the opportunity for being able to wake up and be grateful for who I am and who I am becoming. I recognize that today, You see me for who I am and for who You created me to be. Today, I will begin to disregard the destruction of my past and embrace the creation of my future. I can never truly understand Your wisdom, Lord, but I am grateful You know me. Amen.

# Day 39: Making Connections

Whoever dwells in the shelter of the Most High will rest in the shadow of the Almighty.

—Psalm 91:1 (NIV)

Think back to a time in your life when you were a child, before all the chaos arose, a time when you tried to emulate your favorite Saturday morning cartoon heroes or, better yet, worked so hard in school because you were so focused on a particular career. As kids, these are the secret places we run to in our minds, but what happens when we grow up, and life throws a curveball, and we lose our dreams and our ambitions and our ability to have hope? What happens when we turn out to be the exact opposite of who we wanted to be?

So often, we tend to lie under the shadow of our hopes and dreams to find our self-worth. We cling to the belief that one day, all of our best intentions and goals will take root, and we will fulfill the desires of when we're young. We feel as if our hopes and dreams determine who we are or who we will be.

Today's verse puts all our hopes and desires into perspective, which is that the blessings of God are only for those who are in close fellowship with Him. There is an old saying: If you want to see God laugh, tell Him your plans. Fear and anxiety about your future are a direct result of our lack of faith in God; in turn, they lead to a mountain of self-induced despair. This verse guarantees that if you want peace in all facets of your life, you must surrender all your plans to Him and let Him put those pieces into a new experience for you. We have created an impossible lifestyle for ourselves when we rely on our laurels for success. Don't believe me? Stop and do a quick self-survey of your current condition, and then you can determine for yourself how relying on God will give you peace and rest. Today and every day, God will provide you with peace.

Prayer for the day: Heavenly Father, I continue to successfully fail myself with all the things I think I should be or want to become. Today, I choose to walk beside You and find rest, knowing all is well. Help me to never deviate from Your plans for me, and I promise to serve You by allowing my new life to be a beacon of hope to others. Amen.

# Day 40: Who Is Driving What?

You are blessed because you believed that the Lord would do
what he said.

—Luke 1:45

The man without a purpose is like a ship without a rudder—a
waif, a nothing, a no man.

—Thomas Carlyle

I want you to think back to a month or two ago and ask yourself this one question:
"What was my driving force?" What was it that got you out of bed in the morning
and gave you the feeling of excitement to take the day head-on. Better yet, what
may have been the driving force that used to get you out of bed because you are
regretting having to face the day head-on?

Ultimately, everyone's life is driven by something. In our case, as it pertains to
addiction, we were being driven by a force that felt like someone or something else
was making the decisions for us. There were so many things we wanted to do and
so many different opportunities we wanted to partake in, but we couldn't because
of the obstacles driving us in the opposite direction. Ultimately, we recognize we
were being driven by guilt, always running from regrets and doing all we could to
hide our shame. There was no purpose to the things that were driving us.

Now that we have chosen a new way of life, I want you to ask yourself this
question again: "What is my driving force today?" There is a good chance that
because we are still new in recovery, we have not acquired that force-driven
inspiration that seems to bring people happiness and gives them achievements. We
have put the regrets and shame in the past, and we recognize we no longer want to
rely on our resources, and we want that force-driven inspiration from something
or someone else.

In today's verse, we can find inspiration that drives us by understanding and
having faith in the fact God is going to do what He said He's going to do. Because
of His promises, we are blessed beyond our comprehension. First, we must make
our wants and desires known to God, and from that declaration, we can be filled
with His assurance, which in turn gives us that drive we have been seeking for
so long. Isn't it wonderful to have a life driven by God's purpose? Today, you can
openly declare that God's plan for your life is your new driving force that brings
about your personal happiness.

Prayer for the day: Heavenly Father, for so long, I had been driven by so many different desires, which I thought would bring me happiness. Today, I pray You remain the driving force in my life so I may achieve those things that coincide with Your will for my life. Thank You for this day and the understanding a life driven by God is a life worth living. Amen.

♦

# Day 41: Practical Practices

Love the Lord your God with all your heart and with all your
soul and with all your mind and with all your strength.
—Mark 12:30 (NIV)

I volunteer with the Salvation Army; they receive lots of donations that come in different varieties. Donations that come in the form of food, clothes, automobiles, school supplies; you name it, and it has been donated. What I have come to appreciate are the donations we get from people who ensure that not just the quantity but the quality of the gift is suitable. People who donate genuinely want others to be as blessed as they are. My family and I make it a practice that if we donate, we only give the best we can offer. Anything less is unacceptable and does not adequately lift the spirits of those in need. Ask yourself this question: "When Christ died on the cross, wasn't He giving us His best?" We should do nothing less for those in need.

Today's verse goes right along with that. When we labor in the name of the Lord, we should offer our best physical efforts. When we offer our finances in the name of the Lord, we should remember to give until it hurts. And when we pray, we should offer up prayers that are practical and sincere. Yes, that's right; our prayers need not be repetitive words that we mumble over and over at the dinner table. It should be a thought-out, humble conversation in which we present our whole heart, our complete thoughts, as well as our entire bodies before the Lord.

If you ever wonder if God is truly taking you seriously, ask yourself, are you offering Him sincere prayers? Are you engaged in a Father-to-child relationship, or are you merely offering the bare minimum and convincing yourself that it is good enough? If we are to demonstrate the type of love to our heavenly Father as he has shown to us, it begins by giving him our best, with all your heart and with all your soul and with all your mind and with all your strength. Practice being sincere and giving all you have, and in return, God will continue giving you His best.

Prayer for the day: Heavenly Father, today I asked for Your forgiveness. So many times, I have done nothing more than offer You the bare minimum in my efforts and my prayers and in my works. Today, I sincerely pray for my heart I will do my best to give You my best in all things. Forgive me for my shortcomings in my downfalls, and may I always remember You gave Your all for me.

$\blacklozenge$

# Day 42: Temporary Torment

For our light and momentary troubles are achieving for us an
eternal glory that far outweighs them all.

—2 Corinthians 4:17 (NIV)

Here is a concept that might be hard to grasp: "Every problem has a purpose."
Wouldn't it be wonderful if life's plans were simple, without any of the hiccups and
headaches that are associated with it? Wouldn't it be great if everything was laid out
before us like a blueprint, and all we had to do is follow the directions to a place called
Nirvana? Well, let's determine what life would be like if it were made easy for us.

First, ask yourself, "Have the greatest achievements in my life come from
simplicity or difficulty?" Next ask yourself, "When people ask me for help, is it
because they realize the struggles I went through and want a different perspective
to their current problems, or is it just for an idle chat?"

When you answered the first question, you immediately realized that the
stressful situations in your life taught you the most about who you are and showed
what you cannot achieve alone. It made you aware of your shortcomings and your
strengths. When you answer the second question, you realized that the obstacles
you have overcome are valuable to others so they may achieve their goals without
all the unnecessary detours to get to their achievements. In other words, your past
failures may guide others for future success.

Today's verse helps us to realize that God's most significant achievements in our
lives came when we were at our lowest point. If we are entirely reliant on God, we
understand what it means to have momentary troubles. It means nothing lasts forever,
nothing is more significant than our God, and you can and will do all things through
Christ. So today, I challenge you to look forward to the challenges and troubles you
will face and realize those situations have the most significant impact on your faith
and the success of your future. Sometimes, pains and torment are a good thing.

Prayer for the day: Heavenly Father, I pray today I realize I am not defeated the moment
uncertain situations attack me. Today, I will consciously face my troubles head-on with
You by my side, knowing I will grow stronger. Nothing I face is more significant than
You, and today, I surrender my troubles to You. I pray my problems make me stronger
and the faith I've gained from relying on You brings me strength as well. Amen.

# Day 43: Slower than Slow

My dear brothers and sisters, take note of this: Everyone should
be quick to listen, slow to speak and slow to become angry.
—James 1:19 (NIV)

If I've said it once, I've said it a thousand times, "I wish I had not acted so quickly."
These words resonate in my mind and taught me a valuable life lesson, which is to
always ask myself, "What would Jesus do?"

Quick responses from hurt people end up hurting people. People who are
healthy do not hurt people. People who are genuinely holy do not hurt people.
People whose mission it is to be of service to others do not hurt people. This gives
you an idea of how to answer the question, "What would Jesus do?"

I am amazed at the number of people who are demanding respect from
others but continually act disrespectfully. The first obstacle we must overcome is
known as the tongue. We must overcome the idea that our immediate thoughts
need to be heard by others because as we have seen in the past, it is our immediate
thoughts that should never be spoken. There is nothing wrong with saying nothing
at all. In fact, silence can demonstrate self-restraint, wisdom, and the desire to be
Christ-centered.

If you want to see a perfect demonstration of how we should talk to others,
open the Gospels of the Bible (Matthew, Mark, Luke, and John) and mimic the way
Jesus responded to others: short parables, thoughtful questions, encouragement,
and insightful thoughts.

We live in a world today where your thoughts and ideas can be posted on
Facebook and then become global, possibly having an adverse effect on people
thousands of miles away. Trust me when I tell you, the whole world does not
need to know what you're thinking. In the full spectrum of the universe, we are
not that important. Take your thoughts and give them to God and ask Him how
you can be a positive, meaningful influence on others. Remember, anger-driven
thoughts that are transformed into words can have devastating effects on the lives
of others, as well as yourself. Remember the old adage you grew up hearing, silence
is a virtue? Today more than ever, we should begin to practice what this means.
You will be surprised at how the number of things you wish you had not said will
start to decline.

Prayer for the day: Heavenly Father, today, I can see so many of the problems I am dealing with are a direct link to my responses to a situation. I continue to make things worse, not only for myself but for others, because I am continuously quick to respond. Lord, please help me to be slow to anger and slow to speak. Help me to see that mimicking the teachings of Jesus will demolish the effects of my tongue. Today, I want my actions to be of service and my quick responses to be silenced. In Your heavenly name, I do pray, Amen.

◆

# Day 44: The Greatest of These

If I give everything I own to the poor and even go to the stake
to be burned as a martyr, but I don't love, I've gotten nowhere.
So, no matter what I say, what I believe, and what I do, I'm
bankrupt without love.

—1 Corinthians 13:3 (The Message)

Are you overly bombarded with bright ideas of how you should spend your free
time, your meditation time, when and where you should go to meetings, what
step you're on, and when you will hurry up and get to the fourth and fifth step?
Everyone seems to have a brilliant idea of what you should or should not be doing,
and it can be so discouraging, even if they have the best of intentions.

With all the things that are expected of you so early in recovery, you may tend
to ask yourself if all you are doing is really necessary. Well, that's between you and
God. But if you're asking me personally what my main focus is on throughout all
my recovery, I would have to answer, "Love."

In today's verse, Paul is telling the church of Corinth that although they are
making great efforts and working very hard at becoming Christlike, it is all for nothing
if love is not the driving force. In my first ninety days of recovery, I was working so hard
and doing everything everyone suggested; I felt like I was simply spinning in circles
and achieving nothing. It wasn't until my main focus was on loving others that my
reason for being and staying clean became clear. You can go to 1 million meetings, go
through the twelve steps 1 million times, and attend church seven days a week, but
it is all for nothing if it is not centered around love. It is the same love our heavenly
Father displayed to us when we cried out for help while in our deepest and darkest
despair. The love God has extended to us is the same love we need to extend to others,
and when that becomes the forefront of your recovery, you will have clarity as to why
you are doing the things you do in order to stay clean. The greatest of these is love.

Prayer for the day: Heavenly Father, I work so hard at following instructions
and doing all that is asked of me, but to no avail. Today, I realize the one thing I
may be missing that makes my recovery worthwhile is love. Lord, I will take my
understanding of today's Bible verse and apply it to others. Today, I want to love
others the way God has loved me. Amen.

# Day 45: Just Do It

> But whoever looks intently into the perfect law that gives
> freedom, and continues in it—not forgetting what they have
> heard, but doing it—they will be blessed in what they do.
> —James 1:25 (NIV)

It doesn't matter how young or how old you are, if you are alive and breathing, you've probably seen one of the greatest advertising slogans in sports, whether it be in a magazine or on a billboard that said, "Just do it." The Nike company came out with this slogan while sponsoring many of its pro athletes and encouraging the world to take their dreams and make them happen by being active and intentional.

The apostle James is telling everyone who will listen that merely hearing the Word is not enough. People who only hear the Word and yet do nothing to act on what they heard lead themselves to self-deception. Let me give an example: Have you ever been with a group of friends, and there is always that one friend who tries to encourage you to do something he has only heard someone else talking about but has never truly done himself? He hears what's being said on Sunday but doesn't put what the Bible says into practice for it to make a difference in his life. People who only hear God's Word are soon destined to forget.

The apostle James was adamant about putting into action what he heard. In fact, if you study James, you will discover he was the first apostle martyred for his beliefs. Part of me would like to believe this is because he didn't let anything stop him when it came to spreading the good news of Jesus Christ. He was a "Just do it" type of apostle.

In today's verse, we begin to see the effects of what it means when we take God's Word outside of the church and just do it. The apostle says hearing the Word and doing it leads to blessings. Those who hear the Word and become effectual doers will be blessed in what they do. They look intently at the Word and begin to apply the Word, not just to their outward behavior, but to their heart. From there, they apply the Word so it changes their conduct and character in the sight of God. They also recognize not only the strength in their character and well-being but a strengthened relationship with our heavenly Father. This only happens when you hear the Word and also "Just do it."

Prayer for the day: Heavenly Father, today, I pray I can take the messages you place in Your living Word and put them in action so they may make a difference in my life. I no longer want to be deceived by my thoughts and what I have heard but to be convinced because of the actions I have taken. Help me to be courageous to stand up and take action and be an example to others of what it means to partake in Kingdom living. Amen.

◆

# Day 46: Simple Is Not So Simple

But I have spared you for a purpose—to show you my power
and to spread my fame throughout the earth.

—Exodus 9:16 (NIV)

See if this idea sounds comfortable and practical: "I will get away from all this chaos so others can assist in making decisions for me." Does that sentence sound familiar? Was there a point in your life when this was the only answer that made any sense? You could no longer see a purpose in your life, nor could you focus your sight in any direction God may have been trying to take you. We convinced ourselves, and truly believed, that by taking some time off from this crazy chaos and letting others assist with the decision-making process of life, things could and would get better. But sometimes, simple is not so simple.

One of the most straightforward concepts of recovery to grasp is the concept of "letting go and letting God." It's something we recite over and over but very rarely succeed at, due to our inner desire to take control. We first need to recognize the importance of letting God direct our lives. Why, might you ask? Take a look back to just a few months ago and ask yourself, who do you think directed your life out from the chaos and into your current condition of serenity you currently experience? When everything was lost, and everything had fallen apart, what is the one simple thing you did to change the condition that you were in? The majority of you will say, "I prayed."

It's so simple, isn't it? The simplest thing you did resulted in the most significant results. By taking a chance and letting your Lord and Savior take control, you began to recognize what today's verse in Exodus is all about. By allowing yourself to let go and let God, you acknowledge you have a purpose, and God wants you to fulfill that purpose so bad, He leads you out of Egypt and into His hands.

By looking back, have you been able to recognize God's power and how it continues to impact your life? Make a decision today to keep simple, simple. Make a decision that allows God full control of your life and alleviates your idea of wanting to take control and begin back down that road of destruction. The hardest part of your life was getting to where you are, but today, you see it was your simple prayer of desperation that allowed God to get you here. Only He can do it.

Prayer for the day: Heavenly Father, today I recognize the journey I was on from whence You brought me. The simplest things in life, such as prayer, continue to have the most significant impact. When I begin to trust and have faith that You and only You know what's best for my life, I then start to let go. Help me today to turn over my thoughts and ideas for my life to You. Guide and direct my footsteps down Your path so I may never be lost again. Amen.

◆

# Day 47: Money Where Your Mouth Is

You hypocrites! Isaiah was right when he prophesied about you: "These people honor me with their lips, but their hearts are far from me."

—Matthew 15:7–8 (NIV)

Have you ever thought about taking a sincerity obedience test? It's a test where you sit down with a pad and pen, and jot down those goals you have set for yourself, but you somehow have not been able to achieve. For example, maybe you set a goal for yourself to start exercising. You begin to realize you started with the best of intentions, but after a week, your exercising has diminished. Maybe you set a goal for yourself to lose weight, but after a time of salads and fish, you can't resist the urge to satisfy your sweet tooth. Or better yet, you set a goal to quit smoking, and after putting them down for twenty-four hours, you can't resist the urge anymore and convinced yourself it's okay to have just one. Here's another one: "I'm going to dive deeper into my Bible and begin to know what it means to be truly closer to God." Now it's all you can do to convince yourself to get up and go to church on Sunday.

Tests like these aren't meant to bring awareness to where we are as it pertains to our sincerity. They bring awareness to the fact that whatever goal you set, especially your spiritual goals, you must remain intentional, both mentally and physically. Staying intentional mentally means you need to be prepared for the fact we are all in a constant battle with our thoughts and ideas. We all tend to succumb to our feelings when we entertain those ideas we know are not conducive to our goals and especially our recovery. Staying intentional and aware physically means we don't put ourselves in an environment that eliminates any chance of success.

For example, if you want to lose weight by dieting, then you probably shouldn't join your friends when they go to Krispy Kreme. If you're going to quit smoking, be intentional for the first thirty days to not be around a smoking environment with your friends or in public. If you're going to be closer to God, then be intentional and set a time every day to talk openly and privately with your heavenly Father in prayer. I realize I just described a normal twelve-step meeting environment as it pertains to food and smoking, but do not use this as an excuse to not go to meetings (LOL).

There's nothing more humiliating to your confidence than to verbally proclaim to others your goals and intentions, and then end up unsuccessful. Our spiritual health requires daily maintenance with deliberate plans. The moment we begin to let our thoughts interrupt and disturb our actions with convenient excuses, we are destined to fail. Today, let your only goal be one that allows you to be closer to God and allows Him to direct you to those areas in your life that need the most attention. Once we begin to do that, we begin to conquer those obstacles that always causes us to fail. It's an excellent day to succeed at those things you say.

Prayer for the day: Heavenly Father, I continually fall short of those things I know consciously You want me to do. I am constantly bombarded with my thoughts and humiliated by my failing intentions. Lord, I pray You would clear my mind so I may be focused on you and my next steps will be down a path you would have me travel. Your Word assures me if I do my part, You are faithful to do Yours. Amen.

◆

# Day 48: Get Ready to Live Again

Jesus said to her, "I am the resurrection and the life. The one who believes in me will live, even though they die; and whoever lives by believing in me will never die. Do you believe this?"

—John 11:25–26 (NIV)

Trust is a gift that tends to come with a hefty price. We find ourselves this early recovery having a hard time trusting anyone, and it is not always because others are not trustworthy, but it is because deep down, we still may not trust ourselves. Living a life that is always in survival mode forces us to do and say things that are not always honest and true.

In today's verse, Jesus had just raised Lazarus from the dead and is challenging Martha with a simple question when He asks, "Do you believe?" It is apparent that Martha has no choice but to say yes she believes, due to what she just experienced. She witnessed Jesus completely restore the life of a man whose life was lost entirely. Does this sound familiar to you?

Today, we need to be able to trust where this new way of life is beginning to take us. Jesus wants us to be ready to embrace the fact that our future and our hope is entirely in His hands. Trust that by following Him, all is going to be well and that no matter what we did in the past, our eternity is secure because of His blood. Actual death comes to the ungodly and those who are unwilling to trust at all. The ones who die and cannot truly trust are truly dead.

Today, let's find assurance in knowing when we allow Christ into our lives, He is faithful and true to forgive. He has assured us He will never leave us, and by simply believing in Him, you too can live again. Do you believe this?

Prayer for the day: Heavenly Father, I never knew what to expect when I first came into this new way of life. Today, I want to put my trust entirely in Your hands and allow You to do those things that would give me a new experience again. I pray today You would raise me up from the pits I have fallen into and give me a heart that relies entirely on You. I trust and honestly believe that by doing this, I too can live again. Amen.

# Day 49: All for One

Be wise in the way you act toward outsiders; make the most of every opportunity. Let your conversation be always full of grace, seasoned with salt, so that you may know how to answer everyone.

—Colossians 4:5–6 (NIV)

There is a famous saying in recovery that goes like this: "If you're going to talk the talk, you must walk the walk." Believe it or not, at Day 49 in this new way of life, people are beginning to take notice of the things you say and do. It is incredible to think that in forty-nine days, our heads are no longer in the clouds, our energy is at a new level, and we begin to feel more hopeful than ever before. So how do we act outwardly with this new way we feel inwardly?

First of all, let's begin to remember that we must enjoy life. The whole premise behind recovery is to be able to grasp a new way of living that brings happiness and joy, not only to ourselves but to everyone around us. We no longer want to be viewed as the one who can't be trusted or the one who is always planning to do wrong.

How do you know if what you say is genuinely matching what you do? Here is an old saying you can put to the test for yourself: "A man can be sure of who he truly is by what he will allow himself to do behind closed doors." Our words and behavior need to be genuine and authentic behind closed doors and outside of those doors.

In today's verse, the apostle Paul is telling young Timothy his life outside the church must be a shining example for others to follow. His words should be full of grace and forgiveness. Why is it so essential for us? Because think back to Day 1 of your journey, and remember the grace and the love that was extended to you. Remember that when no one else was willing to trust you, there were men and women ready to extend the loving hand of Christ in your direction to guide you forward. Without this grace or love, not only is it not possible for you to be successful in changing, but ultimately, you will become unsuccessful in recovery.

You are strong enough now to begin to know the difference between purposeful Kingdom living and destructive living. Let the words you speak to others be a shining example of the life you live. If you tell others you are living your life one day at a time and you are genuinely "letting go and letting God," make sure they see that and not just hear it. Remember, not only is God watching, but others around you are watching as well.

Prayer for the day: Heavenly Father, I find it so easy to be able to speak the words that sound good to others. I find it so easy to play the part on a part-time basis, without full-time success. Help me, today, Lord, to overcome these barriers that keep me from being a shining example of the words I speak to others. May my walk be authentic and intentional, with the sole purpose of doing Your will. By being focused on the things You would have me to do, Lord, I can be assured my actions will speak louder than my words. Amen.

# Day 50: Locking the Lips

Do not let any unwholesome talk come out of your mouths, but only what is helpful for building others up according to their needs, that it may benefit those who listen.

—Ephesians 4:29 (NIV)

If you were to stop and take a look at the people around you, you would notice there are more people needing encouragement than there are encouragers. So often, we get trapped into those conversations where people are berating and tearing down a person's character through idle gossip or just utterly destructive conversation. Sometimes, through no fault of your own, you find yourself in these situations, and ultimately, you're left with a choice. Either you remove yourself from the conversation, making them aware of the effects of their discussion, or you can join in their communication. Doing the latter leads to a pattern of behavior that neither glorifies nor benefits anyone.

Believe it or not, idle gossip is old behavior. Sometimes, the reason we are so busy tearing others down is, we want to feel better about ourselves. In today's verse, Paul is directing the leaders in Ephesus to speak only in a way that is edifying to others in good spirit. Having adopted this new way of living for ourselves, we incorporate God's Word in our heart and quickly learn it is our job as disciples to build others up using only the narratives God gives us through His living Word.

Never will you see God take your past behaviors and characteristics, and hold them against you. God reminds us that when He forgives our sins, the slate is spotless, and the focus is on our new way of life with Him. If this is the type of conversation our Savior is willing to have with us, shouldn't we be intentional with the same constructive words with others? When we deliberately bring up past behaviors and use it against them, what we are doing is suggesting they are no better than those past behaviors.

Be a shining example of the same grace and love that has been displayed to each and every one of us. If at times you find it challenging to be able to say something positive, don't worry; for some of us, learning what it takes to be a positive influence takes time and practice. If at times you're not quite sure what to say, or if you think your words may hurt someone, then remember today's title and lock your lips and smile. Smiling goes a lot further than you think and has never hurt anyone.

Prayer for the day: Heavenly Father, I pray today my words may be nothing more than a shining example of what You have done for my life. May I take the grace and love that has been bestowed upon me and share it with others. I pray I can be the one to lift those up who are lost and afraid. May the words from my mouth be directly in line with Kingdom living and the things You would have me to do. Amen.

◆

# Day 51: The Price to Be Paid

> Not only so, but we also glory in our sufferings, because we
> know that suffering produces perseverance; perseverance,
> character; and character, hope.
>
> —Romans 5:3–4 (NIV)

The date is June 9, 2018, and the world sits back and waits. They wait to see the running of the Belmont Stakes in New York to determine a possible new Triple Crown winner in horse racing. On this date, the opportunity of a lifetime is about to happen, but only if the hard work, training, and perseverance pay off. The horse, appropriately named Justify, came out of nowhere and had never made a name for himself until he surprised everyone by winning the Preakness. Not much attention was given to Justify until he won the Kentucky Derby, and then all minds began to wonder. From there, the stage was set for Justify to be able to make a difference in the lives of so many or go back to being a plain ol' racehorse.

You never really know what suffering and perseverance are about until you're placed in a situation that requires constant attention, restraint, and due diligence. So many times, we avoid situations that do not grant us instant satisfaction or a recognizable result. You see, living in a world where most of our problems are solved at the push of a button results in a lack of character as well as having hope for what we can or will become.

What kind of sailor would you have if he never sailed a stormy sea? What sort of racecar driver would you have if he only drove in a straight line? What kind of Christians would we be if God did not allow us to face difficult situations? In today's verse, Paul is telling those who will listen that the golden chain of Christian growth only comes from accepting the path of resistance, not least resistance. Paul is also saying we should rejoice during our tribulation because we have faith that whatever mountain we are to climb or hurdle we are to jump, God will demonstrate through us what it takes to get to the other side.

Commit today to not always look for the easy way out. Have the faith and assurance that all Christians need to accept that whatever it is you're about to go through, God has you there for a reason. You will never grow in your recovery, much less a relationship with God, if you never accept the difficult challenges in life that will make you stronger. If you're facing judgment because of past behaviors, then face them. If you are avoiding the fact that you need to move on and remove yourself from your current condition, then move on. But whatever you do, make sure your first step is to take God with you. Without Him, nothing is possible.

Prayer for the day: Heavenly Father, there are so many things in my life I need to face, and so many fears I need to overcome. Help me today to realize by facing those obstacles head-on, I can begin to grow and see Your work in my life. I have the assurance the plans You have for me are not going to harm me but to give me hope and a future, just like the Bible says. Today, I rest assured in that hope and find comfort in knowing You love me. Amen.

◆

# Day 52: Finding Friends

But I tell you, love your enemies and pray for those who persecute you.

—Matthew 5:44 (NIV)

I would like for you to stop one second and simply read the above verse three times to yourself. Did you read it? Good.

If you would like to sum up the primary focal point of the Bible, as well as the most accurate definition of recovery and Kingdom living, the above verse must be it. Indubitably, some have made it to Day 52, and the pieces of the past are staring them straight in the face in the form of people we have hurt or betrayed.

When it comes to cleaning up the past, I have heard a lot of men and women in recovery say, "Can't they see I'm trying to change my life? Why can't they just forget about what I did to them in the past? I'm a new person now." The problem with this is, the wreckage of the past wasn't rectified simply because I became clean. Being clean allows me to correct the issues of the past. See the difference?

Don't get me wrong; there are those we have harmed who have a heart like Christ and are willing to be more forgiving than others, and we are thankful for them and do our best to demonstrate we have truly changed. For a lot of us in recovery, our biggest persecutor may be the legal system. It is imperative we face our legal responsibilities head-on with God's guidance and remain determined to properly clean slate. Recovery has a better chance of success when we are not bombarded with legal matters.

Who else may be holding your past against you? Your family, your employer, your community, or how about those who have met you for the first time, but once they heard about your past, they were quick to judge and now want nothing to do with you. The list goes on and on, but what does God want us to do? Well, you said you read the verse for today three times, so you already know the answer. The answer is to love them the same way God continues to love you.

It is incredible to watch how God will justify and redeem those things of the past if we are following good orderly direction. Being able to trust God while no one is trusting us allows our recovery to launch into unbelievable, successful heights. Better yet, it creates an even greater Father-to-child relationship between you and God, a link that allows you to forgive those who are determined never to forgive you. It's a hard pill to swallow, but we have to take it.

Prayer for the day: Heavenly Father, today, I realize the problems of the past are going to have to be answered for. I pray for a heart like Christ so I may be willing to truly make amends for the damage I have caused. When I feel the pressure of the past upon me, I pray You guide and direct me entirely to the finish line of freedom. May I always remember to display a Christlike behavior to all those I meet, regardless if they approve or disapprove of who I was or who I currently am. Amen.

◆

# Day 53: Put It to the Test

"Bring the whole tithe into the storehouse, that there may be food in my house. Test me in this," says the LORD Almighty, "and see if I will not throw open the floodgates of heaven and pour out so much blessing that there will not be room enough to store it."

—Malachi 3:10

A once-notorious bank robber was released from prison and had an opportunity to sit down with a reporter to give an interview detailing his history of robbing banks.

The reporter asked him, "When you were caught, it was discovered you hid all the money you stole in your house, versus putting it somewhere safe like a bank; why?"

The gentleman replied, "Because people rob banks."

Let's face it; money is a big issue for most people. For a lot of us, it is a way and a means to an end, whether the end may be paying bills, saving money for the future, sending kids to college, or just going on vacation. There is a love-hate relationship when it comes to money. It always seems like you never have enough, and you constantly feel like you need more. Think back to your past, and try to remember the lengths you would go to obtain more money. If you think about it long enough, it has the appearance of idolatry.

We see our shortcomings with money and how the harder we try with what little we have, it's never enough. In today's verse, God is once again giving His people an opportunity to see how they can become more prosperous, regarding their possessions, by trusting Him. Some of us may have so little as it pertains to money, that simply putting a dime in the offering plate seems disrespectful. Trust me, it's not. What's disrespectful is, we don't believe God can make a difference, even with a little dime. When you were completely lost and had absolutely nothing to offer, wasn't God able to do something with you?

Stop robbing God of what is rightfully His, and realize what He can do when you bring all you have to the offering plate. This type of giving not only enhances and strengthens your faith, but it also allows God to multiply those things in your life you need versus those things you think you need. Today, even if you only have a dollar, give God the 10 percent He asks for, and watch how He will provide you with a 100 percent return.

Prayer for the day: Heavenly Father, today, I realize everything I have is rightfully Yours. I have fallen short in trusting You with what I have, and today, I want to invest in those things You want for me in my life. May I continue to give with an open heart and realize that true happiness does not lie in the possessions I own but in the blessings You continue to provide to me. Give me a heart to give and the faith to trust You with all I have. Amen.

◆

# Day 54: Sharpen Your Ax

Search me, God, and know my heart; test me and know my
anxious thoughts. See if there is any offensive way in me, and
lead me in the way everlasting.

—Psalm 139:23–24 (NIV)

There were two loggers that worked together in the woods. One morning, the
forty-five-year-old logger said to the twenty-one-year-old logger, "I bet that this day
I can cut down more trees than you can." The younger logger thought to himself
that this would be a sure win for him and gladly took the bet. So both men headed
out into the forest and began cutting down trees. The younger logger was chopping
and swinging as hard as he could, with complete assurance that he was winning.
Every hour of the day, the younger logger would look over to the older logger and
noticed that he took a ten-minute break each and every hour. Because the older
logger took these breaks and the younger logger worked full force all day long, he
was completely certain he would win the bet.

At the end of the day, the younger logger counted a total of twenty-five trees
he had chopped down. He approached the older logger with this number and stated
boldly, "You surely could not have cut down more than twenty-five trees today."

The older logger looked at the young boy with a grin and stated, "I cut down
forty-five."

The younger man was in complete disbelief and asked the older logger how
he could have possibly cut down so many trees while taking a ten-minute break
every hour. The older logger stated very kindly he was able to cut so many more
because while he was taking a ten-minute break, he allowed his body to recover,
and while his body was recovering, he remembered to sharpen his ax.

There are so many things in life we can accomplish when we remember to
stop every now and then, and let our bodies recover. When we stop and slow down,
what we really do is allow our minds to remind us of the things that are more
important and to stay sharp in those areas that keep us safe and focused. One of
the things we must do to ensure we are staying sharp is to remember what today's
verse is saying. It simply states we must stop and ask God to remind us of those
areas that need His attention and His guidance.

There are so many times when we get distracted by assuring ourselves we are
being productive because we are working so hard and so fast. We must remember
to slow down, take a deep breath, and ask God to examine those things in our life

that are hindering us from being truly productive in His sight. Remember, people who are most productive are those who rely on God's guidance and not their own.

Prayer for the day: Heavenly Father, there are so many times when I recognize I'm going 100 miles per hour and getting absolutely nowhere and have accomplished absolutely nothing. Help me today to remember to stop and get those directions You would have me to follow. Help me to realize my greatest achievements do not come from how hard or how fast I work but better yet by Who is guiding me in my work. Guide me today, Lord. Lead me in Your way. Help me to ensure that I'm doing Your will. Amen.

---

# Day 55: We Need Leviticus

What shall we say, then? Is the law sinful? Certainly not!
Nevertheless, I would not have known what sin was had it not
been for the law. For I would not have known what coveting
really was if the law had not said, "You shall not covet."
—Romans 7:7 (NIV)

Have you ever noticed you will probably never be pulled over by a police officer for coming to a complete stop at a stop sign or driving under the speed limit? They will never come up to you and say, "Thank you for keeping your driver's license valid," or give you an award for not driving under the influence. Laws, rules, and regulations are all in place for a reason. They remind us of what is unacceptable in our society, as well as unacceptable in Christian living.

A lot of times, we seem to forget why rules are there. For instance, in today's verse, Paul is making it known that the law and rules are good because they inform us how we should live. For instance, how would you know that coveting was wrong if you had not read in the Bible, "You shall not covet"? The law of God is perfect in every way, but there is something that is wrong with us.

So many times, in recovery, we feel because we are obeying the rules and following God's good orderly direction, there is inherently a reward that should be in place. We forget we broke the rules and the law hundreds and hundreds of times and deserve years upon years of punishment, and yet, we have been given a reprieve. It is a very dangerous position to be in if we believe we should be rewarded for something we never should've done in the first place. The fact that we have been given a daily reprieve from the hell we have come from is all the reward we shall ever need, and our urgent desire should be to never break the law again.

You see, the amazing thing is, by continuing to obey God's rules, there is a reward system that is being put in place for you: an eternity of happiness and everlasting love. Just when you thought you would never be rewarded for obeying the rules, along comes Jesus and gives you the greatest reward of all: eternal life. Hallelujah.

Prayer for the day: Heavenly Father, so often I feel I should be recognized for the good things I do but never be held accountable for the things of the past. Thank You, Lord, for forgiving my past with Your grace and reminding me my true reward lies in heaven with You. May I never be rewarded for the things I never should have done to begin with. Thank You for Your infinite grace and all the gifts You continue to give me. Amen.

◆

# Day 56: A Little Knowledge, a Lot of Difference
### ◆ ◆ ◆

> For we are God's handiwork, created in Christ Jesus to do good
> works, which God prepared in advance for us to do.
> —Ephesians 2:10 (NIV)

It's funny how intuitive and smart we think we are. Let me give you an example. One time, I owned a car, and about two years after purchasing this car and making payments on it, I ran across an electrical issue I could not resolve. Now some of you might not know this, but if you look in your glove compartment, you will see this neat little book called an owner's manual. In this owner's manual is a plethora of information that informs you of what your car can and cannot do. Remarkably, not only did I fix my problem with the electrical issue, I also found out my car had a lot more features that could make driving easier than I realized. You see, I thought I knew everything about my car, and I had been invested in this car, and yet I wasn't being fully fulfilled with all this car had to offer.

In today's verse, Paul is telling the church of Ephesus that God has created you and has given you a lot of features and a lot of abilities you may not know you have. He has also given us an owner's manual written by Him in order for you to discover who you truly are. It is very dangerous as Christians to believe we know all there is to know about what God has planned for us. This attitude of thinking we know what is best for us is a direct result of not spending enough time reading God's Word, the Bible.

The more you begin to open God's manual for your life, you will see you know very little about who you truly are, and God has so much more planned for you than you could have ever imagined. When we grasp this concept, we intuitively find ourselves digging deeper and deeper into God's Word in order to assure ourselves what we think and believe is correct and in tune with God's message and direction for our lives. A friend of mine once told me, "A little knowledge is a dangerous thing," and today, I truly know what he means. What I thought I knew about myself was leading me to confusion and ultimately leading me back to devastating situations and chaos.

The message I want to get across to you today is, God has an incredible plan for us, but we should never think we know what that plan is or how we should be truly living. The one thing we know for sure is, God wants us to remain in His will and direction, and the only way we can do that is to ensure that our information is coming straight from His manual and we are reading it entirely.

Prayer for the day: Heavenly Father, today I realize there is a huge gap between what I thought I knew and what I truly know. Help me today, Lord, to be mindful and open-minded, and to realize You created me for a purpose and for a reason. Today, I truly understand I do not know all there is about your plans for me; true knowledge only comes from Your living Word, the Bible. May I be intentional and devoted to reading Your Word and discovering all You would have me to be. Amen.

◆

# Day 57: Hidden Treasures

I have hidden your word in my heart that I might not sin against you.

—Psalm 119:11 (NIV)

We have all heard it said that practice makes perfect, and for most of us, if you have become good at anything, you know this to be true. In fact, studies have shown that when you drive, 75 percent of your reaction is an automatic reflex versus a thought-provoking reaction. Knowing which way to look when making a turn, automatically knowing who has the right-of-way, or even passing through a stop light and then realizing you can't remember if the light was red or green comes from years of repetitive practice and instinctive reflexes.

The same is true in how we react with others. When you are confronted by someone or if something is said that is meant to be provoking, your reaction will be a direct reflection and reflex of the things you hold true to your heart. You may immediately retaliate in aggression, or you may calmly react in a manner that is Christlike and represents Kingdom living. In other words, because you continually submerse yourself in God's Word, you'll intuitively know what to do in all of life's situations.

The psalmist David makes it very clear that as humans, we are programmed to react in a way that is more or less sinful. We truly don't understand the best way to handle confrontation or how to react in a manner that is conducive to what scripture tells us. And the only way to program ourselves so our immediate reaction is biblically sound is to repetitively read God's Word every day. You never knew it wasn't okay to strike someone back who struck you until you read in the Bible to turn the other cheek. You never knew you should treat others how you want to be treated until you discovered it in scripture. Never knew to love your enemies instead of attacking them until you read it in the Bible.

You will never truly know how to properly react to any situation until you base your reaction on biblical scripture, and the easiest model to follow is Jesus and the life He led. His reaction when faced with confrontation is the perfect example of the life you want to lead when people mistreat you or life becomes difficult as a result of others. Our immediate reaction could be the difference between the life of serenity and a life of misery. Today, you must choose.

Prayer for the day: Heavenly Father, today, I realize I often react in a way that is displeasing to You. My life does not seem to be a direct reflection of the life You led or a life You want me to lead. I pray today that I become more aware of the need to bury Your words into my heart, and that begins by intentionally focusing my time in scripture. May I continue to practice being an example of true Kingdom living. Amen.

◆

# Day 58: One Step at a Time

As for other matters, brothers and sisters, we instructed you how to live in order to please God, as in fact you are living. Now we ask you and urge you in the Lord Jesus to do this more and more.

—1 Thessalonians 4:1

On Day 58, there is a good chance you're somewhere between steps 1 and 3, and if so, congratulations, but here is an eye-opener for you: God is not satisfied with our beginning steps. Although it is very good that we are now marching on a new journey, there are bigger and greater steps ahead of us. Just ask yourself, were you completely satisfied after your child's first steps, or were you expecting more? All we have really done is begun the race for what lies ahead of us.

One of the worst things that can happen in recovery is, we can lose that desire to do everything it takes in order to stay clean. Sobriety is a never-ending, constant journey, in which we gratefully take on and willingly accept new challenges each and every day. But we are now at a point in recovery when we need to start taking on spiritual challenges. Step 3 is all about making a decision, and one decision you have to make is if you're willing to take those much-needed next steps by completely relinquishing your will. In other words, are you willing to let your next steps be completely guided by God?

Paul is telling the people of Thessalonica he is pleased they have begun to take those critical first steps, but what today's verse is emphasizing is the importance of taking more and more steps, doing more and more of what God would have you do, preparing yourselves mentally, physically, and spiritually for the journey He wants you to travel on, to be ready for those headaches and heartaches that come with recovery, as well as the blessings and growth that come from living a life in recovery, based on deliberate steps toward spiritual growth and a one-on-one relationship with the Father.

The first step is great, but don't stop after the first step because it's what lies ahead in the next step that God wants you to see and live out. Recovery, as well as life in general, is based on a succession of many steps that require focus and the understanding that our steps in recovery, as well as in life, are never complete until the day our heavenly Father calls us home.

Prayer for the day: Heavenly Father, today, I pray I may take bigger and greater steps toward You. I am blessed and grateful for the joy I experienced in my first few steps, but I pray I willingly take on the challenges of the next steps ahead of me. I pray I never forget in order for me to have success in this life, I must take this journey hand in hand with You, Lord. Give me the strength and clarity of mind to make my next step an even greater step toward You and toward the things You have prepared for me in my life. Amen.

◆

# Day 59: Just a Little Bit Hungry

Do not conform to the pattern of this world, but be transformed by the renewing of your mind. Then you will be able to test and approve what God's will is—his good, pleasing and perfect will.

—Romans 12:2 (NIV)

If you're in recovery, then what I'm about to describe to you might sound familiar. Have you ever passed a beggar on the street with a sign saying, "Hungry, need food." If you are like me, the first thought you have when you see this person is a vision of your former self. Maybe you were once standing on a corner and were truly hungry for food, but you also had another hunger for something else. You were doing everything in your power to satisfy the urges and cravings that paralyzed your very soul and neglecting the physical and spiritual self. Because of this way of life, you are paying a very heavy cost.

When I see people like this these days, I try my best not to be quick to judge but realize I have an opportunity and obligation to offer to them the same thing God gave me: forgiving grace, not in the form of money but in the opportunity to accept a different way of life by presenting God's Word. Don't get me wrong; I offer to take them to a restaurant and get them something to eat. Trust me, people are more receptive to your suggestions when they have a full stomach, but I also look at the opportunity as a way to demonstrate and testify openly that what God has done for me, He can also do for them.

In today's verse, Paul is telling the Romans that allowing the scriptures to guide the way you're thinking ultimately gives God the opportunity to do His will in your life. In fact, Paul is so sure of this, he dares the Romans to try this new way of thinking and see for themselves how God will transform them.

So today, I offer you a challenge: Will you put away the patterns of this world and conform your minds and be transformed yourselves? Will you begin to feed the spiritual body rather than human flesh and desires? Put this new way of life to the test, and if you're not completely satisfied with the results God is giving you, your misery is completely refundable.

Prayer for the day: Heavenly Father, today, I continue to have a spiritual craving only you can fill. Although I have put down the old habits of the past and have become acceptable in society's eyes, I would rather be more acceptable in Your eyes. Help me today to fill my spiritual needs by living a life guided by Your words and scriptures. Today, I commit to putting this promise You have given me to the test, so I may be able to enjoy Your good, pleasing, perfect will in my life. Amen.

---

◆

---

# Day 60: The Need for Reflection

As a prisoner for the Lord, then, I urge you to live a life worthy
of the calling you have received. Be completely humble and
gentle; be patient, bearing with one another in love. Make every
effort to keep the unity of the Spirit through the bond of peace.
—Ephesians 4:1–3 (NIV)

So many times I am asked how I came to be a pastor in the church. I knew I would
be asked this question often, and having had a turbulent past, I often dodged the
subject of recovery and came up with a somewhat pleasing response so as to not
leave an individual with a bad impression of who I am today.

With that being said, I have come to feel there is something dishonorable
about disqualifying who you once were because of the way you arrived in your
current status. I truly believe the way you arrived where you currently are carries
more weight than simply stating your position in the community today. For
example, it's entertaining to watch professional athletes at their peak, but what is
inspiring and motivating is the price they paid to get there.

A lady was inquiring about the church and its programs. At the end of our
discussion, she was curious as to how I became a pastor and what led me to the
ministry. I was on the verge of simply stating I was an employee for a few years
and then pursued leadership, which would've been the soft and safe answer, as well
as somewhat dishonest. Instead, I was led to share my testimony of how I came
to the church through the adult rehabilitation program. I'm not sure why I had
the overwhelming urge to give her my full testimony, but I was glad I did. At the
end of our discussion, she broke down in tears because she had been looking for a
program for a relative who has battled addiction for many years. Apparently, my
testimony gave her the solution she was looking for. It was my past destruction that
gave her strength, not my current achievements. Praise be to God.

In today's verse, Paul uses the word *prisoner* as a visual for the life you should
continue to live in Christ, a life that comes with sacrifices and the ability to say
no when the rest of you wants to say yes, to be intentional toward living a life that
is recognized by others as Kingdom living, to live a life that is peaceful and brings
unity amongst others when all you can think about is your own personal desires.
Never be ashamed to tell the full story of how God brought you from the muck
and mire of your past life into the blissful state of never-ending grace. Remember,

you are not who you used to be, and God continues to mold you into what He wants you to be.

Prayer for the day: Heavenly Father, today, I recognize my past and the grace You have bestowed upon me carries enough weight to overcome my shame of who I was and to assist in changing the lives of others. May I remain determined to continue to make the sacrifices needed to display the same type of grace to others You have given to me. No matter what the cost, no matter how uncomfortable I become, no matter what others may think of me, I will proclaim Your Word and live a life worthy of Kingdom living. Amen.

◆

# Day 61: Destination Somewhere

For I command you today to love the LORD your God, to walk
in obedience to him, and to keep his commands, decrees and
laws; then you will live and increase, and the LORD your God
will bless you in the land you are entering to possess.
—Deuteronomy 30:16 (NIV)

I remember as a kid receiving model cars and airplanes to put together as Christmas
and birthday presents. The biggest problem I had putting these together was that
after I glued a couple of parts together as the instructions had informed me, I
could begin to see its development and convinced myself I knew which parts and
pieces were next. I would lay the instructions aside and begin to assemble freestyle.
I just knew for sure what was next, and I could visualize how it was supposed to
be. Ultimately, in the end, pieces didn't fit the way they should; it was completely
off kilter, and I was left with nothing more than parts and pieces, unable to undo
the damage that had been done, which left me with the question, "How do I start
over?"

There is something very distinctive and reassuring in the message of
today's verse. Simply stated, if you follow God's directions, He will bless
you wherever He has you going. As it states in the verse, you must first love
the Lord; second walk in obedience; and third keep His commands, decrees,
and laws; the result is God's blessing. Now what happens if we take God's
instructions and do them backwards? We would end up like the incomplete
model car or plane, parts and pieces everywhere and unsure of what God really
has planned for us.

We are not always going to know exactly what God has planned for us,
but one thing you can be sure of is, if you remember to do the most important
thing, which is to love the Lord your God with all your heart, with all your soul,
and with all your strength (Luke 10:27), the rest of the pieces of the puzzle will
come together perfectly. There's nothing more satisfying than having a clear
picture of where God has you headed and the life He is developing for you.
Follow God's instructions in the order He laid them out for you, and be blessed
with this new way of life.

Prayer for the day: Heavenly Father, today, I surrender my way of thinking and the false assurance I have given myself as to where I think You want me to be. I see the importance of following instructions in order for Your will to prevail in my life and for me to be grounded in the new land You have waiting for me. May I stay focused, patient, and willing to seek Your good orderly direction in every area of my life; this only happens when I surrender my will. Amen.

◆

# Day 62: Think, Thank, Thankful?

A gentle answer turns away wrath, but a harsh word stirs up anger.

—Proverbs 15:1 (NIV)

I read a story one time that has so much meaning in regards to today's verse and life in general. It goes like this:

You are holding a cup of coffee when someone comes along and bumps into you and shakes your arm, making you spill your coffee everywhere. Why did you spill your coffee?

"Well, because someone bumped into me, of course."

Wrong answer. You spilled the coffee because there was coffee in your cup. Had there been tea in the cup, you would have spilled tea. Had there been water in your cup, you would have spilled water. Whatever is in the cup is what you will spill out.

Therefore, when life comes along and shakes you (which will happen), whatever is inside of you will come out, literally spill out. It's easy to fake it until someone gets you rattled and stirred up.

So we must ask ourselves what's in our cup. When life gets tough, what spills over? Is it the fruits of the spirit: love, joy, peace, patience, kindness, goodness, faithfulness, gentleness, self-control (Galatians 5:22–23), or bitterness, anger, harsh words, and loud reactions?

In today's verse, we once again see the importance of self-control and tolerance in regard to conflicts and disaccord. By remaining full of God's spirit, we begin to see that our first instinctive response to situations is more Christlike than chaotic. We overcome the contagious effect that harsh words and anger bring about when hate and frustration is the first thing that spills out from inside of us.

I challenge you to take notice of the response of others when they are met with love and words of encouragement. Notice what builds amongst them when the words and directions of the Bible are at the forefront of your emotions.

Prayer for the day: Heavenly Father, today, I pray the things that spill out from me are the things that would bring people closer to You. May I be intentional to determine what truly lies within me so as to ensure that good and uplifting words flow out. Amen.

# Day 63: What Are Your Ingredients?

If I have the gift of prophecy and can fathom all mysteries and
all knowledge, and if I have a faith that can move mountains,
but do not have love, I am nothing.

—1 Corinthians 13:2 (NIV)

Has anyone ever asked you, "Why is it you do the things you do?" The majority of
the time, you probably answered, "Because it is what somebody once did for me."
We often have a tendency to duplicate the actions that were once bestowed upon
us. Go to an AA or NA meeting and ask the person who is greeting others at the
door or the people setting up chairs or making the coffee why they do what they
are doing, and they will always say, "Because somebody made sure it was done for
me when I first arrived." You see, the one thing we remember when we were at our
lowest point in our lives is called love.

Love takes on many forms, but if you read the Bible from Genesis to Revelation,
the one thing that sticks out and demands we imitate it is love. In the beginning,
God created the perfect setting to have a loving relationship with Him and gave it
to us. When we fell short and separated ourselves from Him, He gave us love and
accepted us back. When we were determined to live a life that demanded a Savior
in order to atone for our sins, He gave us His Son. All of this made possible by love.

In today's verse, Paul is telling the church of Corinth all their gifts and
knowledge of the scripture is useless if they are unable to display love for others.
*Love* is an action word; it demands we go out of our way to ensure the needs of
others are put before our needs. Where would you be if someone didn't extend a
hand to pull you up after you fell so far down? Where would you be if somebody
said, "Fix it yourself"? Where would we all be if Jesus had not sacrificed His life
in order that we may live? All this was done for one reason.

It is important to remember, we need the help and assistance of others, and
there will be times we need a hand up because we have fallen, but what God
demands we do is to display the same type of behavior to others, realizing that to
love someone else takes effort along with biblical guidance. Rely on the presence of
God and the Holy Spirit in your life to guide you on a path to discipleship, which
requires helping others. Never forget where you came from because the moment
you do, there's a good possibility you will return. So now, when somebody asks
you why you do what you do, you can simply say, "Because God did it for me."

Prayer for the day: Heavenly Father, today, I realize I have so many gifts present in my life, but I pray I continually display the one gift that demands my utmost attention: the ability to honestly love others. Help me to be loving without judging, be loving with no boundaries, be loving sacrificially, and be loving intentionally. Most importantly, help me to love like Jesus so I may never forget the love that was given to me. Amen.

◆

# Day 64: Strange Kind of Joy

Consider it pure joy, my brothers and sisters, whenever you face trials of many kinds, because you know that the testing of your faith produces perseverance.

—James 1:2–3 (NIV)

Here is something a lot of people do not know: The African impala can jump to a height of over ten feet while covering a distance of thirty feet. So I found it odd when I went to the zoo and saw they were kept in an enclosure behind a three-foot-high wall. I asked one of the zoo's staff if they had been trained not to jump over the wall. He quickly informed me the reason they do not jump over the wall is, they cannot see what is on the other side. They will not jump to freedom because of fear. Isn't our faith sometimes like this?

Think for a moment how much joy you may be missing because of fear. Is your lack of faith hindering you from traversing to the other side? So many times, we let difficult situations and little obstacles hinder us from receiving what God wants us to have. In fact, many obstacles in life are made a lot bigger than they truly are simply because of our level of faith.

In today's verse, the apostle James is assuring us that regardless of the obstacles you may be facing (court, divorce, bankruptcy, sobriety, etc.), pure joy comes when you jump over that three-foot wall standing in front of you. The moment you pray, "God, I do not know what lies in store for me when I cross this wall, but I am assured that together, we will persevere," you will find pure joy. When we take this type of leap of faith, two things happen: 1. We realize that with God in our life, we can conquer anything successfully. 2. Our ability and desire to place all our assurance and security in God becomes evident to others and is our first line of defense in all our situations.

Stop denying yourself the joy that comes from a faith-based relationship with your heavenly Father. This can only happen when we realize that problems are guaranteed to arise, stressful situations are lying in wait for us, and no matter how hard we try to avoid pain, we will inevitably experience it once again. It is pure joy to know we can do all things through Christ Who strengthens us (Philippians 4:13).

Prayer for the day: Heavenly Father, today I know that pure joy comes when I rely entirely on You. May I learn how to find joy in the things I fear the most. Today, I choose to confront the walls in my life head-on, with the assurance You will bring me to the other side stronger and more reliant on You. Amen.

◆

# Day 65: Love Me, Love Me Not

> Do not love the world or anything in the world. If anyone loves the world, love for the Father is not in them. For everything in the world—the lust of the flesh, the lust of the eyes, and the pride of life—comes not from the Father but from the world.
> —1 John 2:15–16 (NIV)

Haddon Robinson points out that one old recipe for rabbit started with this injunction: "First catch the rabbit." Robinson says, "The writer knew how to put first things first." That's what we do when we establish priorities: We put the things that should be in first place in their proper order.

Day 65 is a pivotal point in one's recovery. We have just gotten over the excitement that sixty days of continuous sobriety can bring, our physical well-being is better than ever, we have our strength back, and our minds begin to convince us it's okay to explore new options that could be lying ahead. Day 65 will enlighten us as to where our priorities indeed are and what we value as important in our lives. Some people feel they are ready to mend damaged relationships with loved ones. Others are convinced what brought them to recovery will never happen again, and they are prepared to tackle the world. You are constantly riddled with stinking thinking, and your recovery community begins to tell you to slow down.

I would like for you to read today's verse very carefully. There is a good chance you fit into one of the categories listed in the verse. Are you lusting after the flesh, undressing others with your eyes, or even worse? Have you convinced yourself you can tackle anything life throws at you? The point of today's verse is this: Anything you put before God, you will lose, and you will lose it with the assurance that it will be a more significant loss than any loss you have suffered before. Satan is waiting to tickle you with grandiose thoughts and ideas that your problems and your current situation is only part-time and it's okay to tackle the world alone.

Remember the recipe for the rabbit? First, you must catch the rabbit before you can even think about cooking it. The same is true as it pertains to your relationship with God. You must first let God catch you, and He will begin to show you the rest of the recipe He has for your life. It will be simple, clear, and with the assurance that it is the best plan for you. On Day 65, slow down with all the things you're convinced you're ready for, and become confident that you're prepared for a relationship with your heavenly Father. Be convinced today He loves you and is waiting for you. Blessed be the Lord.

Prayer for the day: Heavenly Father, I am filled with so many grandiose ideas of the direction my life should be taking. Help me to be mindful of my shortcomings and how easily I fell in the past with my perfect scenarios for my life. Today, I pray You take control of the direction I'm heading and make clear the plans You have for me. I pray I put aside anything I may place before You and become completely patient and willing to follow good orderly direction. Amen.

◆

# Day 66: Shhh!

A gentle answer turns away wrath, but a harsh word stirs up anger.

—Proverbs 15:1 (NIV)

In the spring of 1894, the Baltimore Orioles came to Boston to play a routine baseball game. But what happened that day was anything but routine. The Orioles' John McGraw got into a fight with the Boston third baseman. Within minutes, all the players from both teams had joined in the brawl. The warfare quickly spread to the grandstands. Among the fans, the conflict went from bad to worse. Someone set fire to the stands, and the entire ballpark burned to the ground. Not only that, but the fire spread to 107 other Boston buildings as well.

—*Our Daily Bread*, August 13, 1992

Oh, what a perfect world we would live in if only everyone would act and behave the way we wanted them to. But fortunately, or unfortunately, that world does not exist; therefore, we must be mindful of how we come across when confronted by others. If there is one thing I have learned in recovery, it is I never want to do or say anything that would cause harm to others. You never know what they may be going through at the time, and your words can be the final straw that breaks them and sends them over the edge.

I want to share with you a couple of sayings that help me to stay grounded and humble, which in turn keeps my tongue in check:

1. Whatever another person thinks or feels about me is none of my business.
2. If people think ill of you, don't be angry with them, for you are genuinely far worse than they think you are.

Today's verse is a remedy and extinguisher of all conflicts you may face. There will always be a part of you that feels justified by lashing out and using harsh words when you think or feel you have been wronged by someone else. Trust me when I tell you, you will never find true serenity and peace in your life until you can meet hatred with kindness. Plain and simple, it's about doing the opposite of what you have been accustomed to doing, which is tearing someone apart with your words the first moment someone looks at you wrong.

In the opening paragraph, I can imagine that what started the chaos on the baseball field was the exchanging of a few demeaning words. Those words led to a confrontation, and the confrontation led to so many others being hurt. Think back and remember when you were at your lowest and worst; somebody met you with loving and open arms and a desire to lift you up rather than tear you down. That's what Kingdom living in recovery is all about.

Prayer for the day: Heavenly Father, I pray today I may meet my adversaries with a loving heart and kind words. Today, I choose to remember when our Savior Jesus Christ was met with hatred, He used words of love and kindness to say what needed to be said. I pray I may be a living example of how to react in a Christlike manner. Amen.

◆

# Day 67: Ready, Set, Redeemed

> Then Abraham bowed down to the ground, but he laughed to
> himself in disbelief. "How could I become a father at the age of
> 100?" he thought. "And how can Sarah have a baby when she
> is ninety years old?"
>
> —Genesis 17:17

Experiencing a life-changing faith, having a close relationship with God, and desiring to please God above all else are strong earmarks of belief for born-again Christians, according to a recent poll comparing America's religious attitudes. A lot of us genuinely believe God is solely responsible for getting us to where we are but lack faith and assurance He will carry us to the next step.

It is apparent in the lives of most everyone, not just people in recovery, that people's assurance and confidence in the success of their future comes from how assured they are of themselves and their abilities. In other words, if people have been living lives that are not designed to prepare for the future, they are apt to feel their future will be in shambles. Your thoughts may sound something like this: *I will never be able to have a fulfilling future because of my actions in the past.* In other words, you believe your past dictates what lies ahead in your future.

In today's verse, Abraham is an example of how God fulfills His promises in His time. God has promised all who believe and trust in Him shall have the desires of their heart (Psalm 37:4). Abraham was unsure how he could be the father of many nations without having a son to fulfill the promise and, better yet, at the age of a hundred and his wife at ninety. To make a long story short, God demonstrates He can do anything in your life when you choose to follow Him, regardless of your age and regardless of what you have done in the past. The problem arises when we want to step in and give God assistance to ensure the desires of our heart come to fruition. Remember what Sarah did to ensure Abraham would have a child? She intervened and allowed Abraham to sleep with her maidservant because they were both so sure God's plan was not going to work. Do you continue to try to intervene and assist God in His work?

God desires to give you complete redemption, but that requires your willingness to be redeemed entirely, and to do that, you must completely surrender your entire life. You must let God work in His time and be willing to accept, like Abraham and Sarah should have done, that when the time is right, and you are ready, you will see God's complete glorious plan in your life. First, make your desires known to God, and pray that His will be done. Secondly, patiently wait and do not attach any strings or ultimatums to God's plan. Some of God's most magnificent plans in our lives have been shattered when we chose to interrupt what He had begun.

Prayer for the day: Heavenly Father, my goal today, as I make You aware of the desires of my heart, is to allow You to bring Your plan to fulfillment. Today, I realize to do that, I must step aside and be sure You're hard at work in my life. May I never let my past problems such as financial, legal, or spiritual issues, stand in the way of my assurance that You can overcome my past to give me a prosperous future. Thank You, Lord, for giving me the confidence I am wholly redeemed and You are giving me back those things I have lost. Amen.

◆

# Day 68: The World in His Hands

What, then, shall we say in response to these things? If God is
for us, who can be against us?

—Romans 8:31 (NIV)

Fans of the American Wild West will find in a Deadwood, South Dakota, museum
this inscription left by a beleaguered prospector: "I lost my gun. I lost my horse.
I am out of food. The Indians are after me. But I've got all the gold I can carry!"
This type of scenario will make a person wonder, "What does he truly have?"

If there's one thing I know, it's that after being clean and sober as long as I
have, nothing came quickly, nor did it come easily. Early on in recovery, I used
to believe people should be forgiving and understanding; they should dismiss my
past actions and behaviors. Don't they know I am sober now and changing my life?
Don't they know I am sincere? What right do they have to judge me?

So many times, we lose sight of the fact that if we had honestly gotten what
we deserved in life, we would be locked up behind bars forever. With that being
said, I began to realize Somebody did forget about my past behaviors; Somebody
was looking after me the whole time: God. I thank the Lord I never got what I
truly deserved, but that is not to say I am not still eligible for a life of misery if I
continue down that path I had been on before. For all of us, misery lies just around
the corner and is completely refundable.

In today's verse, Paul is telling the Romans that regardless of what you're faced
with or how much adversity awaits you, you are not defeated, nor should you ever
give up. The problem we have is a lack of assurance that God is in control of our
lives. On Day 68 in recovery, we begin to feel as if things are not happening quickly
enough in our lives; we are not progressing forward as quickly as we would like. If
we succumb to this trap long enough, we will lose the one tool that is imperative
to have to stay spiritually fit in recovery: our gratitude. Without gratitude, we are
unable to see how far we have come from Day 1 and indulge in a pity party that
can lead us right back to a life of misery. Rest assured, you will probably always be
faced with obstacles brought on by others, but rest assured, God is in your corner
and is fighting for you. Sometimes, all God wants to do, before He reveals His
next blessing for you, is to see how you will respond to your current situation by
staying focused and, most importantly, by proving you trust Him.

Prayer for the day: Heavenly Father, not a day goes by where I am not faced with an obstacle that seems to stand in the way of my current plans for my life. I am overwhelmed and so many times very lonely and confused. I fall short of the assurance You are looking after each and one of my needs. Thank You, Lord, for the life I currently have and the life You have planned for me. With You in my corner, nothing can stand in my way. Amen.

◆

# Day 69: You Can't Fake It

> But he said to me, "My grace is sufficient for you, for my power is made perfect in weakness." Therefore I will boast all the more gladly about my weaknesses, so that Christ's power may rest on me.
>
> —2 Corinthians 12:9 (NIV)

People often get entangled with the question, "Who am I in Christ?" We often see our shortcomings and then question whether we are on the right path or not, or if we are, indeed, disciples. For instance, you can sleep around and still be a great architect. You can tell a white lie and get whatever you want. You can cheat on your spouse and still manage a successful restaurant. You can alter your testimony when talking with others to not feel humiliated about yourself, and still keep your sobriety. But you cannot do these things and truthfully tell others you are a true believer and follower of Christ. You must begin to come to grips with who you are in recovery. Your relationship with Christ demands there be no deviation from Kingdom living behavior.

On Day 69, it is way too early to determine what you will be successful doing. Our grandiose ideas stand in the way of reality and convince us we should achieve success no matter how morally corrupt or dishonest it may cause us to be. In other words, we need to be okay with who we are in Christ and ourselves and not who we are in the eyes of others.

In today's verse, Paul makes it clear to the church of Corinth that if they focus on their weaknesses and shortcomings, and correct those defects, there is a higher chance for God to prevail and amplify their gifts and talents. All too often, we are caught up and concerned with how everyone else views us. We don't want to be known as the recovering addict or the morally challenged. We want all our past wiped away and for others to view us with our fictional vision of ourselves. When we do that, we are willing to act, speak, and behave in a manner that renders us foul as disciples.

Be willing today to accept who you are in Christ and know God can use the shortcomings in your life to help others, which in turn gives you purpose and a mission. Only God can take the devastation and destruction of active addiction and turn it around and use it for good. The moment you decide to focus on your shortcomings, which are real and evident, rather than how you want others to see you, which is fake and devious, you will begin to see the glory of God working in your life. Don't surrender your godly morals and behaviors to pacify your lack of confidence of who you are. Confidence and assurance of who we are begins with our shortcomings.

Prayer for the day: Heavenly Father, the real character of who I am comes from how You see me and not how I want to be seen by others. Please help me today to focus on those things that would separate me from You. Wanting to be celebrated in the eyes of others has kept me from being worthy in Your eyes. May I focus and boast gladly today on my weaknesses so You may be glorified in my life. I genuinely believe Your powers are made perfect in my infirmities, and through my shortcomings, I remain a true disciple. Amen.

◆

# Day 70: Confess What?

> Therefore confess your sins to each other and pray for each other so that you may be healed. The prayer of a righteous person is powerful and effective.
>
> —James 5:16 (NIV)

Have you ever asked someone their true feelings about you and had them grade you on the way you respond to others? Sometimes, looking at yourself in the mirror and self-evaluating who you are is not enough. We need the honest opinions of others to be sure we are who we think we are or who we should be. Is the unbiased view of others significant to you, and do you display integrity when expressing your opinion of others to them?

There is one thing we all need, but we all try to avoid, and that is constructive criticism. Constructive criticism shows consideration for other people's feelings and invites their suggestions and cooperation. Why would you want to start any conversation without knowing how to criticize something constructively? If this is something you're not gifted at doing, then the wisest course is to keep your opinions quiet. Criticism that starts by attacking people and making them defensive often turns small problems into big ones and is usually done so these critics can feel good about themselves. Typically, the best way to start is with simple, friendly questions and queries that give people a chance to explain their position without being offended and without shutting down.

In today's verse, the apostle James is declaring the importance of confessing our shortcomings to one another. It can render us healed when done lovingly but can tear us down when done with aggression and judgment. Holding each other accountable is more about being a good listener. So often, when we begin to declare our problems openly to each other, we can see the answers right before our eyes, and our opinions are not always necessary. Constructive criticism allows an atmosphere that is conducive to recovery and healing, holding each other accountable in a loving Christ-like manner.

Prayer for the day: Heavenly Father, today, I pray I allow myself to be held accountable by others. I pray I use the opinions of others as a tool to become a better person and not to be offended so easily. I also pray I approach others in the same loving manner so we all may be true disciples for You. Amen.

# Day 71: Common Cure

I have told you these things, so that in me you may have peace.
In this world you will have trouble. But take heart! I have
overcome the world.

—John 16:33

Either you deal with what is the reality, or you can be sure that
the reality is going to deal with you.

—Alex Haley

I have come to believe those who are early in recovery for the first time deserve the stone-cold truth and the reality of their current dilemma. The truth is, not everyone who seeks this new way of life will recover. Relapse is a reality that is often ignored, and a lot of people tell themselves, "This will not happen to me. I am stronger this time; my situation is different from yours." Everyone wants to focus on the cure and ignore the cause, and the statistical fact is, if we are not consciously aware of what got us here, then we are destined to repeat.

Today's verse reminds you where you came from and gives you the blessed assurance there is hope for change. We need to accept the fact that mental and physical cravings are a reality we need not run from, but face them head-on with the assurance that Jesus has overcome greater things so you may find peace in Him. You either deal with the reality of who you are and what you need to become in Christ, or let your past deal you the cruel hand it always gives you. It's like being told you have cancer and refusing to deal with it and hoping it goes away.

We have been told as individuals in recovery there is no cure for our disease, but this is not true. Our remedy is in Christ when we remain assured of who we are and that through Him anything is possible, including never-ending sobriety.

Prayer for the day: Heavenly Father, today I realize who I am and take comfort in knowing You have the best planned for me. May I never forget the hell that brought me here and that if my heart and mind are not focused on You, my hell will become my reality once again. I commit myself completely to You and pray that my past remains my past. Amen.

# Day 72: Love Me Not

But I tell you, love your enemies and pray for those who persecute you.

—Matthew 5:44 (NIV)

God is more concerned about our character than our comfort. His goal is not to pamper us physically but to perfect us spiritually.

—Paul W. Powell

If there is one thing I love about recovery more than anything else, it's that it asks us to act the exact opposite of what we are comfortable doing. Our whole life and character have been designed to take care of, and love, one person and one person only: ourselves.

At this phase of our recovery, there probably has been a time or two where you have encountered people with a set of problems and circumstances you don't recognize, nor do you know how to handle. They lash out at you and treat you with disdain and persecute you for no reason. I am here to tell you that believe it or not, the majority of people in this world have problems in their lives, which has nothing to do with addiction, either past or present. Not everybody has the excuse of past active addiction to justify their behavior.

We come to recovery to put down past behaviors and to begin to learn how to function and socialize with those around us in a productive manner. But guess what? Just because we are behaving differently doesn't mean everyone else is doing the same.

So what do you do when the average Joe belittles you or tears you down? You love them. When your employer skips over you for that promotion, you love them. When you are falsely accused, and you know you are innocent, you love them. When your family is not ready to take you back, you love them. When someone consistently stands in your way and keeps you from moving forward, you love them.

Most importantly, always remember the one person you should love most is yourself. It is vital to show others the same love you want to be confirmed, but to do that, we must value who we are. Remember, those who persecute you need the one thing you cherish the most: God's love. Show those who torment you that God's love is the only answer.

Prayer for the day: Heavenly Father, I am constantly bombarded with people and circumstances that are overwhelming and leave me wanting to lash out in anger. I pray today I may have the strength to recognize situations that can tear me apart from You. May I be more apt to listen rather than speak, love rather than hate, pray for others rather than judge them. May my actions today be a shining example of the love You have shown to me. Amen.

◆

# Day 73: Have Fun

I can do all things through Christ who gives me strength.
—Philippians 4:13 (NIV)

General Mark Clark was one of the great heroes of World War II. He led the Salerno invasion that Winston Churchill said was "the most daring amphibious operation we have launched, or which, I think, has ever been launched on a similar scale in war." When Clark was promoted to lieutenant general, he was the youngest man of that rank in the US Army. He graduated from West Point in 1917. At the top of his class? Nope. He was 111th from the head in a class of 139.

If there is one point I try to tell everyone and try to remember for myself, it's that God can use you regardless of your limitations or your talents or lack thereof. The Bible is filled with stories where God has chosen less-than-perfect people to achieve great success. Just look at King David and Saul of Tarsus.

I say that to say this: Without a doubt, you are going to sell yourself short due to a lack of confidence in who you are and who you are becoming. You are going to limit your job search to places of employment you are familiar with. When you evaluate yourself, you will base your future efforts by remembering nothing more than your past achievements. Stop selling yourself short, but most of all, on Day 73, I want you to begin to have fun.

Recovery is meant to be enjoyable and to experience new avenues and new talents we never knew we had. To do this, we must get out into public, make new friends, and experience new hobbies. God cannot work in our life if we're stuck in a room, hiding away from everything life has to offer us. The way the Holy Spirit intercedes in our life is when we become present in our communities and introduce ourselves to new people, and it never fails that God will use someone else to make an impactful statement in our life.

If there's one thing I've learned about our Lord and Savior, it's that He loves to show off His abilities by transforming those things we have determined were completely lost into success. In today's verse, God has declared there is nothing you can't do or accomplish if you remain in Him. Just remember, your past behaviors are not keeping you from doing great things; only you are. Go with God, and be all He wants you to be. There is a whole new life waiting for you.

Prayer for the day: Heavenly Father, today, I choose to see myself not through my eyes but through Yours. I pray You intercede in my life so I can see who You want me to become. I pray I continue to make myself present and accountable in society so You may use me in a new and purposeful way. Show me my new talents, Lord, and I promise to use them for Your glory. Amen.

---

# Day 74: Cross Control

Then Jesus said to his disciples, "Whoever wants to be my disciple must deny themselves and take up their cross and follow me."
—Matthew 16:24 (NIV)

To choose to suffer means that there is something wrong; to choose God's will even if it means suffering, is a very different thing. No healthy saint ever chooses to suffer; he chooses God's will, as Jesus did, whether it means suffering or not.
—Oswald Chambers

Self-denial can either be an easy or difficult concept to grasp. Take this devotional you are reading, for instance. You had to make a conscious choice and intentionally read today's message or, you could have done something else that seemed more pleasing to you at the moment. In the beginning, self-denial is an easy concept because all we want to do is put down and deny ourselves of the evil substance that brought us here. But on Day 74, are we allowing ourselves to be tempted with little intricate pleasures that in time will grow into uncontrollable urges that we can't say no to?

In recovery, we should all have a memory verse in the Bible. Today's verse is one of the best memory verses of them all. The disciple Matthew is instructing us to practice self-control and self-denial by taking up our crosses and carrying them. This means that we do the right thing even when it makes us uncomfortable, and it is something that seems hard to bear. We have never been very good at telling ourselves no. We have always allowed ourselves to experience anything that will change the way we currently feel and gives us a false assurance of hope. God is demanding that we say no to these false pleasures and rely on Him to fill us with the confidence that only He can give us.

Today, I want to give you a sense of hope and to ask you to rest on the assurance that God has prepared the ultimate plan for your life. If you're thinking about cutting back on your support group meetings, don't. If you're uncertain and juggling with the idea of jumping into a relationship right now, don't. If you feel that this new way of life is too tough and you're ready to run, don't.

I have exciting news for you, and I want you to hold on and never leave this journey. I promise you there is a cure for addiction, but I will not reveal what I have found and experienced until later on. On Day 74, you deserve to know God has given us a cure, and before we get to Day 180, I will share it with you. I may share it with you tomorrow on Day 75, or I may wait until Day 179. Whatever day I choose to share it with you, keep denying yourself those things that would separate you from God and be ready to receive His gift. Practice a little "cross control" today.

Prayer for the day: Heavenly Father, there are times in recovery when my cross seems too heavy to bear, and I want to lay it down. Lord, help me to remember it is the struggles that make me stronger and not my comforts. Help me to deny myself those things I deem important and realize with You, I can face my troubles head on. Today, I choose to be a disciple. Grant me the fortitude and strength to carry my cross throughout this whole journey. Amen.

◆

# Day 75: Great Gifts

Every good and perfect gift is from above, coming down from the Father of the heavenly lights, who does not change like shifting shadows.

—James 1:17 (NIV)

But Jesus did not run from rejection. He knew God always has a purpose for the pain, and He willingly embraced it.

—Tony Evans

The most beautiful thing about the book of James is that it is short, sweet, and to the point, and it emphasizes the importance of one thing and one thing only: faith. When you look at today's verse, you may automatically think "good and perfect gifts" are all those things in our life that bring us joy and self-fulfillment. But can good and perfect, pleasing gifts strengthen our faith? The answer is no. Good and perfect gifts are those events in your life that are confusing and uncomfortable, and force you to rely on God for the answers. The greatest gift you can receive is a closer relationship with God. How can your faith strengthen if everything is always going your way?

Some of the best gifts I have received are the gifts of a life learning experience that was not always pleasant. Recovery is the same way. If recovery was a natural path with no bumps or bruises, then it is safe to say everybody would be doing it successfully. It's when we deliberately face our difficulties head-on and have faith in God's outcome that we grow exponentially and assuredly.

Today is an excellent day to reevaluate our definition of a "good and perfect gift." May we look at the difficulties life gives us as a perfect gift of assurance that will strengthen our faith and force us to rely even more on our heavenly Father. Have faith that God does not waver or change His perfect plan for you, regardless of what life throws your way.

The cure for addiction is still on the way.

Prayer for the day: Heavenly Father, today, I pray for wisdom to recognize the true gifts in my life. Help me to recognize my discomforts have the ability to bring me closer to you. Grant me the wisdom and strength to never look for an easy way out when life throws me a curve ball and to find comfort in uncomfortable situations. Amen.

◆

# Day 76: A Little Knowledge
## Is a Dangerous Thing
### ♦♦♦

If any of you lacks wisdom, you should ask God, who gives generously to all without finding fault, and it will be given to you. But when you ask, you must believe and not doubt, because the one who doubts is like a wave of the sea, blown and tossed by the wind.

—James 1:5–6 (NIV)

In a recent chapel on campus, Chuck Swindoll listed the following six reasons why it is essential to pursue knowledge of the Scriptures: 1. Knowledge gives substance to faith. 2. Knowledge stabilizes us during times of testing. 3. Knowledge enables us to handle the Word of God accurately. 4. Knowledge equips us to detect and confront error. 5. Knowledge makes us confident and consistent in our walk with God. 6. Knowledge filters out our fears and superstitions.

—*Kindred Spirit*, Vol. 22, No. 1, Spring 1998, 8

When I was young, a good friend of mine gave me the most magnificent piece of advice I ever received. You see, I had a habit of thinking I knew everything, and therefore, I refused outside information and instructions. Someone would say, "Let me show you how it's done," and I would respond, "I already know how to do it." On one occasion, I made the statement, "I know what I'm doing," to a good friend, who was sure I was going to fail at what I was about to attempt, and when I did fail, he said, "Wayne, a little knowledge is a dangerous thing."

The six points of knowledge Chuck Swindoll made in the above statement do not say we are born with vast knowledge and need to apply it. It's quite the opposite; we gain knowledge because we first seek it. If you lack the expertise and know-how to do something, you must first ask and seek after it. The same is true with today's verse as it pertains to wisdom. James is telling us the greatest wisdom one can obtain is the wisdom given to us by God.

You will inevitably find assurance in your internal instincts, but the point that needs to be made is, they are not always correct and, in fact, can lead to self-destruction. People who have the wisdom to seek God's knowledge will have a life that will grant them fulfillment and accomplishment. If you are under the impression you know everything and the assistance of others is not needed, then I challenge you to stop and ask yourself, "Isn't my best way of thinking and knowledge responsible for where I am today?"

On Day 76, the smartest thing we all can do is to humbly kneel down and ask for God's wisdom to take us to the next phase of our life. Remaining teachable is the one correct way of gaining knowledge and God's wisdom. Now that you have read this, do you now understand how a little knowledge is a dangerous thing? The moment you think you have all the answers is the moment you need to stop and ask for help. And oh, yeah, the cure for addiction is still coming.

Prayer for the day: Heavenly Father, today, I realize the greatest wisdom and knowledge comes when I patiently wait on You. Help me to seek Your guidance, Lord, and disengage my old way of thinking so I remain teachable. May I remain firmly grounded in Your guidance so I may attain all those things You want me to have. Thank You for what You are about to show me and for the wisdom I will gain. Amen.

---

# Day 77: Desires Aside, Please

Those who belong to Christ Jesus have crucified the flesh with its passions and desires.

—Galatians 5:24 (NIV)

Compassion can't be measured in dollars and cents. It does come with a price tag, but that price tag isn't the amount of money spent. The price tag is love.

—J. C. Watts Jr.

There is an old saying about why bank robbers do not put their stolen money in the bank. It's because they have a fear of their bank being robbed. They are always suspicious of others and can never be at peace with themselves. They cannot trust others because they know they cannot be trusted.

The same is true with the desires of the flesh. The most challenging thing to do is to evaluate what our motives are when we are seeking companionship. When you are engaging a person in a conversation, is your mind focused on how you can assist them and show them compassion, or is your mind undressing them and concentrating on how they can fulfill your needs? In other words, are you still trying to use and manipulate people to satisfy your desires?

On Day 77, there's a good chance our minds are running amok with thoughts of physical satisfaction and gratification. Let me challenge you today to focus on the consequences of those actions and the long-term effect, versus the short-term gratification. Just because we are not meddling in our active addiction doesn't mean we do not have the ability to practice selfish, self-centered behavior. It is our self-centeredness and the desire to take care of our own needs first that makes us unable to be of service to others.

Paul's message in today's verse is informing the Galatians if they are genuinely following Christ, they will have to bridle their lust of the flesh and inner desires. The marvelous thing about this type of practice is that saying no becomes easier and easier, and saying yes to showing Christlike compassion toward others seems to drown out our selfish wants and needs. The most important thing to remember about love is, first and foremost, you must be lovable. Once we begin to mimic Christlike love and behavior, we obtain an attraction others seek to follow.

Prayer for the day: Heavenly Father, the greatest love I can mimic and give to others is the love You continue to show me. To put the desires and needs of others first and separate myself from my selfish wants is the greatest love I can display today. Give me the strength to put my desires of the flesh aside and realize in time, even those desires can be expressed in a way that is pleasing to You. May I love with no strings attached. Amen.

◆

# Day 78: Have a Heart

For it is with your heart that you believe and are justified, and
it is with your mouth that you profess your faith and are saved.
—Romans 10:10 (NIV)

Who are you? Where are you, what are you doing, where are you going, and why
are you doing it? Who are you talking to, what are you telling them, why are
you saying what you are saying? What do you believe in? What is your purpose?
What is your mission? What are you trying to succeed at? If you want to be able
to evaluate the desires of your heart and measure your intentions and future plans,
then all you have to do is ask yourselves the above questions.

Everything comes from the heart: how you feel about others, whether you like
yourself, where your confidence lies, and if you genuinely believe you can succeed.
Your heart tells others if you know how to love and can be loved. Your heart reveals
the path you are on and if you're capable of being trusted. But most importantly,
your heart reveals whether Christ is present within you or not.

To continue on this journey of recovery, we need to make a pitstop and ask
ourselves, "Where is our heart leading us?" There's a good chance it is leading you
right back to the devastation and destruction from whence you came, and you were
not even aware of it. Or it may be in tune with the plans God has for you, and you
may be right on track. Whatever the case may be, you need to have certainty in
your life that the desires of your heart are strengthening or destroying your faith
as well as your future.

In today's verse, Paul is telling the Romans there is a good possibility whatever
is coming out of their mouth was influenced by the desires of the heart. Are you
lifting people up and declaring positive and spiritual feedback, or are you overly
judgmental and tearing people down? Are you associating with specific individuals
only because you have ulterior motives and selfish wants? Think about the words
Christ spoke whenever He was approached by others. His statements and answers
99 percent of the time were in parables and uplifting. His words gave a direct
insight into what was in His heart. Ask yourselves today, "What is my heart
made of?"

Prayer for the day: Heavenly Father, my heart is heavy with uncertainty, first and foremost, uncertain of what I want or who I truly am. I pray today for a cleansing of my heart that I may be filled with Your spirit and be a living example to others, an example of a heart filled with sincerity, compassion, love, and adoration. Amen.

◆

# Day 79: 1 + 1 = 2

◆ ◆ ◆

> Two are better than one, because they have a good return for
> their labor: If either of them falls down, one can help the other
> up. But pity anyone who falls and has no one to help them up.
> —Ecclesiastes 4:9–10 (NIV)

Do you ever watch a movie on television and envision yourself having a similar lifestyle, to have a perfectly chiseled body, great athletic ability, unwavering fearlessness, and always with a happy ending? Sometimes, it's fun to envision ourselves being perfect.

Although the above statement is not a declaration of what we are currently trying to live up to, it is a scenario we often take part in. For example, there may be a tendency for you to admire the accomplishments of others around you while trying to imitate their actions. Has anyone ever accused you of trying to act like someone else? Has anyone ever told you to be yourself? You are so in awe of the success and accomplishments of others, you feel less than adequate at what you're trying to do. You will never be able to appreciate the movie God is producing in your life if you are so busy concentrating on everyone else's highlight reels. So first and foremost, be yourself.

With that being said, do not do it by yourself. It is imperative on Day 79 to begin to appreciate the talents and gifts God has given you and to surround yourself with people who can strengthen those gifts, to find those individuals with like-minded goals and desires. People who have strength and hope can expound on your talents and your talents alone. These people will be there for you during your most significant achievements as well as your inevitable mistakes.

You will never find in the annals of recovery a document that states, "One must take this journey alone." In today's verse, Solomon shows us the value of human relationships, especially when both parties are like-minded and evenly yoked. There is a greater value and return on your efforts when you intentionally join forces with those who are after the same goals and desires. Don't sit back and admire the accomplishments of others who are achieving the things you want. Humble yourself and ask them how they got there, and then pray God will start creating some highlight reels in your life. Continue to stay partnered up with Christ, and remember the importance of partnering with others; 2 is always better than 1.

Prayer for the day: Heavenly Father, help me today, Lord, to appreciate who I am in the movie You are producing in my life. Help me to realize I am surrounded by those who genuinely want to support me and help me to achieve greater things and to be successful. Help me also to be an individual who is willing to recognize the skills I have been given in order to be of service to others. Help me to remain a friend. Amen.

◆

# Day 80: You Are What You Speak

It's not what goes into your mouth that defiles you; you are
defiled by the words that come out of your mouth.

—Matthew 15:11

There's an old saying that goes like this: "It's better for someone to think you're
ignorant than to open your mouth and prove them correct."

I am still amazed to this day how my visual mind convinces me how
superior some people are based on their appearance. For example, if I see
a gentleman walking downtown with a fresh haircut and a new suit, I
automatically assume he is a standout citizen and an admirable individual,
one I'd like to associate with. That's until I discover he's on the way to court
facing embezzlement and physical assault charges. Funny how appearances are
so impactful yet so deceiving.

It goes without saying it is crucial we take care of our bodies and are in
tune with what activities we are partaking in. Our objective and goals are to
be able to strengthen our physical self and to feel good about our new way of
life. But don't let the obsession for physical fitness override the necessity for
our spiritual fitness.

In today's verse, Matthew's statement cannot be misconstrued for anything
else other than you will be judged by what you say and how you act, and not
by how you look or appear. The wisest men and women I know, the people I
look up to the most, are not six foot six with a chiseled body like an Adonis
and wear name brand clothes. They are the ones who speak the truth as wise
counsel and are more concerned about my well-being and growth than I am.
They do not appear to be healthy because of the physical presence but prove
they are healthy by their words and actions. Be mindful today of what you
value the most. A rose is only beautiful for a moment, but the memory of its
beauty and sweet smell lasts a lifetime. Let the impact of what you say and do
make a positive impact on all those around you. That's the most magnificent
appearance of them all, and oh, yeah, hang on, the cure for addiction is still
on the way.

Prayer for the day: Heavenly Father, I pray today if I must obsess over something, let me obsessively speak and behave in a way that is pleasing to You, oh, Lord. Let me be mindful of my words and how I am impacting others. May I feel as good about my inner self as I do about my new outer self, and may they both line up with Your will and what You would have me do. Help me to be uplifting to all I come into contact with today. Amen.

◆

# Day 81: Why Worry?

For the entire law is fulfilled in keeping this one command:
"Love your neighbor as yourself."

—Galatians 5:14 (NIV)

An average person's anxiety is focused on 40% things that will
never happen, 30% things about the past that can't be changed,
12% things about criticism by others that are mostly untrue,
10% about health which gets worse with stress, 8% about real
problems that will be faced.

—Source Unknown

If you are anything like me, you tend to be overly concerned about a lot of different
scenarios that are unimportant in the scheme of things. I once asked a friend what
fictional character would describe me perfectly. He said, "The rabbit in *Alice in
Wonderland*." The rabbit worried about everything. Worried about people, about
the weather, about whether or not he was late, about the thoughts of others as it
pertained to him, always thinking of ways to make the world a better place. The
rabbit and I have wasted a lot of time with all these unnecessary concerns.

There is a chance you are looking for a way to stop the roller coaster of
thoughts and emotions that are going through your mind and leaving you tired,
tired of realizing all your concerns and efforts are being misguided because you
can't pinpoint what is most significant for the here and now. For the majority of
us, we are overly concerned if our thoughts, words, and actions are in tune with
what Christ would have us to do. This way of thinking and living is so stressful
and tiring.

In today's verse, Paul has given us the answer concerning assuring ourselves
we are currently in tune with how our Lord and Savior wants us to behave and
where we should focus our concerns. It's so simple, it's so glorious, and it eliminates
all our stress and anxieties and worries. Simply stated, Jesus wants us to focus our
attention and love on others and less on ourselves. If we remembered the needs of
others and their struggles, we would be less worried about our own wants and needs
and fears. Demonstrating this type of behavior shows God you are content and
assured of who you are in Him, which in turn allows the blessings He has for you
to come to fruition. With this type of assurance in Christ, you truly have nothing

to worry about. Oh yeah, don't worry; no pun intended: The cure for addiction is still coming. Tell a friend.

Prayer for the day: Heavenly Father, I surrender all my thoughts and worries to You, oh, Lord. I'm tired of being concerned about how others view me or what they think of me. Today, I want the assurance You are happy with me and I am doing things that are pleasing to You, Lord. Today, I take comfort in knowing by helping others, You are pleased and all my situations are in Your hands. May I focus my actions and thoughts on others to allow You to work assuredly in my life. Amen.

◆

# Day 82: Too Many Limbs

He cuts off every branch in me that bears no fruit, while every branch that does bear fruit he prunes so that it will be even more fruitful.

—John 15:2 (NIV)

Success is a lousy teacher. It seduces smart people into thinking they can't lose. And it's an unreliable guide to the future. What seems the perfect business plan or latest technology today may soon be as out-of-date as the eight-track tape player, the vacuum-tube television or the mainframe computer.

—Bill Gates

If you are like me, there's nothing more disturbing or disheartening as when I spend hundreds of dollars on the latest smartphone, and it becomes obsolete in a matter of a year. You want to hold on to your old phone as long as you can and continue using it, but all of a sudden, the new phones have features your old phone doesn't, and you can't access the latest apps. It's like having a fifty-dollar flip phone and thinking it will be enough to keep you in touch with the rest of the world.

The same is true with people in recovery. We can remember the gifts and talents we had before and what worked and didn't work back then. But now that we are on this new journey of life, we are well aware the talents we possessed ten years ago are not sufficient. All of us have said at one point we need to go back to school and brush up on our skills. It's out with our old talents and in with the new. The same is true on our spiritual journey.

In today's verse, the apostle John is making clear that God is busy enhancing those gifts you already possess. Our Lord and Savior is pruning and conditioning us so our talents may be beneficial rather than pointless. The only way to ensure our talents are beneficial and useful to others is to allow God to continue to prune and strengthen those things He determines to be useful. He is the vinekeeper, and we are the vines.

Prayer for the day: Heavenly Father, today I give You all of me in order that I may be pruned, shaped, and strengthened into a fruitful child. Lord, continue to make me aware of those things in my life that need strengthening. Help me to eliminate those branches that no longer bear the fruits of Your spirit. Amen.

◆

# Day 83: Little Light of Mine

In the same way, let your good deeds shine out for all to see, so
that everyone will praise your heavenly Father.
> —Matthew 5:16 (NIV)

Be not angry that you cannot make others as you wish them to
be since you cannot make yourself as you wish to be.
> —Thomas à Kempis

Have you ever asked yourself what you would do if you won the lottery? Once
you began to ponder this idea, did you recognize that your first instinct was to
eliminate all your debt and problems before thinking about cruises, cars, and
houses? Did you sense the security that came with the assurance of what you think
money can do for your life?

There's a reason why they say, "Money is the root of all evil." First and
foremost, it eliminates the need to engage your talents and gifts God has given you
to succeed. The worst part is, it gives you the assurance you will shine brightly in
the eyes of others and gain their acceptance not because of who you are in Christ,
but because of the way money has determined your self-worth.

Jesus assured His disciples they would be able to change the lives of others by
the presence of the Holy Spirit in their lives, not by the presence of money in their
pockets. In today's verse, Matthew is telling us we may be letting our light shine
to glorify our good works and to glorify ourselves. Oh, aren't they wonderful? Oh,
did you see they gave that family a sum of money to eliminate their problems? Oh,
aren't they marvelous because of what they said and how they reacted? It is easy to
do beautiful and magnificent things when everyone is watching, but when no one
is watching, it is an entirely different story. Your motives change.

Everyone wants a pat on the back, but today's verse is telling us that everything
we say and do is to glorify and to shine upon our Lord and Savior. We need to find
assurance we can accomplish great things, not by the size of our bank accounts,
but by the strength God gives us to do His work. Great things happen when
we do things on behalf of our Lord. We see lives changed, spirits uplifted, and
impossible scenarios rectified. When people see your good deeds, do they see you
lifting yourself up and shining, or do they see the presence of God through the
gifts He has given you? Check your motives every day to ensure God's light is the
one that shines the brightest.

Prayer for the day: Heavenly Father, I pray today I resist the urge to use my gifts and talents to glorify myself. For as soon as I misuse those gifts You have given me, they will surely be taken away. May I remember the grace and love bestowed upon me to lift and position me where I am today. May I be mindful of displaying the same grace and love, through my gifts and talents, to others so Your name may be glorified. Today, I will do all things so others may see You, oh, Lord. Amen.

◆

# Day 84: Who's Watching Who?

Therefore, my dear friends, as you have always obeyed—not only in my presence, but now much more in my absence—continue to work out your salvation with fear and trembling.
—Philippians 2:12 (NIV)

1. How's your thought life?
2. How are you handling the balance between work and home?
3. Have you been in the Word over the last few days?
4. What has God been teaching you recently?
5. How are you doing in handling God's provision of time, talent, and money?
6. Are you being responsible for protecting your eyes, hands, feet, and mind with those other than your spouse?
7. Are you shooting straight in answering the above questions—or trying to blow smoke?

In 1990, a study conducted by the Roper Organization for High Adventure Ministries found the moral behavior of born-again Christians actually worsened after their conversions. Examined were incidences of illegal drug use, driving while intoxicated, and marital infidelity. The problem can be solved, says one researcher, with a new commitment to accountability and discipleship (*New Man*, November/December 1994, 13).

In six days, you will be recognized for achieving 90 days of continuous sobriety from your local support group, family, and friends. It is a way of proclaiming openly you have been acting and behaving in a way that is conducive to a healthy recovery. But have you?

The more and more sobriety time you get under your belt, the more you begin to notice you're being entrusted with a lot of responsibilities you didn't previously have, such as being accountable for appointments, geographical hangouts, associates, what you listen to, what you watch. All these little freedoms we are beginning to obtain need to be scrutinized for their positive or negative influences. If you're not trembling in fear because of these new responsibilities, you should be. Remember, the small things can induce relapse way before we get to the large ones.

Ask yourselves, are you following God's instruction to the fullest? How are you behaving behind closed doors? Are your thoughts uplifting and supportive, or degrading and destructive? A life of recovery from the past and for the present is a matter of checks and balances. Nobody is getting it right 100 percent of the time. It's not what you do in front of people that defines you; it's what you do behind closed doors that defines you. Remember to attack your salvation and commitments with the idea that today could be your very last day. Your recovery depends on it because you are one step closer to the cure for addiction.

Prayer for the day: Heavenly Father, I pray I never become too comfortable in my current conditions or where I am at in recovery. May I always remember the eyes of others may not always be upon me, but You see all my actions and behaviors. May I always keep a healthy fear of what is to come and how I may or may not react. I pray my actions in public as well as behind closed doors display true Kingdom living. Amen.

---

# Day 85: Action Steps

> Therefore everyone who hears these words of mine and puts them into practice is like a wise man who built his house on the rock.
>
> —Matthew 7:24 (NIV)

The doctor to the patient, "You are in terrible shape. You've got to do something about it. First, tell your wife to cook more nutritious meals. Stop working like a dog. Also, inform your wife you're going to make a budget, and she has to stick to it. And have her keep the kids off your back so you can relax. Unless there are some changes like that in your life, you'll probably be dead in a month."

"Doc," the patient said, "this would sound more official coming from you. Could you please call my wife and give her those instructions?"

When the fellow got home, his wife rushed to him. "I talked to your doctor," she wailed. "Poor man, you've only got thirty days to live."

By now some of you may be on or may have completed step 3. You have decided to turn your will and your life over to the care of God as you understand Him. You may even hold the third step prayer close to your heart: "God, I offer myself to Thee. To build with me and to do with me as Thou wilt. Relieve me of the bondage of self, that I may better do Thy will. Take away my difficulties, that victory over them may bear witness to those I would help of Thy Power, Thy Love, and Thy Way of Life."

These are some incredible and powerful words of truth. They go hand in hand with today's verse, which assures us if we are diligent in practicing these truths, our foundations for life will be formidable and strong.

It is only human to seek assurances for ourselves. We want to know with a definitive answer that what we are doing is positive and proactive in achieving the success we desire. But what is success? What is it you're really going after? Is it really God's will for you? Let me ask you this: Have you really turned your will and your way of life over to the care of God if you are always in battle with these questions? Maybe not.

The scriptures are what's known as the definitive truth. You can rest assured by following God's direction, you will achieve a level of success that is unfamiliar to you but is pleasing to your heavenly Father. You can rest assured God has your best interest at heart when you completely surrender your will and your way of life over to Him. But remember this: God can do nothing for those who are not willing to completely surrender. You can't yield 50 percent of your will and control the other 50 percent yourself. Your relationship with God is similar to recovery. You're either 100 percent in or 100 percent out. There's no in between. The cure for addiction cannot be achieved by those who will not wholly surrender their all. Those foundations crumbles quickly.

Prayer for the day: Heavenly Father, I have uttered the words and declared so many times I have surrendered my will over to You, but inside, I still have reservations. I pray today I may find the assurance when I surrender 100 percent of myself, You will rebuild 100 percent of me. May I obtain the confidence and assurance needed to trust and obey fully. I declare my assurance in knowing Your will is the best for me. From this declaration, I give You my all. Amen.

◆

# Day 86: A Little Discernment Goes a Long Way

Carry each other's burdens, and in this way, you will fulfill the law of Christ.

—Galatians 6:2 (NIV)

Everybody thinks of changing Humanity, and Nobody thinks of changing himself.

—Leo Tolstoy

Some of us have this uncontrollable urge to take what we've learned and our gifts, and be endowed to change the world. Let me be the first one to say there is not a more excellent demonstration of brotherly love than when we feel the urgency to help others, but we first must be discerning. Discernment is a gift that comes from life experiences. It knows helping sometimes ends up hurting, and it is not always our responsibility to carry someone else's baggage. The first thought that should be at the forefront of your mind before helping others is, *God, what would You have me do?*

First and foremost, you need to be grounded and assured you are following God's good orderly direction yourself. There is nothing more damaging than a hypocrite who is trying to help; ultimately, what ends up happening is the individual with the problem will bring you down before you can raise him up. The end result can be relapse.

Take today's verse, for example, and see how wise and discerning you are. By only reading verse 2, you are doing what's called proof-texting. You have taken one single verse and assured yourself of its meaning and application, and now you're ready to go out and save the world. But let's look at what came before verse 2 and after. Let's look at verses 1 and 3 to get the complete picture of what Paul is saying:

1. Brothers and sisters, if someone is caught in a sin, you who live by the Spirit should restore that person gently. But watch yourselves, or you also may be tempted. 2. Carry each other's burdens, and in this way, you will fulfill the law of Christ. 3. If anyone thinks they are something when they are not, they deceive themselves.

Today more than ever, it is imperative you discern if you are qualified to lift up your brothers. Satan wants nothing more than to confuse us with false assurances that stem from not evaluating our own personal attributes. The most significant help you can begin to give others is to be 100 percent certain you are obeying and following God's Word. Should we always have the desire to want to be there to offer help when needed? Of course. But remember, it is just as essential to be assured you have something to offer. Bury God's Word deeply within your heart, and He alone will qualify you to be of godly service to others.

Prayer for the day: Heavenly Father, thank You for giving me a heart of compassion and a willingness to be of help and of service. I pray today I accept all I am; all I can offer can only come from You. I pray for the gift of discernment to know when I am qualified to be of service to others. May I also continue to recognize when I myself am in need of help. Amen.

◆

# Day 87: Here, We Grow Again

The seed that fell on good soil represents those who truly hear and understand God's word and produce a harvest of thirty, sixty, or even a hundred times as much as had been planted!
—Matthew 13:23 (NIV)

A farmer hired a man to work for him. He told him his first task would be to paint the barn and said it should take him about three days to complete. But the hired man was finished in one day. The farmer set him to cutting wood, telling him it would require about four days. To the farmer's amazement, the man finished in a day and a half. The next task was to sort out a large pile of potatoes. He was to arrange them into three piles: seed potatoes, food for the hogs, and potatoes that were good enough to sell. The farmer said it was a small job and shouldn't take long at all. At the end of the day, the farmer came back and found the hired man had barely started.

"What's the matter here?" the farmer asked.

"I can work hard," the hired man explained, "but I can't make decisions."

—Source Unknown

A question we so often ask ourselves when self-evaluating is, "Why don't I feel like I am growing? I feel like I am giving my best, but I do not see the results." It's like being on a strenuous diet, and at the end of the week, you only lost 3 pounds when you expected to have lost 7. It leaves us asking ourselves, "What am I doing wrong? What is it I am missing? Can I ever get it right?"

Today's verse has an agricultural feel, as it pertains to seeds and how things should grow. But I think the point Matthew is trying to make is, for us to be a good cultivator of seeds, we must first have those seeds within us and understand how they grow. Through trial and error, the gift of experience allows us to see where our efforts can have the most significant impact. A lot of times, in recovery, we are being led and guided by others as to the decisions we need to make. We find comfort in allowing others to make all our decisions and choices for us, in order to have the most exceptional outcome. The problem with this is, we never fully grasp hold of our decision-making skills, which allows us to evaluate success and failure.

It's easy to ask someone where your efforts might produce the greatest results, but wouldn't you rather have the assurance that the decisions you made were giving you your greatest results?

By intentionally staying grounded in God's Word, you can be sure you'll never make mistakes with irreversible ramifications. God allows us to get tripped up to determine what works and what doesn't in a relationship with Him. Find out today what actions and behaviors produce the most significant fruit in your life as well as others. Plant your seeds on solid ground that is richly fertilized with God's spirit.

Prayer for the day: Heavenly Father, today, I recognize there are areas of my life where seeds cannot grow. Because of my inability to let go or surrender my control, things are not growing in my life as I feel You would have them to. I pray today for the assurance that regardless of my inability to see growth, You are continuing to change me for Your good each and every day. Today, I pray for fertile ground that is rich in Your Word. Amen.

---

◆

# Day 88: Language of Love

If I speak in the tongues of men or of angels, but do not have love, I am only a resounding gong or a clanging cymbal.

—1 Corinthians 13:1 (NIV)

Real generosity is not determined by the amount that we give but by our hearts. When Jesus saw the widow give two mites in the Temple, He responded, "Verily I say unto you, That this poor widow hath cast more in, than all they which have cast into the treasury" (Matthew 12:43). The sacrificial gift she gave demonstrated how much she loved God and His work. The best way to determine what we love most is not by our words but by how we use our time and our money.

—*Chicago Tribune,* June 13, 1995

Here's a disturbing statistic: Depression is substantially higher for those in a secular society. Suicide rates, anger, bitterness, and hopelessness are higher. All these are prevalent in a secular society, and because of this, there is also a disturbing fact. People living in a secular society are missing one ingredient that would overcome these problems: the love of God. When we take our life into our own hands, we tend to seek those things that soothe our egos, forcing us to strive to get ahead and ultimately causing us to lose hope. Once again, the critical ingredient that is missing is the love of God.

Let me give you an incredible statistic: If you made it clean and sober to Day 88, then you are the by-product of God's grace and are now able to appreciate the above statistics and what it takes to overcome them. You have a gift so many in society do not have. You're beginning to see how God is being able to use something as horrible as active addiction and allowing it to become a tool for a positive lifestyle. Only your heavenly Father has the power to reverse the devastating effect of addiction and turn it into something positive. You can see God's great hand in your life. You know what real depression and anger are all about and how, on this day, they are dissolved and diminished. God has taken this horrible thing Satan has placed on you and flipped it to work in His favor. And all this can be attributed to and recognized as love.

In today's verse, Paul is informing the church in Corinth that the love that is needed is not mere words, but an intentional act. Everything you know about

God is pointless if it is not expressed in the same type of love He has displayed for you. God has been so active in your life and making intentional changes for you. You have been given the tools needed to grab those who are coming into recovery for the first time and let them know the love of God. Tell them all the things the secular world has to offer are nothing compared to the love God is waiting to give them. You have enough of God's grace and glory within you today to be able to fulfill what 1 Corinthians 13:1 is trying to tell you. Don't just know God's Word; live God's Word. Oh yeah, hang in there; the cure for addiction is still coming.

Prayer for the day: Heavenly Father, thank You, Lord, for the wonderful insight as to how You are so active in my life. Thank You for allowing me to appreciate that this world has so little to offer me, and You have so much. I pray I know what it truly means to love someone else, to recognize the greatest love I can give is when I apply Your words in my life, to be of service for others. I can memorize the Bible from Genesis to Revelation, but if I do not demonstrate to others the love You demonstrated to me, it is all for nothing. Amen.

◆

# Day 89: Please Stay

As Paul talked about righteousness, self-control and the judgment to come, Felix was afraid and said, "That's enough for now! You may leave. When I find it convenient, I will send for you."

—Acts 24:25 (NIV)

There has never been, and cannot be, a good life without self-control.

—John Milton

People are curious when they first come into recovery. Some people are desperate to understand it and will grab hold of anything and everything, while others will take a little longer to convince. Don't be discouraged. There is a tendency for those of us with a little clean time under our belt to be offended if somebody doesn't act quickly upon the advice we give. Just think for a moment how many times you disregarded good, sound advice others had given you. Get the picture?

Many people coming into recovery will respond to the Gospel in the same way Felix did, by delaying their decision to commit to Jesus Christ. What's important to remember is that it is not okay to delay, because to delay accepting Jesus is to deliberately reject Him. The Bible tells us to come to Jesus in repentance and faith today: "Behold, now is the accepted time; behold, now is the day of salvation" (2 Corinthians 6:2).

On Day 89 and as believers in Christ, we should tremble in fear for those who declare openly, "I'm not ready for Christ right now." How many times have we seen people fall who could have been saved? How many lives were lost who did not know the love and grace of God, but yet they were given every chance in the world? How many times have we heard, "I will try attending church next week"? It is not okay to force God to wait on you until it becomes convenient. Self-will allows you to make these types of decisions, but remember, self-will will not guarantee you tomorrow.

Let's always remember never to do things when they are merely convenient. God has a purpose and a plan for all of us, right here and right now. To delay God's will for your life is to ensure you are missing so many of the blessings He has in store for you. Call upon God today and every day as if your life depends on it.

Prayer for the day: Heavenly Father, today, I realize You are not an easy convenience for my life. You continue to be the answer to my physical freedom as well as my eternal salvation. May I never forget You are first, and everything else is unimportant. May I never be discouraged when others reject You, but may I always bounce back with a resilient force to ensure Your Word reaches all those who are in need. Amen.

◆

# Day 90: ½ way 2 180

My feet have closely followed his steps; I have kept to his way
without turning aside.

—Job 23:11 (NIV)

The story is told of a new bank president who met with his
predecessor and said, "I would like to know, what have been
the keys to your success?"

The older gentleman looked at him and replied, "Young
man, I can sum it up in two words: Good decisions."

To that, the young man responded, "I thank you immensely
for that advice, sir, but how does one come to know which are
the good decisions?"

"One word, young man," replied the sage. "Experience."

"That's all well and good," said the younger, "but how does
one get experience?"

"Two words," said the elder. "Bad decisions."

—*MBI's Today in the Word,* November 1989, 23

Today is a milestone as it pertains to your 180-day adventure to freedom. To
recognize you are halfway there allows you time to focus on the past eighty-nine
days and to self-evaluate. Take time to jot down some of the mistakes you have
made, as well as some accomplishments. For example: how you overcame the urge
to run away. How have you allowed Christ to intercede on your behalf? Can you
recognize the obstacles God has brought you through? How is your family? How's
your serenity? How is your desire to want to pass on to others what God has been
doing for you? And so on.

It is imperative to know how we came to where we are before we can understand
where we are headed. One of the hardest things we need to do is to ask others for
their opinion of ourselves. Today's verse leaves us with some great questions: Are
my feet closely following His steps? Have I kept to His ways without turning aside?
Remember, you are halfway through this initial phase of the rest of your life. Don't
lose focus; stay in step, and get ready for what the next ninety days have to offer.

Prayer for the day: Heavenly Father, only You could have gotten me to where I
am today. I give You all the praise and glory of meeting this milestone in my life.

Today, I choose to stop and recognize all the ups and downs that have taken place and give You all the praise and glory for the success I feel inside. May I continue to grow, with You leading my every step in my every way. May I remember never to look left or right nor behind, but to remain focused on what's ahead and the plans You have for me. Thank You for this glorious day in my life. Amen.

◆

# Day 91: Be Assured

Whoever gives heed to instruction prospers, and blessed is he who trust in the Lord.

—Proverbs 16:20 (NIV)

Relationship building is a process that takes time; when that time is invested, trust and vulnerability grow. We offer these questions as part of this building process, knowing that when used in love and wisdom, they will help men and women open their hearts to each other.

1. Have I been with a man or woman in the past week who could be viewed as compromising? 2. Have all my financial dealings been filled with integrity? 3. Have I viewed sexually explicit material? 4. Have I spent adequate time in Bible study and prayer? 5. Have I spent quality time and given priority to my family? 6. Have I fulfilled the mandates of my calling? 7. Have I just lied to you?

—*Discipleship Journal,* 11–12/92

There's nothing worse than thinking you know God and come to find out when it's too late that you don't. We live in a world where we automatically assume God requires our righteousness, and we seek it because God has placed this instinctive feeling within us. At this point in recovery, you probably have a checklist of what is right and what is evil. You wake up day after day, trying to squash the evil thoughts in your mind with spiritually sound biblical inspiration, which can leave an individual feeling hopeless and in despair and often with the question, "What am I doing wrong?"

Let's face it; there's a good possibility your efforts are futile in a world where you are surrounded by negativity and chaos. God does not want you quarreling or fighting with the things of this world, and if you are behaving good or bad, but rather possessing a heart that has an open-door policy for Him to invade.

In today's verse, we must first recognize that to give "heed" to instruction, we must first become submissive. A submissive heart conquers the urge to want to fight so hard at being good. It alleviates the constant battle that goes on with the thoughts in your mind. A submissive heart allows you to be malleable so you can be molded into someone who knows how to trust. You see, it's not always the worldly issues that bother us; it's the fact we don't trust ourselves with worldly matters.

Today more than ever, you need to be assured you're doing the right things. You need to be asking yourselves essential questions, such as the ones listed above. But most importantly, assure yourself that you are submissive, with an open heart, with the assurance God is molding you into what He envisions you to be. Having this type of warranty extinguishes the overwhelming concerns of being good or bad.

Prayer for the day: Heavenly Father, I have woken up many days feeling uninsured and defeated. I recognize I also evaluate goodness based on the acceptance of this world. Lord, today, I open my heart and my soul as a submissive servant and child of the one true King. I will trust completely that You are in control of my eternal salvation, eliminating my fears of my current condition. May these thoughts remain at the forefront of my mind. Amen.

◆

# Day 92: I See You

Since, then, you have been raised with Christ, set your hearts on
things above, where Christ is, seated at the right hand of God.
—Colossians 3:1 (NIV)

Humility does not mean thinking less of yourself than of other
people, nor does it mean having a low opinion of your gifts. It
means freedom from thinking about yourself one way or the
other at all.

—William Temple, *Christ in His Church*

Never has there been a more accurate statement made than when I heard someone
say, "It's never been about me." If there's one thing I have come to learn, it's that
God hates pride. He absolutely loathes it. Scripture teaches us that it is pride that
led Satan to fall from heaven, and it leads to our fall as well.

Here's a little food for thought I would like you to chew on: What if one
of the main reasons for you coming to recovery was not so you could stop your
suffering, but so God could use you to end the suffering of others as well. What
if you accept the fact you are just a mere pawn who is needed to do great things
to fulfill God's purpose. Do these types of questions bring you to a better
understanding of humility? Do they eliminate your pride? When we eliminate
pride, we allow ourselves to be concerned with how God sees us and not how
society sees us.

In today's verse, Paul has made it clear that when we became Christians,
we first had to become humble. So being humble is not as tricky as continuous
humility. It's when we lose that humility that pride steps in, and we begin
sidestepping the things God wants us to do. We refuse to take a look at ourselves
from the inside and evaluate our importance based on the way others view us
and not the way God views us. Pride is like a pair of blinders on a horse; it only
allows you to see a small part of the bigger picture God wants you to see. Take
off the blinders called pride and see yourself as God sees you, which is one of
His own.

Prayer for the day: Heavenly Father, so often I have viewed my level of
importance based on my pride and my current conditions. Many of the
solutions to my problems can be overcome when I concentrate on the needs

and concerns of others. Today, may I swallow my pride and see myself the way You see me and humbly make known my shortcomings so I may remain a true servant to You. May I be grounded and comforted by the blessings You have bestowed upon me, and may I continue to be a humble servant to others. Amen.

◆

# Day 93: Who's Will Is It?

Teach me to do your will, for you are my God; may your good Spirit lead me on level ground.

—Psalm 143:10 (NIV)

Someone says, "The will of God which we sometimes think so hard, is, if we only knew it, just the softest pillow to rest upon." If we recognized that there was no choice but God's, no aim but such as had Him for its object, how it would take the worry and care from our lives! Have we learned that we are only safe, happy, right, when He chooses?

—*Gospel Herald*

January 20, 2019, is a day few football fans will ever forget. It was the NFC championship between the New Orleans Saints and the Los Angeles Rams, playing at the Mercedes-Benz Superdome in New Orleans. As predicted, the game was very close, and the Saints had an opportunity to gain a first down and run out the clock for the win. The score was Rams 20 and the Saints 20, with a 1:48 seconds left in the fourth quarter. Drew Brees threw another one of his beautiful passes to Tommy Lee Lewis, but out of nowhere, Lewis was struck down and hindered from catching the pass. What was clearly pass interference was called an incomplete pass, and the Rams would go on to win the NFC championship game and play in Super Bowl LIII. The referees missed a call, which made a game-ending tragedy for the Saints. The next day, I heard someone say, "It just wasn't God's will for the Saints to win."

Let's be realistic; our Lord and Savior is not up in heaven, making decisions on who wins football games or any other sporting event. If the truth is known, I don't think the Lord would encourage us to intentionally put ourselves in a position to receive concussions and broken bones. Those are choices we make our own. But the truth is, God gives us the most beautiful gift that no other creature possesses: the gift of free will.

You see, free will allows us to decide whether we choose to follow God or not. It allows us to incorporate a lifestyle that is pleasing to Him. God allows us to pursue those things we believe are important to us and we view as a blessing. He provides for those things we choose to bring us joy and for us to understand that sometimes, our decisions bring us pain. So what is the point in all of this free will?

The point is this: Whatever you decide to do, your Lord and Savior asks that you take Him with you. If you want to try a new job and a new career, take God with you. If you're going to move to a new location, take God with you. If you want to seek new friendships, take God with you. In all the things you do, take God with you and understand He will be with you, regardless of the outcome you experience. If it is a beautiful outcome, give God the praise and glory. If it's a disappointing outcome you didn't expect, still give Him the praise and glory because you are assured He will see you safely through.

The good Lord didn't determine the outcome of the NFC championship; it was a referee. It will be you who determines the outcome of your life, based solely on the decision to choose to incorporate God in all the things you decide to do.

Prayer for the day: Heavenly Father, today, I recognize that sometimes, the outcome in my life is for the better. Regardless if I feel the outcome was appropriate or not, today, I choose to believe it was the best. I may not have received the job I wanted because You may have had a better job in mind. I may not be where I want to be, but You have me where I should safely be. Deciding to incorporate You in my life means I am accepting of Your will for me. I accept all my outcomes, whether good or bad, with a clear understanding that all things are in Your time. Amen.

# Day 94: Short but Sweet

With the tongue we praise our Lord and Father, and with it we curse human beings, who have been made in God's likeness. Out of the same mouth come praise and cursing.

—James 3:9–10 (NIV)

Don't break a bird's wings and then tell it to fly. Don't break a heart and then tell it to love. Don't break a soul and then tell it to be happy. Don't see the worst in a person and expect them to see the best in you. Don't judge people and expect them to stand by your side. Don't play with fire and expect to stay safe. Life is about giving and taking. You cannot expect to give bad and receive good. You cannot expect to give hate and receive love. So, if you're willing to see a positive change in your life, you must be willing to be that change itself.

—*The Minds Journal*

Never has a verse brought more clarity into my life than when I read, "Do unto others as you would have them do unto you" (Luke 6:31). On Day 94, I do not think it's necessary to fill two or three pages with words of inspiration to bring clarity to what you just read. If today's quote as well as the verse that coincides with it does not bring clarity or hasn't begun to resonate in your heart, then you are in a spiritual danger zone. If there's anything I would want people to remember from today's message, it is this: "Treat others better than you would treat yourself."

Prayer for the day: Heavenly Father, thank You for the biblical verses in my life that need no explanation in order to understand Your message. May I be intentional and deliberate on ensuring the love and grace You have bestowed upon me is displayed tenfold to others. Cleanse my heart, free me from the bondage of self, and guide me in the direction of others. Amen.

# Day 95: Lacking Just a Little

If any of you lacks wisdom, let him ask God, who gives
generously to all without reproach, and it will be given him.

—James 1:5 (NIV)

Don't let what you expected from God keep you from what He wants you to
experience.

Let's face it; due to our past experiences, we have a tendency not to expect
much from ourselves these days. The problem with self-reliance is, we often fall
short of achieving the visual expectations in our minds. We have grandiose ideas
of success and achievement as well as inflated or deflated ideas about our abilities
and talents.

We tend to pray, "God, help me to be my best in everything I do." Do you
see the conflict you're facing with this type of prayer? Can you see that relying on
self is our most significant dilemma? What does Jeremiah 29:11 say? "'For I know
the plans I have for you,' declares the Lord, 'plans to prosper you and not to harm
you, plans to give you hope and a future.'"

With that last verse, it is probably safe to say you are not experiencing God's
best because you didn't expect His best to begin with. One of the hardest things for
us to do is to sit back and not rush down the path God has us on. Don't visualize
the journey God has you on and decide it's safe to make a left turn to see what lies
ahead of you on a different path. You will never experience the incredible joy God
has planned for you if you continue to focus on your plans.

In today's verse, James once again informs us the wisest thing we can do for
ourselves is to continue to look up and ask our heavenly Father for His best in our
life. There is nothing wrong with a prayer of confidence aimed at our Lord, stating
we are patiently waiting for His best in our life. Today, we can expect God's best,
and because of these new expectations, you should also get ready for the most
beautiful experience you have ever had. Hallelujah.

Prayer for the day: Heavenly Father, today, I am made aware I have not received
Your best because I did not expect Your best to begin with. Today, I realize the
quarrels and troubles I continue to face are because of the expectations I have of

myself. Help me, Lord, to see the wisdom in relying on You and having the faith and assurance that Your plans far exceed all of my limited expectations; may I experience the incredible new life You have waiting before me. Today, I choose patience and wisdom to persevere. Amen.

◆

# Day 96: What to Do, What to Do?

For we are God's handiwork, created in Christ Jesus to do good works, which God prepared in advance for us to do.
—Ephesians 2:10 (NIV)

Everything continues in a state of rest unless it is compelled to change by forces impressed upon it.
—Isaac Newton, First Law of Motion

I am going to take a punt in the dark and guess it is safe to say on Day 96, you have begun to think of a million different things you would like to do (or at least like to try) as they pertain to the workforce. You are guessing and even second-guessing your abilities and skills. You are not sure and scared of trying something new. You see so many different people doing so many different things, but you don't have a clue which option is the best for you. Am I correct?

First, I want to state being grounded in God and recovery is a gift and a skill in and of itself. The majority of the hundreds and hundreds of people you see who are successful will tell you their most significant achievements came after they developed a relationship with God. Philanthropists will say to you the reason they remain rich is they continue to give it away. Some of the world's greatest thinkers will tell you their most magnificent ideas were scripturally based and not something they conjured up themselves. Do you see the biblical significance?

You see, on Day 96, you should recognize that to change, you must first put change into motion. We have all heard the saying "Nothing changes if nothing changes," and for us, this has never been more relevant than now. If the highest achievers in this world rely on the guidance of something greater than themselves, then wouldn't it be safe to say we should too? Once we begin this type of change, we will automatically see what today's verse is telling us.

Prayer for the day: Heavenly Father, I am still bombarded with grandiose ideas of who I should be and what I should be doing. Guide me to be compelled to rely on Your handiwork and the plans You have for me. Keep me on a path that allows me to see the future You have in store for me, in the comfort in knowing I do not have to make the biggest decisions in my life. You are doing that for me. Amen.

# Day 97: Rose-Colored Glasses

I keep asking that the God of our Lord Jesus Christ, the glorious
Father, may give you the Spirit of wisdom and revelation, so that
you may know him better. I pray that the eyes of your heart
may be enlightened in order that you may know the hope to
which he has called you, the riches of his glorious inheritance
in his holy people.

—Ephesians 1:17–18 (NIV)

A man was looking at a couple, and he said to his wife, "Look
at them, they look so happy. They look like a happy couple."

She said, "Don't be too sure, they're probably saying the
same thing about us."

—Tony Evans, *Illustrations*, 202

In recovery, we do a lot of second-guessing. Guessing who we should hang out
with, guessing who we can trust and who we can't, guessing if what we are reading
is safe, and guessing if the music we are listening to will trigger a craving. We
second-guess our abilities and talents, and we are always concerned about the
opinions of others. The only thing I can tell you is, it is what it is and nothing is
going to change it."

On Day 97 in recovery, we can see our problems, but what gives us fear is
that we do not possess clarity for the solution. There is nothing complicated about
listing our shortcomings. There is nothing difficult about remaining in fear and
drowning in hopelessness. There is nothing complicated about second-guessing
every step that we take. What is difficult is embracing God's assurance and
recognizing how He is at work in your life.

Seeing clearly takes time, and for most of us, it takes more than just 97 days.
There is a tendency for us to jump after and grab any shiny object that lies before
us, not knowing the devastating results that may lie ahead. In today's verse, Paul is
praying for the church of Ephesus in hopes they begin to think with clarity from
their hearts, which God encompasses, and less with their minds, in which He is
not present. If you have received Jesus as your Lord and Savior, then I challenge
you to think and see clearly from your heart from which He resides. You will be
amazed by how the heart sees more clearly than the mind. Oh yeah, the cure for
addiction is still on the way, and I hope you will see it clearly soon.

Prayer for the day: Heavenly Father, I admit openly my vision is blurred and my thoughts are a mess. I ask, oh, Lord, for Your presence in my life by encompassing my heart with Your love and guidance. Help me to know and recognize clear solutions instead of attacking the obvious problem. Give me the patience to wait courageously on Your solution with the assurance of victory over my current situations. Amen.

◆

# Day 98: Problems or Pleasure?

> But he said to me, "My grace is sufficient for you, for my power is made perfect in weakness." Therefore I will boast all the more gladly about my weaknesses, so that Christ's power may rest on me.
>
> —2 Corinthians 12:9 (NIV)

> In most church services, people attending can hear because of the process of amplification. Amplification takes a weak signal and makes it powerful. It takes what would otherwise be unintelligible or soft or complicated and now allows it to make sense. What an amplification system does for a weak signal, God does for weakness in your own life.
>
> —Tony Evans, *Illustrations*

We have all been to the doctor, and the one thing we have come to understand is, doctors cannot help us if they don't understand the problem. We have to be able to identify those things bothering us and what doesn't seem to be working for us to receive help. Nobody goes to the doctor to discuss how good they're feeling or to inform them they do not have a problem.

In today's verse, we see God operating a little differently. You see, sometimes the load may be substantial, but in time, it can bring about a positive change. Paul was informing the church of Corinth he was desperate in his desire to find relief from this burden. God could've removed the load Paul was carrying, but where would Paul's strength have come from if he didn't participate in carrying the weight? If the problem was eliminated, then why would he need to rely on God? Our debilitating problems keep us relying on His grace and His strength, and not ours.

Think about this: God wanted Paul, as well as you and me, to remain in Him and for us to recognize our problems and weaknesses ultimately give us strength. In other words, our problems are finally our greatest blessings if we seek God's guidance to get us through. Don't be so quick to run from your weaknesses but rather take delight in them, to be given the assurance that God's power will continue to rest in you. Our recovery depends on it.

Prayer for the day: Heavenly Father, today, I recognize the source of my strength can be found in my weaknesses. I pray I always delight in those things that strengthen my relationship with You. I pray I always remember Your grace and love are sufficient in all my circumstances. Today, I boast of my weaknesses so I may continue to rely on You. Amen.

◆

# Day 99: It Takes a Little Time

This is the confidence we have in approaching God: that if we ask anything according to His will, he hears us.

—1 John 5:14 (NIV)

Jesus prayed briefly when He was in a crowd; He prayed a little longer when He was with His disciples; and He prayed all night when He was alone. Today, many in the ministry tend to reverse that process."

—Rev. Billy Graham

What is your prayer time like? Do you wait till the end of the day, right before bed, and quickly ask God to bless those in your life, and then ask Him to forgive your sins, and then make known one or two of your problems, and then it's off to sleep? This type of praying doesn't allow for much time of response from our heavenly Father. So often we don't hear a response to our prayers because we are not willing to remain on our knees and give Him time to provide us with the answer.

Would it be shocking if I told you God hears all your prayers and is ready to give you His response, if only you would remain in prayer just a little longer? Allow Him to whisper His answers in your ear. Give Him the chance to respond to the desires of your heart by giving him your time. Listening is something that does not come easy, especially for those of us in recovery. We are always on the run, looking for a quick answer and solution, and never have time for anyone. This is why we lack clarity in our direction and where we are going. God has heard our prayers, but we have not listened for His answer.

In today's verse, John has affirmed that everything you bring before God in prayer, He hears, and if He hears and it is in His will, His response is assured. Make your prayers and the desires of your heart known to your Lord and Savior, but in return, remain still and in place so you may receive His response. You never know, for the first time, you may hear His glorious voice whispering in your ear.

Prayer for the day: Heavenly Father, if I am guilty of one thing, it is I have robbed You of time with me. I have robbed You of the opportunity to speak with me so I can clearly hear Your voice. Today, I see that not only do I rush everyday situations, but I am continuing to rush my relationship with You. May I remember to slow down, make my prayers known in reverence, and wait to hear Your voice. Amen.

◆

# Day 100: Sufficient Sin

Now listen, you who say, "Today or tomorrow we will go to this or that city, spend a year there, carry on business and make money." Why, you do not even know what will happen tomorrow. What is your life? You are a mist that appears for a little while and then vanishes.

—James 4:13–14 (NIV)

There is a fascinating word I came across the other day. I came across it when I was trying to make some plans and ensure I accounted for all the possibilities that could interrupt or disrupt those plans. I was telling somebody about the plan I was making and asked if he could assist in assuring it went smoothly, and he responded, "Your humanistic mindset will never allow you peace of mind without assuring yourself that your plan is God's will."

So I looked up the word *humanism,* and he was correct. Webster's defines *humanism* as "an outlook or system of thought attaching prime importance to human rather than divine or supernatural matters. Humanist beliefs stress the potential value and goodness of human beings, emphasize common human needs, and seek solely rational ways of solving human problems." My friend was correct. I was trying to be self-sufficient on my own, not accounting for the problems that will always arise in life.

We don't speak about this enough, but I genuinely believe self-sufficiency is a sin. On Day 100, you have probably begun the process of planning and constructing the blueprints for your future. There's nothing wrong with making plans; what is wrong is when we make those plans and forget to include God in them. Why should God be at the forefront? Because whatever plans you make, there will always be a situation you didn't plan for, such as the prognosis from a doctor you didn't expect, the car wreck because somebody fell asleep at the wheel, your job ended because it went overseas, and so on.

In today's verse, James is telling us you have no control over what will happen in the future, and that is why we need God more than ever to pick us up and reroute us when our plans began to crumble. We live a life faced with endless possibilities for chaos and disruption, and no matter how much planning you do, you will never be able to account for the unknown opportunities. Only God can be there to help us stay on course when our plans appear to be destroyed. Whatever you plan to do, just remember to take God with you.

Prayer for the day: Heavenly Father, today, I recognize I pride myself on being too self-sufficient, always having an answer for my problems, always thinking I know best when the unexpected happens. Today, I pray I rely completely on You, Lord, and accept that when my plans go awry and start to fall apart, You will be there to guide me through those disasters I never planned for. Amen.

———————————— ◆ ————————————

# Day 101: Giving to Receive

Jesus answered, "If you want to be perfect, go, sell your possessions and give to the poor, and you will have treasure in heaven. Then come, follow me."

—Matthew 19:21 (NIV)

The story is told that one day, a beggar by the roadside asked for alms from Alexander the Great as he passed by. The man was poor and wretched and had no claim upon the ruler, no right even to lift a solicitous hand. Yet the emperor threw him several gold coins.

A courtier was astonished at his generosity and commented, "Sir, copper coins would adequately meet a beggar's need. Why give him gold?"

Alexander responded in royal fashion, "Copper coins would suit the beggar's need, but gold coins suit Alexander's giving" (source unknown).

Do you still find yourself measuring your self-worth or value by your possessions and what you own? It's truly an essential question for us to delve into. What if I asked, "Would you be happy with two pairs of pants, one pair of tennis shoes, one pair for dress shoes, one suit for Sunday, five pairs of socks, five pairs of underwear, one short-sleeve shirt, and one long-sleeve shirt?" You're probably not too sure how to answer that question because you are visualizing the contents of your closet, which includes six pairs of jeans, four pairs of slacks, ten long-sleeve dress shirts, fifteen short-sleeve polo shirts, six pairs of shorts, six pairs of tennis shoes, three pair of dress shoes, five fall coats, two winter coats, and enough items to start a small Salvation Army thrift store of your own.

I say all that to say this: Having things isn't bad, but when we begin to measure our value and self-worth based on how others view us because of what we own, then it becomes idolatry, plain and simple. In today's verse, the parable of the rich man has a sad ending because even when Jesus told him what it took to be perfect, he still couldn't relinquish his possessions. The reason we can't do it is, we do not value ourselves the same way Jesus values us.

On Day 101, it is imperative to begin to evaluate what is essential in your life. You can do this by asking yourself, "Are the needs of others more important than my self-indulgence of needless items?" Are you going out of your way to be of service to others? Better yet, are you still so grateful for the small things you had on Day 1 that accumulating things doesn't cross your mind? When you think about it, it's all about gratitude. The key ingredient to recovery and the heart of Jesus is gratitude.

Remember this: You will never receive the treasures God has in store for you by hoarding items here on earth and neglecting people in need. Don't ever forget the day you were an individual who had absolutely nothing, and it was because somebody obeyed this verse so you might have a chance at a new way of life. Plain and simple, we were once the poor and lowly in the spirit that today's verse speaks.

Prayer for the day: Heavenly Father, as I evaluate my surroundings, I see clearly I have more than I need. I have been selfish. Today, I recognize I need to see myself the way You see me, and I should see others the way You see them. Help me to begin to realize that in Your eyes, I am already priceless, and that my job on Day 101 is to ensure that others come to know You. Amen.

◆

# Day 102: Becoming a Teacher

Teach these new disciples to obey all the commands I have given you. And be sure of this: I am with you always, even to the end of the age.

—Matthew 28:20 (NIV)

The yoke and the cross are twin symbols of Christian experience. The cross speaks of leaving the world for Christ; the yoke speaks of learning in the world from Christ. The one speaks of sacrifice; the other service. The disciple must bear both; he cannot choose to take one and leave the other.

—*The Prairie Overcomer*

In the beginning of recovery, it was all about being teachable, all about complete surrender, all about us finding out what Jesus wants us to do and how He wants us to live. But eventually, we need to recognize the gifts we have been given, the hurdles we have overcome, and the sacrifices we have made and start to share them with others. It's time to start leaving the nest.

In today's verse, the disciples were in the same position you are currently in. They have seen and experienced true freedom and God's love. They have been given a new life and a real understanding of what it means to be happy. They have the tools and resources to guide people to the same experiences and freedom you currently feel. In other words, it's like the old saying you hear in the twelve-step programs: "You can't keep what you have unless you give it away." Today, it's crucial for you to realize Jesus is saying the same thing. Share with others the gifts God has given you and your new-found knowledge of life.

The gift of sobriety and recovery is so priceless and precious, you will never feel its complete gratifying effects in your life until you share its unbridled potential to change the life of someone else. If you keep this precious gift to yourself, you will never understand its full power. The same was valid with the disciples. The ultimate goal is to lead people to Christ, regardless of their situations and circumstances. In other words, congratulations. It's time to take ownership of your discipleship. On Day 102, you have so much to offer to so many people, and when you make the priority and concerns of others your priority, you begin to see, in heavenly detail, the path God wants you to be on. Your life will have a new meaning and will become straight.

Prayer for the day: Heavenly Father, for so long, I have had an inner feeling of uncertainty, the uncertainty of what I am called to do and how You want me to do it. Today, I have learned my priority is to share my experiences with others, to speak Your words into life, and to be a disciple for You. I pray You will guide me and direct me through the difficult times so I may never surrender my discipleship and remain true and faithful to the calling You have placed in my heart. Amen.

◆

# Day 103: Know What You Know

The Lord is not slow in keeping his promise, as some understand
slowness. Instead he is patient with you, not wanting anyone to
perish, but everyone to come to repentance.

—2 Peter 3:9 (NIV)

There's a story about a proud young man who came to Socrates
asking for knowledge.

He walked up to the muscular philosopher and said, "Oh,
great Socrates, I come to you for knowledge."

Socrates recognized a pompous numbskull when he saw
one. He led the young man through the streets, to the sea, and
chest deep into water. Then he asked, "What do you want?"

"Knowledge, oh, wise Socrates," said the young man with
a smile.

Socrates put his strong hands on the man's shoulders and
pushed him under. Thirty seconds later, Socrates let him up.
"What do you want?" he asked again.

"Wisdom," the young man sputtered, "oh, great and wise
Socrates."

Socrates crunched him under again. Thirty seconds passed,
thirty-five. Forty. Socrates let him up. The man was gasping.

"What do you want, young man?"

"Air," he screeched. "I need air."

"When you want knowledge as you have just wanted air,
then you will have knowledge."

—M. Littleton, *Moody Monthly*, June 1989, 29

There is an old saying that goes, "You don't know what you know until you
know what you know." On Day 103, you may have come to a point where
you are wondering if God has heard your prayers or if He has denied you your
prayers because He is taking so long. It's a little arrogant of us to think we should
immediately receive the desires of the heart based on our assurance that what we
want is what we truly need. Let me give an example: It took me twenty-five years
to become serious about recovery and give my life to God. What makes me think

I can repair all the damage and get the desires of my heart in 103 days? Get the picture?

The point is this: God is the only one Who is sure of the things you are prepared for. He knows if you're ready to move out on your own or if it may be better for you to have a roommate in recovery. He knows which jobs will bring you success and keep you safe, and which ones will take you right back to your tumultuous past. He knows how much money you can handle and how much is too much.

In today's verse, Peter is reassuring us God hears our prayers and wants us to have those desires of the heart that fit into His will. God is concerned for our safety and well-being, and when we can show our Lord and Savior we can be patient, this assures Him we are ready. If you are in the hospital and needed life-saving surgery, would you prefer doctors who work fast and carelessly, or would you want doctors who take their time and give you their best effort? This is the way God is performing in your life. He is taking things at a pace that ensures you will not return to that old lifestyle from whence you came.

Oh, yeah, be patient; the cure for addiction is still on the way.

Prayer for the day: Heavenly Father, I pray today I may be able to see the importance of being patient and realizing things happen in God's time and not in mine. I can see where I have a tendency to move too fast and to move ahead of You, Lord. Today, I pray I recognize You are preparing a beautiful table for me to enjoy, not only with myself, but with others. Thank You for the wisdom You continue to give me. Amen.

◆

# Day 104: Are You Well?

> When Jesus heard this, he said, "Healthy people don't need a doctor—sick people do."
>
> —Matthew 9:12 (NIV)

What they say: "It could be one of several things." What they mean: "I haven't the foggiest idea what's wrong with you." What they say: "Are you sure you haven't had this before?" What they mean: "Because you've got it again." What they say: "I'd like to run that test again." What they mean: "The lab lost your blood sample." What they say: "Insurance should cover most of this." What they mean: "You'll have to sell your house to cover the rest." What they say: "These pills have very few side effects." What they mean: "You may experience sudden hair growth on your palms." What they say: "Why don't you go over your symptoms with me one more time?" What they mean: "I don't remember who you are." What they say: "There's a lot of this going around." What they mean: "And we'll give it a name as soon as we figure out what it is."

—David Grimes, in *Sarasota Herald-Tribune*,
quoted in *Reader's Digest*, May 1994, 112

At this stage of your recovery, ask yourself this question: "Is it more important to be physically fit or spiritually fit?" Most of us would probably say we want to be fit in both departments, physically and spiritually. The problem is, we tend to focus more on the physical rather than the spiritual.

In today's verse, Matthew tells us about Jesus meeting with tax collectors and sinners, and we can see these individuals are not physically sick, but it is their spiritual sickness Jesus wants to attack. For so many of us, we may not be able to recognize how spiritually ill we are. We often have the mindset that feeling good means we are living good. Not true.

Never once does the scripture mention you must be a physical Adonis to enter the gates of heaven, but it does say you must be in tune with God and accept Jesus Christ as your Lord and Savior. Now more than ever, we need to find a healthy balance in our physical well-being as well as our spiritual. Our physical well-being allows us to think clearly and to seek boldly the spiritual remedies needed for our soul. On Day 104, you should have begun feeling physically well, and your mind should be clearer. Now, be determined in your spiritual fitness and be sure you are gaining spiritual knowledge and strength from the living Word of God and His direction.

Prayer for the day: Heavenly Father, no matter how physically fit I become and how well I treat my flesh, I continue to notice there is something inside I am missing. Today, I pray I may begin to conquer my spiritual deficit and strengthen those spiritual attributes that would please you and keep me spiritually fit. Strengthen me today, Lord, in this area of my life, that I may ensure my eternal salvation with You. Amen.

---

# Day 105: Unassured Assurance

I have told you these things, so that in me you may have peace. In this world you will have trouble. But take heart! I have overcome the world.

—John 16:33 (NIV)

The woman at the insurance office inquired as to the costs, amounts paid, and so on.

"So," she concluded, "if I pay five dollars, you pay me a thousand if my house burns down. But do you ask questions about how the fire came to start?"

"We make careful investigation, of course," the agent replied.

The woman flounced toward the door disgustedly.

"Just as I thought," she called over her shoulder. "I knew there was a catch in it."

—Source Unknown

So many of us in recovery try so hard to cling to assurances that aren't there. It would be wonderful if we could be assured we'll never go back to that old way of living. It would be great if we were convinced the temptation or the thought to use would never cross our minds or we may never endure another craving. On the contrary, if you want to be assured of anything, be assured trials and tribulation will always be in front of us. There is no getting around it.

In today's verse, Jesus tells the disciples the one thing they could be assured of is the friction and turmoil that would lie ahead from preaching the Gospel. But regardless of the storm, they would always be able to find peace in Christ.

We must remember, Jesus did not promise peace; He offered it. Jesus made way for us to find peace with God through the assurance of our salvation through His blood on the cross. But regardless of what we are facing or what we have done in the past, we can find peace through Him. What a blessed assurance for all of us to have, that with the travesties of our past and the guarantee of the trial and tribulations that are to come, Jesus already claimed the victory for us. For those of you who are still fighting, I say, "Peace unto you from our Lord Jesus Christ." That is one assurance you can count on.

Prayer for the day: Heavenly Father, I constantly seek to cling to those things that give me false hope of assurance in this life. I constantly grapple with the idea that one day, all of my mental anguish and worldly troubles would just vanish and disappear because I have changed my life. I recognize today this is not true, and the only assurance I have is You paved the way for my peace and happiness. May I remember when trouble finds me, I will be intentional to find You. Amen.

◆

# Day 106: Enough Is Enough

So don't be afraid; you are more valuable to God than a whole
flock of sparrows.

—Matthew 10:31 (NIV)

A reporter once asked the world's richest man what he was worth, to which he
replied, "In whose eyes, man's or God's?" He told the reporter, "In man's eyes,
I'm worth $4.8 billion, in God's eyes, I am worth all the treasures of the world."

Our Father holds us to this same value, which should make you feel pretty
good about your future. The problem we face is, we currently value ourselves
by whether or not the Lord has answered our prayers and whether we can see
definitive answers to our future. A good friend of mine once told me a little
knowledge is a dangerous thing. The reason is, our ways are not God's ways, and
God's thoughts and plans are not our thoughts and plans.

In today's verse, Matthew wants us to stop and realize all the crucial things
in our life are being met. If God can meet the needs of the sparrow, then why
wouldn't He give His children even greater attention? If you can stop and marvel
at all the things around you and how they work perfectly, you will have an
appreciation for where you are right now.

Your heavenly Father brought you out of the chaos and quagmire of addiction
so you may live abundantly. Stop trying to live beyond your means and realize
the things you need to worship and have a relationship with your God have been
taken care of. What are those items, you may ask? Well, let's keep it simple. All
you truly need is food, shelter, and clothing. The rest of life is nothing more than
just icing on the cake.

Prayer for the day: Heavenly Father, so often I do not see the value in myself the
way You value me. So often self-worth is based on an abundance of things that
will never bring me happiness. Help me today to realize to be loved by You is the
greatest gift of them all, and help me to appreciate all my needs have been met.
Continue to grant me those things You want me to have, and I will use them to
better serve Your Kingdom. Amen.

# Day 107: Real or Fake?

Praise the Lord. Praise the Lord, you his servants; praise the name of the Lord. Let the name of the Lord be praised, both now and forevermore.

—Psalm 113:1–2

It is quite easy (and human) to be proud of one's goodness and if the goodness isn't real, to fake it. That sort of thing goes on all the time with those who say one thing and live in a way quite different. It's even worse with us. We know the rules and can fake it better than people who don't know the rules.

—Steve Brown, *Christian Life*

Praising the name of the Lord sounds good and often it makes us feel good, but what does it really mean to you? Our heavenly Father has many different names all throughout scripture. I would like for you to think of the name you refer to your heavenly Father with and treat it as if it were a priceless diamond you would never lose or destroy, to never say or do anything that would cause you to lose it or have it taken from you. Now ask yourself, are these your feelings when you're praising God?

We often see individuals praising the name of our heavenly Father on Sunday and quickly defile that type of worship with their actions and their words. We want people to think we are okay by being belligerently vocal with our praise and worship, but it doesn't take long before our hearts are truly revealed. Don't be a fake. It only leaves you in bad standing with your community and separates you even further from your heavenly Father, for He truly knows your heart, regardless of your words.

In today's verse, the psalmist reminds us God is holy and eternal. The facet of this diamond is so brilliant, we cannot even glimpse it with our own eyes. Realize God's holy name has many facets within a diamond. The facet of sovereignty, the facet of omniscience, the facet of omnipresence, and the facet of omnipotence. This is Who we are praising, and this is where we find peace, comfort, and grace. Don't forget, it was only 107 days ago we were accursed and outcast due to sin, but God's grace brought us in. What a wonderful name it is. Be real when it comes to praising your heavenly Father.

Prayer for the day: Heavenly Father, today, I realize there are many areas of my life where I lack sincerity. One area could possibly be how I praise Your name. I pray I may never take for granted Who You are and all You have done for me. I pray I remain reverent in every area of my life and my heart speaks the same reverence as my lips. May I never attempt to praise Your name in order to be appealing to others. Amen.

♦

# Day 108: Worry Wart

Jesus replied, "Your mistake is that you don't know the Scriptures, and you don't know the power of God."
—Matthew 22:29

One witty individual wrote, "A dentist's mistake is pulled out, a lawyer's mistake is imprisoned, a teacher's mistake is failed, a printer's mistake is corrected, a pharmacist's mistake is buried, a postman's mistake is forwarded, an electrician's mistake could be shocking."

There's an incredible saying that states, "The greatest mistake a person could ever make is to not learn from his or her mistakes." There is a tendency to be justifiably concerned if we are doing things right or not. For a lot of us, we understand mistakes can have detrimental ramifications that can be life-changing. So what do we do to ensure we are on the right path? How do we find comfort and peace that we are sure-footed in our steps and not about to slip? What is the biggest mistake we could be making and not realize we are making it?

In today's verse, Matthew is informing us our biggest mistake is not being grounded in scripture to ensure ourselves of Who God truly is. We worry because we do not understand God's strength. We suffer because we are unsure if He is guiding us. We worry because relying on ourselves has always proven to be catastrophic. We worry because worrying is all we have ever done. We worry because a recovering addict's mistakes can be deadly.

On Day 108, you need to grasp hold of the assurances you currently have in your life, the confidence if you remain steadfast and true to what the scriptures are telling you, you will be embraced in God's arms. You realize mistakes are inevitable but not life-threatening. You no longer worry about the ramifications of simple errors. You have comfort in knowing your recovery is safe, and for the majority of us, all we've ever wanted is to be safe in recovery. Continue to hold on, and do not worry; God is supplying the cure for all our strongholds each and every day.

Prayer for the day: Heavenly Father, as I continue to evaluate how I spend my time, I realize I am not as grounded in Your Word as I should be. I am still threatened with the impending doom I am going to slip and fall back into an old pattern and lifestyle. Help me today to realize mistakes are inevitable, but if I remain assured and confident in Your living Word, then I will have peace in knowing You will pick me up and have me continue on this path of recovery. Amen.

———————————————◆———————————————

# Day 109: Rightfully Rewarded

I the LORD search the heart and examine the mind, to reward each person according to their conduct, according to what their deeds deserve.

—Jeremiah 17:10 (NIV)

We are afraid that heaven is a bribe, and that if we make it our goal we shall no longer be disinterested. It is not so. Heaven offers nothing that a mercenary soul can desire. It is safe to tell the pure in heart that they shall see God, for only the pure in heart want to.

—C. S. Lewis in *The Problem of Pain*

I have come to believe we are born with the presence of the Holy Spirit in our lives. At a very young age, we can decipher the difference between right and wrong. On my first trip to the candy store by myself without my parents, I knew instinctively that whatever I picked up was not mine until it was paid for. Knowing right from wrong is an instinctive behavior that is a quality given to us by God, which ensures us that we are His children.

Having said all this, you are qualified to examine your heart to determine if you are sincere or not. There is no guessing, and there's no confusion; there is no doubt if you were living a life that does not resemble Kingdom living. You know your thoughts, you know your intentions, and you know if you are sincere. You have this ability not because you were born a genius, but because as children of God, we are made in His image, and in that image, we instinctively know what is right and what is wrong, who is sincere and who is not, who is being authentic and who is lying.

In today's verse, the prophet Jeremiah confirms God perfectly knows the heart and the mind of each of us, and because of this knowledge, His judgment of every one of us is true and accurate. Don't let the feelings of the heart and the thoughts of your mind fool you into thinking you are safe and secure when your godly instinct is telling you to change. Be willing to condemn those things God finds disapproving and do the things that assure you your judgment before God will bring security in your salvation.

On Day 109, there are so many thoughts and ideas that are threatening your recovery. Be sure the only answers are found in scripture and let the living Word of God guide you to your rightful reward that only He can give. Freedom from active addiction and the lifestyle of absolute chaos are just one of the gifts He has for us by following Him.

Prayer for the day: Heavenly Father, I have instinctively known for so long if my actions were sincere or not. Today, I recognize this instinct is a gift You have given me. May I resolve to remain steadfast in listening to the heavenly instinct you have given me and not to my deceitful heart and mind. Help me to find my answers in the living Word of the Bible and not in the chaotic calamity of my mind. You know me best, oh, Lord, and You know my heart. Today, I pray when the day comes for me to be judged, You find a pure heart and a clean spirit, deserving of the rewards You have in store for me. Amen.

◆

# Day 110: Blessed Assurance

Blessed are those whose transgressions are forgiven, whose sins are covered.

—Romans 4:7 (NIV)

Two hunters came across a bear so big they dropped their rifles and ran for cover. One man climbed a tree while the other hid in a nearby cave. The bear was in no hurry to eat, so he sat down between the tree and the cave to reflect upon his good fortune. Suddenly, and for no apparent reason, the hunter in the cave came rushing out, almost ran into the waiting bear, hesitated, and then dashed back in again. The same thing happened a second time.

When he emerged for the third time, his companion in the tree frantically called out, "Woody, are you crazy? Stay in the cave till he leaves."

"Can't," panted Woody, "there's another bear in there."

—Source Unknown

So often we find ourselves in situations that are nothing more than never-ending problems. We want to be able to walk away scot-free, but once again, problems appear before us. We fixed one problem, another one pops up. We grasp and harness and extinguish one dilemma, only to be met with another. No matter how hard you try, life can be nothing more than a never-ending curveball of problems.

The reason I say all that is to emphasize better what today's verse means. The apostle Paul is quoting King David from one of his psalms emphasizing how blessed we are when our problems and dilemmas and sins are entirely covered. There is not one individual who can handle the consequences of sin and make it justifiable. No one who can walk away from their transgressions and set themselves apart from their wrongdoing. Only God can take the dilemmas and consequences of sin and cover them so they may no longer hinder your salvation.

On Day 110, there are two assurances you need to be made aware of: 1. The problems and situations you are faced with during everyday life can be conquered and dealt with when you rely on guidance from God. 2. You should never have to worry about the problems and dilemmas of the past that resulted from sin if you surrender your life to Christ. Issues of today can be handled if you walk with God, and your sins and transgressions of the past can be dealt with through God if you declare your sins and ask for forgiveness. If your transgressions are forgiven, then what problems do you really have?

Prayer for the day: Heavenly Father, every day, I feel as if I am being dealt a bad hand. As soon as one dilemma is dealt with, another one arises. I pray today that regardless of my current problems or condition, I can find peace and rest in the assurance the transgressions and sins of my past are forgiven. Today, I realize my problems are nothing more than simple hiccups in life and are defeated when I walk with You. Thank You for forgiving my sins and guaranteeing my salvation after all the problems I used to create for myself and others. Amen.

———————————— ◆ ————————————

# Day 111: The Greatest Thing

And now these three remain: faith, hope and love. But the greatest of these is love.

—1 Corinthians 13:13 (NIV)

Compassion can't be measured in dollars and cents. It does come with a price tag, but that price tag isn't the amount of money spent. The price tag is love.

—J. C. Watts Jr.

Love is a four-letter word that no matter how it is to be expressed or shown, it comes at a price. Whether it be your time, finances, personal belongings, or wisdom and insight, love is only truly expressed when there is a recipient. Think for a moment when you realized you were loved. It's straightforward and easy to understand. You were able to feel what someone else gave you. It doesn't have to be a solid object or something you see, but a connection through an inner desire to share a godly experience with someone else.

The whole foundation and basis for the Christian religion is nothing more and nothing less than love. Everything our Lord and Savior Jesus Christ did was an expression of love. Every move He made, every word He spoke, could change someone's life for the better. This is how we should behave. Don't think you have to have a pocket full of money to change someone's life or some shiny object to make a difference. When you deliberately engage another individual in hopes you can share the message of Jesus Christ for His words to impact their situation, this is love.

In today's verse, Paul is telling the church of Corinth there are three things we need to have to display Kingdom living. Faith, hope, and love are the essentials for this kind of life, but if for some reason you're having difficulty obtaining all three fruits, then concentrate on love, and faith and hope will surely follow. Without love, our recovery will surely die and fade away. On Day 111, remember to have faith in the unimaginable, display confidence when things seem hopeless, and always love the unlovable. That's authentic Kingdom living.

Prayer for the day: Heavenly Father, today, I recognize I fall short in displaying Christlike behavior to others. Help me to love without reservations, to find faith in those who are lost, and to be hopeful for the lives that seem hopeless. I know I may never be able to love like Jesus, but I pray the love of Jesus helps me to overcome those hurdles that keep me from displaying true Kingdom living. I pray for the freedom of love so I can share it freely with all those who are willing to receive. Amen.

◆

# Day 112: A Gift Is a Gift

Anyone who has been stealing must steal no longer, but must work, doing something useful with their own hands, that they may have something to share with those in need.

—Ephesians 4:28 (NIV)

Charles Spurgeon and his wife, according to a story in the *Chaplain* magazine, would sell the eggs their chickens laid, but they refused to give them away,. Even close relatives were told, "You may have them if you pay for them." As a result, some people labeled the Spurgeons greedy and grasping.

They accepted the criticisms without defending themselves, and only after Mrs. Spurgeon died was the full story revealed. All the profits from the sale of eggs went to support two elderly widows. Because the Spurgeons were unwilling to let their left hand know what the right hand was doing (Matthew 6:3), they endured the attacks in silence.

There is one thing about addiction we come to realize when we are on the path of recovery. The one fact that resonates the loudest is, we took and took and took and took until people would not let us take any more. This resonates so loud that on Day 112, we are overly conscious of this past action, and we have a recognizable urge to want to give back and help others. This is an admirable desire, but make sure your motives are in check.

Some people early in recovery will have a tendency to give because they want others to think they are genuinely getting better. Others may offer because they want to feel assured they can rely on the recipient's help in the future. The list goes on and on and on, but for a gift to be a true gift, it must be genuinely given. In other words, there can be no strings attached. To give a gift for any other reason is nothing more than our old and ugly behavior.

In today's verse, Paul is telling us to be completely rid of our old habits and be intentional in doing something useful with the newly recognizable gifts God is giving us. Make it a point today to change the life of someone else, without them knowing it was you. Without expecting a pat on the back, without trying to secure friends for the future, and without expecting anything in return. That is what makes a true gift truly a gift. And oh, yeah, the gift of a cure is still coming.

Prayer for the day: Heavenly Father, today, I recognize there are times when my motives are not in tune with what You would have me to do. May I always remember to weigh the desires of my heart against the message of the Gospel to ensure my motives are pure and in accordance with Your will. May my desire to be of service to others bring nothing more than the assurance of their happiness and a smile on Your face. I pray I may be a true giver of gifts. Amen.

◆

# Day 113: Are You Sure You're Sure?

And everyone who calls on the name of the Lord will be saved.

—Acts 2:21 (NIV)

Even if they try to kill you, you develop the inner conviction that there are some things so precious, some things so eternally true that they are worth dying for. And if a person has not found something to die for, that person isn't fit to live!

—Dr. Martin Luther King Jr.

The word *relapse* seems to be at the forefront of our minds and tends to dominate our own personal image of ourselves. I myself relapsed so many times, I accepted it as a way of life and could not get around it. I was who I thought I was, and I lived with the belief I could never change. It wasn't until I accepted who I was in Christ that I could relinquish and dismiss the idea of ever relapsing again, and because of this new identity in Christ, I refused to let it go. I am who I think I am, and I believe who I believe I am in Christ, which is saved.

On Day 113, we need to know not everyone has the same understanding or is in the same relationship as you are with your Lord and Savior. People are going to relapse and fall short. Do not let this deter you or cause you to feel you will follow in their footsteps. By now, you have made a conscious decision to call on the name of Jesus Christ as your Savior, and today, you have the assurance you are saved. You are not who you were in the past, but you are who you say you are in Christ, Jesus. That you can count on.

In today's verse, Paul wants you to be assured if you intentionally call on the name of the Lord Jesus Christ as your personal Savior, and you have faith and believe He died for your sins, then you are saved. If you're more confident in relapsing than you are in your salvation, then I hope on this day, you will humbly fall to your knees and ask Jesus to come into your heart. Have the assurance of being saved, and go forth this day in faith that you are a child of God and you refuse to let anything or anyone steal that from you. Your salvation is worth staying sober for.

Prayer for the day: Heavenly Father, my life has been filled with so many disappointments and failures, I find it hard to have complete faith in my future. Help me today, oh, Lord, to have the assurance my life is not a revolving door of chaos and calamity, but a purpose-driven, Christ-centered plan of action. I call on the name of the Lord today with the confidence I am saved and my past has not determined my future. Amen.

◆

# Day 114: A Mimicking Mindset

Now that I, your Lord and Teacher, have washed your feet, you also should wash one another's feet.

—John 13:14 (NIV)

Don't judge people and expect them to stand by your side.

—Najwa Zebian

Have you ever known someone who can always clearly state what your problem is, but they never have clarity in giving you a solution? They are the first one to say what you should or shouldn't do, but you never really see them doing it themselves. They love giving advice but can never display any physical act to support their opinion. Annoying, isn't it?

In today's verse, Jesus clearly states we are to be more than verbal mouthpieces of His Word. Jesus demands we show the same humble, sacrificial love to one another as He did when He washed His disciples' feet. Jesus requires we not only be encouraged by what we say but we demonstrate our encouragement with what we do, even if that means washing the feet, assisting the elderly, giving of our time and talents in any arena necessary, and so on.

It's quite simple: being a disciple and teacher of God's Word means we mimic what Christ did for others. We are to recognize what He has already done in our lives and declare it in our testimonies and then physically implement what you feel God is calling you to do. The only way for someone to truly receive the message of Jesus Christ is by first seeing you physically live it. You might be the closest thing to the Bible someone sees. So be more than just a speaker of the Word but also a doer of the Word. What an awesome responsibility on Day 114.

Prayer for the day: Heavenly Father, I recognize it is so easy to simply tell others what they should do, without them seeing me do it myself. When it comes to being a true disciple, there are never any shortcuts. I must walk a path of righteousness and physically display a Christlike behavior in all I do and say. Help me today to be a living example so I may be of true service to others. Amen.

# Day 115: Wings of a Dove

He will cover you with his feathers, and under his wings you will find refuge; his faithfulness will be your shield and rampart.

—Psalm 91:4 (NIV)

The restraining hand of the Lord was felt recently in Pohang, Korea, during a terrible fire where twenty houses were burned to the ground. One of the believers from the church, and a faithful Christian from a Presbyterian church lived in that district, and the fire came right up to both of their houses and then stopped, so that they were unharmed in any way. This incident has had a remarkable effect, for not only do the Christians feel that this was the hand of the Lord, but the unsaved have also been made to say that it was the Lord, the God of the *Christians.*

—*Oriental Missionary Standard*

The psalmist David knew what it meant to be safely under the wings of his Lord and Savior. He knew what it meant to be faced with adversity because of his sins and to witness God's intercession in his life. He knew what it meant to make a covenant and promise with God, only to end up breaking it and sinning one more time. In other words, regardless of David's actions, God kept him safe.

We, in recovery, have unique stories and situations to talk about. Because of our behaviors, we have put ourselves in situations that were dangerous and borderline insane, and had it not been for our heavenly Father's intercession in our lives, we would probably be dead. How do I know this? Because there are so many times when I look back on my life and declare openly that I shouldn't be alive today. It is only by the grace of God I am still on this earth.

Even in recovery, you can rest assured life is going to throw a curveball, and you will be staring into the face of a dangerous and deadly situation. But know this: God still has you under His wing and is shielding your path so you may safely arrive at the destination He has planned for you. How can you be assured of this? It's simple. Reflect on the times in your past where you determined there was no explanation as to why you should still be on this earth, that because of some of the scenarios and situations you have been a part of, you should not be alive reading this devotion. That's how you know God was looking after you.

What's more encouraging is, we realize today if God was willing to protect us while we were so deep in sin, it's only comforting to be assured He is still protecting us in recovery. Hallelujah, for the refuge of God is yours today. And oh, yeah, hang in there; that cure for addiction I keep writing about is on the way.

Prayer for the day: Heavenly Father, I praise Your Holy name and give thanks for Your continued refuge and protection. I shout for joy in knowing I was as important to You then when I was deep in sin, as I am to you now in my new way of life. Thank You, Lord, for never giving up on me and for seeing in me what I could not see in myself. Continue to protect me, Lord, safely under Your arms as I intentionally stay on this new way of living. Amen.

◆

# Day 116: Promises, Promises

"For my thoughts are not your thoughts, neither are your ways my ways," declares the Lord. "As the heavens are higher than the earth, so are my ways higher than your ways and my thoughts than your thoughts."

—Isaiah 55:8–9 (NIV)

God hath not promised Skies always blue, Flower-strewn pathways all our lives thro'; God hath not promised sun without rain, joy without sorrow, peace without pain. God hath not promised smooth roads and wide, swift, easy travel, needing no guide; never a mountain, rocky and steep, never a river turbid and deep: But God hath promised strength for the day, rest for the labor, light for the way, grace for the trials, help from above, unfailing sympathy, undying love.

—Annie Johnson Flint

As I continue to work with the church, I'm always faced with individuals who are in a state of crisis or have recently come out of one, and the one question that is all too familiar is, "If God loves me, why has He let this happen to me?" Even for those of us in recovery, we would love to think God is pleased with what we are doing in this new way of life, and therefore, we should be exempt from any future turmoil. Our recovery is not grounds for dismissal and gives us no exemption status from adversity, but it does allow us to understand how to conquer it successfully when we are hit with trouble.

The answer is not always pretty, but God does not promise us exclusion from tough times based on the quality of our character or the type of life we have led. But I have to ask you, "Aren't your current problems and situations more manageable now that God is in your life? Hasn't it been nice to be able to conquer your problems with God versus making your problems worse without Him?"

In today's verse, the prophet Isaiah is confirming God has a plan for every single adversity you are going to face, and furthermore, He is reassuring us God's plan is so much greater than our current problems and difficulties. You see, one of the things I have come to learn is, my relationship with Christ has become stronger because of overcoming these adversities with Him. Had it not been for some of my misfortunes, I would not have clarity toward the path I need to take.

So remember, sometimes a little difficulty is a good thing, and it's God's way of growing closer to you. Hallelujah.

Prayer for the day: Heavenly Father, today, I want to take on the mindset of welcoming adversity and how I can overcome it with Your help. Today, I take assurance in knowing I can do all things through You, Who give me strength. I take comfort in knowing my current situation is not a problem as I would view it, but a tool to providing clarity and strength in this new way of life. Today, when life presents its problems, I choose to present those problems to You, and together, we will both be conquerors. Amen.

———————————————◆———————————————

# Day 117: No Labels Needed

How great you are, Sovereign LORD! There is no one like you,
and there is no God but you, as we have heard with our own ears.

—2 Samuel 7:22 (NIV)

We are living in a society where social acceptance trumps biblical direction. In other words, people are now convinced that if an act, regardless of what it is, is lawfully and socially acceptable, then the Bible should conform to our ever-changing lifestyles to fit society's laws. Lord, help us.

We have so many different labels we apply to ourselves, it may become hard to know who you are in God's eyes. And if this is true for you, then look at what the prophet Samuel is saying in today's verse. He is saying God's law is the only law, sovereign law. The basic definition of sovereignty is, one possessing supreme and ultimate authority and power. So if there is One final authority and power, there is no scenario that constitutes conformity to any other rules or regulations.

I find it funny how society's laws regularly change, but God's law has remained the same. You will not go into your local bookstore and find the Bible written in the seventies saying anything different than a Bible printed in 2020. It can't be changed because of God's sovereignty; therefore, the laws remain the same, and you are who God says you are, which is "His child." I love it because it is so clear and impactful, and squashes all unnecessary labels. We may be a recovering addict in society's eyes, but in God's eyes, you are His child. No labels needed.

Today, let's remember that as children of God, we are required to conform to the Bible and not for the Bible to conform to us, to make it be known to others that just because society says it's okay, does not mean it is okay. Be determined to know who you are in Christ, and you will surely find all the confusing labels and all of society's laws have a place under God's sovereign law and not above it.

Prayer for the day: Heavenly Father, today, I continue to commit my life to the law You have set down before me. Today, I will do my best to follow the laws You have written, and when society confronts me with its never-ending dilemmas, I will quickly find my answers in Your Word versus accepting society's declarations. Give me the strength to continue to conform in a manner that is in tune with the life You would have me live and for society to see clearly Whose laws I follow. Amen.

# Day 118: I Think I Can, I Think I Can

"It is beyond my power to do this," Joseph replied. "But God can tell you what it means and set you at ease."

—Genesis 41:16

One New Year's Day, in the Tournament of Roses parade, a beautiful float suddenly sputtered and quit. It was out of gas. The whole parade was held up until someone could get a can of gas. The amusing thing was this float represented the Standard Oil Company. With its vast oil resources, its truck was out of gas. Even though Christians have access to God's omnipotence, if we do not avail ourselves to it we will run out of power.

—Source: Lee McGlone, *The Minister's Manual*

Today, you are just two days shy of four months of continuous sobriety. Congratulations. A lot can happen in 118 days. Your health is probably at an all-new level, your understanding of what needs to be done to start maintaining healthy daily living is evident, and you are surrounded by people who give you confidence they will support you in some of your decisions. There is probably also the feeling that in a couple of months, you will be graduating from this six-month program and have begun asking yourself, "What will I do to support myself?"

Today, I'm going to tell you to do something I wish someone had said to me on Day 118 in my recovery: Slow down, and stop thinking about the future. God is infinitely more capable of accomplishing things in one hour than you can think up and plan in one year. God already has it worked out where He wants you, and He is going to make it very obvious to you when the time is right. One thing I have come to understand is, our self-will can get us off course and on a different path quickly. After seven years of sobriety, I still have to remember to slow down and breathe.

In today's verse, Joseph makes it clear he does not have all the answers, but he is telling Pharaoh God does. Joseph could've come up with some brilliant analysis of Pharaoh's dream and appeared to be a hero, but instead, he said, "I don't know, but God has all the answers." Today, I want you to do what Joseph did. I want you to say, "I don't know what I will be doing when I graduate in two months, but what I do know is, God will reveal what He wants for me when the time is right."

On Day 118, let it be evident to others you are relying on God to have you accomplish what you currently think is impossible. God doesn't want you to be a cashier in some company; He wants you to be in charge of it.

This last quote by A. W. Tozer says it all: "God is looking for people through whom He can do the impossible. What a pity that we plan only the things we can do by ourselves."

Prayer for the day: Heavenly Father, I realize one of my biggest character defects is not being able to let go and let God. Not being able to admit I do not have a clue on where I will end up on this new journey. What I do know is, You have an amazing plan already set out for me, and I pray I will slow down and be in place when it is time to receive Your instructions. May I live this day with the assurance You're in control. Amen.

———————————————◆———————————————

# Day 119: Time and Season

Though the fig tree does not bud and there are no grapes on the vines, though the olive crop fails and the fields produce no food, though there are no sheep in the pen and no cattle in the stalls, yet I will rejoice in the LORD, I will be joyful in God my Savior.

—Habakkuk 3:17–18 (NIV)

Researchers have found almost no correlation between income levels and happiness. Between 1957 and 1990, income levels in the U.S. doubled. Yet at the same period, people's levels of happiness did not increase. In fact, reports of depression actually increased tenfold. Incidence of divorce, suicide, alcoholism and drug abuse also rose dramatically.

—Jim Loehr, *The Power of Full Engagement*

In the first year of my ministry, I went through a period of about three weeks when I felt a complete separation from God. One day, I woke up and felt disconnected and distant. As someone who is in recovery, the first thing I thought was, *Is this the beginning of the end? Am I going to fall victim to relapse once again?* As I said, it stayed this way for about three weeks, and nothing I said or did felt like it had any meaning to it. I couldn't hear God's voice, and nothing I did seem to produce any good works or fruit for others. I began to doubt my calling as a leader and minister, and I wondered if God was still beside me on this journey.

We will all have to face a time in this new way of life when God says, "You have been given the tools; now, I need you to rely on them." Think for a moment how Jewish people must have felt during the four hundred years of silence that is noted between the Old and New Testament.

I say all that to say this: There will probably come a time where all the excitement and security from God you currently feel may seem lost. You may feel as if God has dropped you off on an island all by yourself; nothing makes sense, and productivity in your life has come to a halt. When and if this happens, you must evaluate how far you have come and know our Lord and Savior wants to see how far you really want to go. As it says in today's verse, regardless of what happens, "I will rejoice in the Lord, I will be joyful in God my Savior." And oh, yeah, when I came out of that three-week drought I was feeling, God had the most incredible blessing waiting for me after that time of separation was over. God is so faithful.

Prayer for the day: Heavenly Father, I know there will be times when I will begin to feel as if I have no use for anything or anyone. Lord, when these feelings come upon me, may I grasp hold of the assurance You have given me the tools to see me through any obstacles I may face. I take assurance today that even though I may not be able to hear or feel You for a moment, I truly know and believe You are with me for a lifetime, regardless of what I am going through. Amen.

$$\blacklozenge$$

# Day 120: Real or Unreal?

> But when you pray, go into your room, close the door and pray to your Father, who is unseen. Then your Father, who sees what is done in secret, will reward you.
>
> —Matthew 6:6 (NIV)

> Robert Redford was walking one day through a hotel lobby. A woman saw him and followed him to the elevator. "Are you the real Robert Redford?" she asked him with great excitement. As the doors of the elevator closed, he replied, "Only when I am alone."
>
> —Source Unknown

It is natural to want others to witness how well we are doing. Some of us have been such a disappointment to ourselves and others, it is helpful for others to see our new way of living with approval. The problem that comes into play is when we are so desperate for recognition, our actions and prayer life become fake and resemble showmanship.

The relationship between you and the Father takes on genuine sincerity when we eliminate those actions that are pretentious and fake. You do not need the approval of others to confirm who you are in Christ. God hears the voice of the righteous and humble, who are alone and one-on-one with The Creator. Shouting prayers or words of wisdom publicly does not constitute a personal relationship with God. Remember, personal relationships are entirely personal and one-on-one.

Today's verse is a good reminder if we desire this type of one-on-one bond. Are you excited when you get to spend personal time with the Father alone, or is your prayer time set aside only for public appearances? We need to set aside time in our day when there is no one around, and we can empty our hearts truthfully to the Father. Why? Because God knows this time alone with Him is when you are the most sincere.

Prayer for the day: Heavenly Father, I pray today for an even stronger and more meaningful relationship, now more than ever. May the words from my mouth and actions of my body resemble a life of Kingdom living. I pray the approval of my heavenly Father continues to outweigh my desire for public approval and that my personal relationship with You remains personal. Amen.

# Day 121: I Am Where I Am

The Lord is close to the brokenhearted and saves those who are crushed in spirit.

—Psalm 34:18 (NIV)

John Climacus, a seventh-century ascetic who wrote Ladder of Divine Ascent, urged Christians to use the reality of death to their benefit: "You cannot pass a day devoutly unless you think of it as your last," he wrote. He called the thought of death the "most essential of all works" and a gift from God. "The man who lives daily with the thought of death is to be admired, and the man who gives himself to it by the hour is surely a saint." "A man who has heard himself sentenced to death will not worry about the way theatres are run."

—Gary Thomas, in *Christianity Today* (October 3, 1994, 26)

There are so many different guarantees we are faced with during recovery. Not to say we weren't faced with the same guarantees before recovery; it's just that now, we have to approach things differently in how we respond. One of these guarantees is losing loved ones and friends.

The world does not stop for anyone, regardless of your current condition. If you haven't already, you will be confronted with the most heart-wrenching circumstances. Losing a friend or loved one to natural causes, such as old age, is not as complicated as losing someone who is in active addiction. We find when we live a Spirit-filled life, we suffer differently for those we can relate to, and we have a sudden epiphany realizing, "There but for the grace of God go I." We understand, had it not been for God's love and grace, it could have been us friends were grieving for.

Losing a loved one who is in active addiction crushes our spirit because we realize there is a way out. There is an answer. There is a cure. There is God. This feeling of assurance reinforces the importance of our recovery and consecrates the assurance that without God, we are all completely and utterly lost as well as spiritually devoid. Not everyone will surrender and accept this new way of life before it's too late. That feeling we used to have of invincibility while on the streets was nothing more than a façade we no longer cling to.

The psalmist David assures us God is with us during times of grief, when we are so vulnerable to relapse. Lean on Him and learn how to cycle through life successfully when life throws us a curveball, such as death. We must all do our part as disciples to present God's message to those in need and pray they accept it before it is too late. Let not your hearts be heavy, and remember to thank your Lord and Savior for another day of genuine sobriety.

Prayer for the day: Heavenly Father, today, I walk with the assurance I am not promised tomorrow. Help me to be grateful for my current condition and never to forget it is by Your grace I am where I am. Help me to understand even in the most difficult times, such as the loss of a loved one, I must rely solely on You. Thank You, Lord, for helping me overcome the difficult obstacles I continue to face. Everyday life will guarantee me days of turmoil, but you have given me the guarantee of triumph over troubles. Amen.

◆

# Day 122: Surgically Precise

For the word of God is alive and active. Sharper than any double-edged sword, it penetrates even to dividing soul and spirit, joints and marrow; it judges the thoughts and attitudes of the heart.

—Hebrews 4:12 (NIV)

As dangerous as it is to cross paths with a mother bear and her cubs, the Bible tells us that it is even more dangerous to cross paths with a fool.

—Chicagotribune.com, July 8, 2011

Have you ever stopped to wonder why there are times when a preacher's message cuts deep to the core of your soul and has such an incredible impact on your current situation? Times when it feels as if a sermon was written specifically for you? Don't dismiss this feeling. This is the power of God's Word and His message for you.

God's Word diagnoses our current thoughts and condition with a surgeon's precision. It lays open our hearts and discerns our spiritual health. It informs us if we are acting in an appropriate or inappropriate manner and if we are truthful or devious. In the case of those individuals the Hebrews first addressed, they were too ready to follow in the failure of the children of Israel and give up their strong living faith, rather than adhere to the convictions God's Word had on them. Have you felt the confidence of God's Word in your life lately?

When the Word of God exposes our weakness and unbelief, it demonstrates its inherent power, sharpness, and accuracy. Today's verse refers to God's Word as a double-edged sword, meaning both sides will cut deep to the core of our current situation, problems, and way of thinking. We realize God is determined to meet us in His Word; therefore, we will never be able to get around the impact that the message of the Bible can have on our lives.

Today, we realize we submit ourselves to the Word of God because we have witnessed the transforming power the Word has in our own lives. In other words, on Day 122, we acknowledge it was the message of our sword, the Bible, that brought awareness and understanding of the detrimental life we once lived. The message of the Bible allows us to recognize our shortcomings and convicts us every day. May we all continue to feel the presence of God's Word in our lives and act swiftly and accordingly. Not conforming to the message God is currently giving you is like crossing paths with a bear cub and not expecting to feel the wrath of its mother.

Prayer for the day: Heavenly Father, I often dismiss my inner convictions and live according to my own ways and means. Today, I will recognize those convictions as Your way of speaking to me and guiding me down the correct path. May I always remember the entire message of the Bible is applicable to my life and should be used accordingly. Help me to rely on the words of the scripture rather than my own personal way of thinking. Amen.

◆

# Day 123: Who Is Greater Than?

You, dear children, are from God and have overcome them, because the one who is in you is greater than the one who is in the world.

—1 John 4:4 (NIV)

President Lincoln had an early political rival named Edwin Stanton. He called Lincoln the original gorilla. When Lincoln was elected President, he chose Stanton to be his secretary of war because he believed he was the best man for the job. At Lincoln's funeral Stanton said, "There lies the most perfect ruler of men the world has ever seen." President Lincoln had learned not to take insults personally.

*—Abraham Lincoln: The Observations of*
*John G. Nicolay and John Hay*

No matter how you slice it, dice it, flip it upside down, or try to get rid of it, your past will always be at the forefront of somebody else's mind. Your actions and behaviors from days long ago will be more important to others than your current achievements and successes. It's a hard pill to swallow, but it is so true. You want to get ahead, and someone seems to want to bring you down. You want to forget and move on, and someone wants to keep reminding you and holding it against you.

It's important not to become discouraged and upset with the way others view us. There are some people I know who can tell me they have changed their lives and are entirely different, but until I see it for myself, I don't have the assurance needed to believe them. The one person who needs to be assured they have changed is you. This type of guarantee can give you great confidence and spiritual power. For those who were able to walk in this truth, there is the assurance of victory over the judgment of others. Why? Because your confidence is a definite statement, not a wishful hope. It means you no longer fear the opinion of others because just like the verse says, "The one who is in you is greater than the one who is in the world."

We never want to forget our past or where we came from, and we do not need to place so much value on the opinions of others and feel as if we will never become successful at anything. God's plan and purpose for you will rise to the forefront if you remain determined to stay grounded. The evil one will come at you in so many different directions, and one of those directions is the harsh judgment of others. Continue doing what God wants you to do, and people will see you in a completely different light. And oh, yeah, another good reason to hold on is because the cure for addiction is right around the corner.

Prayer for the day: Heavenly Father, I put way too much value in the judgment and opinions of others. May I go forth this day with the assurance that Your opinion and Your judgment is what's imperative in my life. May I begin to convince others by my actions I am no longer who I once was and I am living a life centered in Christ. Amen.

◆

# Day 124: Mix It Up

For we are God's handiwork, created in Christ Jesus to do good works, which God prepared in advance for us to do.
—Ephesians 2:10 (NIV)

Cement, in order to become concrete, must be mixed with sand and water. If bags of cement in a store are never stirred in with water, that cement will never become concrete. Water and sand must be married if you want to get something that is cementable. In order for God to make your life concrete, you're going to have to learn to mix it. You've got to take faith, mix it with works, and watch God lay some concrete in your life.
—Tony Evans, *Illustrations*

On Day 124, you can probably smell the completion of your six-month program right around the corner. It's coming so close, you can visualize your completion date. There's just one dilemma: You have a hard time visualizing where you will be going when it's time to move on. We want to have the advanced assurance our concrete foundation is going to hold our future plans without crumbling. We want our battle plan blueprint for life to be stamped with the approval of others and the assurance that all will be well. Guess what? If this is at the forefront of your mind, then your foundation could very well need a little more mixing for it to strengthen. In other words, we are not quite where God wants us to be, and He is still at work in our lives.

This next statement might sound a little crazy, but it is an incredible tool for success. If you are feeling a bit uncertain as to the direction you're going and you're trying to figure out God's plan in your life, then it's a good idea to freeze and not move at all. More damage can be done to your future when you are in a state of confusion and uncertainty as it pertains to God's plans for you. The only thing you will end up succeeding at is traveling down a path God has not intended for you.

There comes a time in everyone's life when there is instant clarity and understanding as to what God wants us to do and where He wants us to go. How or when will this happen for you, nobody knows. Everyone's paths are different, but you can rest assured when God makes evident His plans for you, you will have a life mixed with faith, assurance, and love, which are all the ingredients for a perfect foundation in your life. So today, if you recognize you are trying and thinking too hard about your future then stop, God is still mixing the ingredients for your solid foundation.

Prayer for the day: Heavenly Father, too often my thoughts and my worry force me down a path of uncertainty followed by calamity and leaves me a crumbled mess. Help me today to mix together those things that will assure me of a concrete spiritual foundation. Help me to know it's okay to be still and understand You are God and You are in control. May I no longer find the need to force a scenario into my life that is not meant for me. Today, I choose to wait on You, Lord. Amen.

◆

# Day 125: Source of Our Success

> I am the vine; you are the branches. If you remain in me and I in you, you will bear much fruit; apart from me you can do nothing.
>
> —John 15:5 (NIV)

Temporary success may often crown the efforts of the godless, but even their greatest achievements cannot bring complete satisfaction. That was Solomon's theme when he said, "The expectation of the wicked shall perish." If unrepentant sinners should view their most brilliant accomplishments in the light of eternity, they would find them to be as lasting and as valuable as bursting bubbles.

*—Our Daily Bread*, January 31

Have you ever noticed certain institutions or organizations run more effectively and efficiently when everybody knows their place and respects the authority of upper management? When you work in this type of environment, where people show respect for each other's positions, you appreciate the part you play and respect the parts other people have. Everyone realizes they cannot achieve their company's goals all by themselves and everyone answers to a higher authority.

Take today's verse, for example. John is declaring that Jesus is the ultimate authority, or as the verse states, He is the source from where we get our instruction and direction. As long as we remember Who the final authority is, our lives have meaning and purpose and a clear path. The moment we practice self-sufficiency and become our bosses, we find ourselves detached and eventually lose direction and begin looking for that authority figure one more time to get us back on course.

In recovery, we must know someone or something higher than us will always be in charge. If you are in the courtroom, there will be a judge; if you are in the workforce, there be a boss. Even the boss who sits at the top of the company ladder has someone to answer to, and that someone is Jesus Christ. Without Him in your life and part of your recovery, you can do nothing. He is the source of all our success.

Prayer for the day: Heavenly Father, it doesn't take me long to see every time travesty occurred in my life, it was because I was not walking alongside You.

I was not attached to Your words the Bible gives me, nor was I relying on Your sovereignty. Help me today to remember that without You, I can do nothing, and my life will produce nothing if I'm separated from You. I am not the ultimate authority of my life, and today, I decide to give You control once again. Amen.

◆

# Day 126: I Want What I Want When I Want It

> There is a time for everything, and a season for every activity
> under the heavens: a time to be born and a time to die, a time
> to plant and a time to uproot, a time to kill and a time to heal, a
> time to tear down and a time to build, a time to weep and a time
> to laugh, a time to mourn and a time to dance, a time to scatter
> stones and a time to gather them, a time to embrace and a time
> to refrain from embracing, a time to search and a time to give
> up, a time to keep and a time to throw away, a time to tear and
> a time to mend, a time to be silent and a time to speak, a time
> to love and a time to hate, a time for war and a time for peace.
> —Ecclesiastes 3:1–8 (NIV)

Have you noticed everybody wants to do things a little better and a little faster? When I was a child, I thought it was amazing I could receive a handwritten letter from my grandmother through the Postal Service in three days flat. Today, using the Postal Service seems almost unheard of and an inefficient way of doing things. We no longer understand the meaning of patience, nor do we approve of it. If I need an answer to a question, I Google it and get an instant response. If I want to communicate with someone, I text them and expect a quick reply in return.

This type of lifestyle leaves no room for the natural order of life to take place. It doesn't allow us to appreciate those things that take time and effort. It also affects how we value our recovery. It takes time to have a clear understanding of who you are and where you're heading in this new way of life. It takes time for people to come back and trust you once again. It takes a conscious effort on your part to listen rather than always wanting to be heard. It takes time to mend those broken hearts by remaining sober and spiritually fit. In other words, in recovery, everything takes time, and there are no quick fixes or answers. Recovery is not accomplished by doing a Google search.

In today's verse, there is not much room for misunderstanding. There is a time for every single scenario in your life, and the most important thing you can do today is to "give time … time." Be ready and willing to be patient and to let God present those things to you in His time when He sees fit. Be prepared to know that in time, you will face controversy without having to look for it. In time, you will sense an abundance of gratitude and happiness you can't explain. In time, you will know when it's time to move on to the next leg of your journey. In time, you will have clarity and understanding. All of these things take time, so please, give yourselves the gift of time, and wait to see what God reveals to you. And oh, yeah, the cure for recovery is still coming, in time.

Prayer for the day: Heavenly Father, I am forced into a world where the value of my success is based on how quickly I can respond, how quickly I can come up with the answers, how quickly I can meet the needs of others. Help me today, Lord, to slow down and realize everything happens in Your time. Everything comes together exactly when it is supposed to. Help me to keep the main thing, the main thing, and to realize my recovery is a day-by-day process that never ends. Amen.

◆

# Day 127: The True Cost

Wherever your treasure is, there the desires of your heart will also be.

—Luke 12:34

It took less than ten seconds for Jamaican sprinter Usain Bolt to cover the one-hundred-meter distance on the Olympic track and win the gold medal in London. Those few seconds cemented his status as the "fastest man alive" and placed him on the winner's podium once again. But the race was not won in those seconds—it was won by hours and hours of practice, workouts, weightlifting, special diet, and coaching. The race was not won in the performance but in the preparation. It is our desire for something greater that causes us to sacrifice some things, even some good things, for the sake of things that are better.

—Belmont and Belcourt Biographies,
*Usain Bolt: An Unauthorized Biography*

There's a misconception so many people have as it pertains to recovery. A lot of times, people are under the impression recovery consists of not picking up another drug or having another drink. This is far from the truth. Putting down the drugs and alcohol allows us to be in a perfect position to truly comprehend the amount of work necessary to achieve successful sobriety.

There's a common characteristic a lot of us have. We have a natural craving to want the achievements other people have, minus doing what it takes to achieve it. In other words, we want the success without the hard work and sacrifice it takes to get it. This type of thinking has no place in recovery. Recovery is, without a doubt, hard work driven by a sincere desire from the heart.

In today's verse, Luke informs us whatever is driving the desires of your heart is where you apply your most significant efforts. If your heart desires to be the world's fastest runner, then you will sacrifice and do whatever it takes to achieve this. If your heart desires money and fame, then you will do whatever it takes to get it. If your heart truly desires recovery, then you will sacrifice any and everything to receive it.

There are no free rides in successful sobriety. You must be willing to sacrifice friends, places, and material items to achieve a new way of life. We must all spend time investing in others while we would rather be entertaining ourselves. Recovery is just one big sacrifice after another, with life-changing rewards. Some of the most spiritually fit men and women I have met in recovery will tell you the quality of an individual's recovery is built upon their heart's desire to be of service to others, to make sure others freely receive what was so freely given to them, no matter what it costs. Your recovery comes with a cost.

Prayer for the day: Heavenly Father, today, I pray for a sacrificial heart that desires to assist and help with the needs of others. I realize today the success of my recovery can be measured by my heart's desire to help others. May I always be sacrificial in my actions and behavior, and may I be willing to sacrifice my wants and desires in order to help others so Your grace may shine as brightly upon them as it is shined upon me. Amen.

# Day 128: The Cry of a Winner

> When he had received the drink, Jesus said, "It is finished."
> With that, he bowed his head and gave up his spirit.
> —John 19:30 (NIV)

> One day George Muller began praying for five of his friends. After many months, one of them came to the Lord. Ten years later, two others were converted. It took 25 years before the fourth man was saved. Muller persevered in prayer until his death for the fifth friend, and throughout those 52 years he never gave up hoping that he would accept Christ! His faith was rewarded, for soon after Muller's funeral the last one was saved.
> —*Our Daily Bread.*

A simple phrase can change everything. A phrase such as "Not guilty" in a court of law changes everything. When you're unable to play great, but you play "fair" on the playing field, it changes everything. When a woman says yes to a marriage proposal, it changes everything, for a lifetime. "Goodbye" can break a heart and can change everything. There has never been a single phrase spoken that impacted history more than what Jesus said in John 19:30. It is finished.

Sometimes, it can be confusing to know when we have given our best. Parts of us would like to give up and call it quits or better yet convince ourselves we've done enough. The truth is, if our Lord and Savior had this type of attitude toward us, He would have given up on us a long time ago. It is God's persistence to see things to the end that allows us to live our lives so freely today.

In today's verse, Jesus knew what He had to do to complete His mission. He knew it would be difficult, and being in human form, I'm sure He was tempted with the idea to quit. I think there are two important messages from this verse, the first being, as long as we don't quit on Jesus, He will never quit on us. The second: Be willing to go the distance for those who are in need. We should never be quick to judge or assume the worst in others. What Jesus did for us, we should have the mindset and desire to mimic ourselves to be of service to others. The only quitting people in recovery should ever do is something you've already done, which is quitting past behaviors. Let God be the one to tell you when "it is finished."

Prayer for the day: Heavenly Father, I have always had a bad habit of never seeing things through, never keeping my promises with my friends, or never being present when I was supposed to with my family. Help me today, oh, Lord, to recognize Jesus never gave up on me, and therefore I should be willing and determined to finish this race, the race that says, as long as I am in Christ, I can do all things. Amen.

$$\text{\textdiamond}$$

# Day 129: Wonder Bread

Then Jesus declared, "I am the bread of life. Whoever comes to me will never go hungry, and whoever believes in me will never be thirsty.

—John 6:35 (NIV)

A little girl came to her grandmother and noticed that her grandmother's ring was big and gaudy and ugly looking.

She said, "Grandma, those rings back there when y'all got married were so big and heavy and gaudy looking."

Her grandmother replied, "Yeah, cause when I got my rings back in the day, they were made to last."

—Tony Evans, *Illustrations,* 203

Why are we so determined to invest in things that give us a false sense of security and never last? Take, for example, people who want to lose weight. They will immediately go online and try to find the newest pill or diet that will guarantee them weight loss. Inevitably, the only thing they lose is their money and their desire to do the things necessary to lose weight. And the same goes for our money. We want a satisfying option that will allow us to get rich quick and to feel successful.

The same is true when we try to fill the spiritual void we sometimes encounter. We listen to false prophets and felonious preachers who sell heresy and fake remedies for your spiritual needs. You work so hard to satisfy that hunger and spiritual craving, only to be left starving for more.

In today's verse, we see there is only one real source that can feed our spiritual hunger, and that is Jesus Christ. In recovery, we may feel overly anxious as it pertains to our spiritual hunger and what we can consume to satisfy it. We are like little kids in a bright new world, ready to grab anything to see what type of effect it will have on our spiritual cravings. Don't be fooled. Once you begin to digest the bread of life, you will find that certain spiritual cravings are fulfilled and no longer leave you dissatisfied and searching for more.

Prayer for the day: Heavenly Father, every day, I hunger and thirst for those things that will bring complete satisfaction in my life. I continue to look in all the wrong directions to find a quick remedy and continue to end up with a void in my life. Help me to understand today's verse and what it means to "hunger and thirst to know more." Today, I choose Your message to feed my spiritual cravings in order that I may be filled completely. Amen.

♦

# Day 130: The Whole Truth

> "Teacher," they said, "we know that you speak and teach what is right and are not influenced by what others think. You teach the way of God truthfully."
>
> —Luke 20:21

On Day 130, you're probably aware not everybody is doing what they're doing for the right reasons or for the same reasons you may be doing them. Some people are in recovery to please others, some to please the court, and some want a short and temporary reprieve from what they were experiencing before they return to past behaviors. Be aware of these individuals and their motives. Be mindful of your surroundings. Most importantly, be completely aware of what you read and how you react. You never want to get drawn into somebody else's chaos.

When we read the Bible, we need to make sure that we are not doing what's called "proof-texting," which is when we read one small verse in the Bible and assume we have it figured out. People who want a justifiable reason to do something biblically incorrect will take one single verse and decipher it to their favor to feel good about what they want to do.

Let's look at today's verse, for example. Merely reading this verse by itself, one would assume that it was the disciples giving praise to Jesus, and therefore, you move on without understanding the complete story. If this is your current method of understanding scripture, one verse at a time, you are missing the entire message and how it could impact your life.

Let's look at the whole text, starting at verse 20–22:

> So they watched Him, and sent spies who pretended to be righteous, that they might seize on His words, in order to deliver Him to the power and the authority of the governor. Then they asked Him, saying, "Teacher, we know that You say and teach rightly, and You do not show personal favoritism, but teach the way of God in truth: Is it lawful for us to pay taxes to Caesar or not?"

When we read the complete verse, we understand verse 21 is not about disciples giving praise to Jesus; it has to do with spies trying to trick Him. The point is, be careful of those who are around you. Be sure the ones you are taking advice from have read the complete scripture passage and are giving you good orderly direction, versus those who simply proof-text and can lead you astray. Be completely grounded in God's Word, and never let others lead you astray by using only one verse from the Bible. Be sure you have the complete message.

Prayer for the day: Heavenly Father, I pray today for the peace and comfort the complete and entire Bible can bring me. I pray I never find comfort or try to find assurances by minimizing Your Word. May I always be mindful of the ones who are around me and put what they are teaching me to the test. Guide me and direct me safely down the one true path of righteousness. Amen.

◆

# Day 131: Never Surrender

But the one who endures to the end will be saved.

—Matthew 24:13

One of the biggest boxing matches of the twentieth century took place on November 25, 1980, at the Superdome in New Orleans, Louisiana. It was a rematch between Sugar Ray Leonard and Roberto Duran. Duran had won the previous fight and was the favorite the second time around. He had a record of 72 wins and just one loss and he had won his last forty-one fights. That is some winning streak. The rematch was a close fight. Only a point or two separated the two fighters on the judges' scorecards. But then something unthinkable happened in the eighth round that no one expected. Roberto Duran turned to the referee and spoke two words: "No Mas." "No more." He quit. He wasn't injured. He wasn't cut. He was frustrated and he'd had enough. Here is a fighter who was one of the best to ever step into the ring. He won a total of 103 fights, but when anyone mentions his name today, the first thing that comes to mind is "no mas." People remember the day he quit.

—Source Unknown

One simple act can spark the greatest change in our lives. In recovery, we only have to make one of two decisions every day: 1) Stay focused on the path God has us on, or 2) give up and quit. It's that simple. Staying focused and on the path God has you on assures you of what today's verse clearly states: "You will be saved." Giving up and quitting this journey guarantees a life of chaos and death.

Unfortunately, quitting is the easiest thing to do and the one thing everybody else seems to remember the most. No matter how hard we try, each time we give up on God and ourselves, it makes a lasting impression on others. It makes it that much harder for people to believe in us, and the worst thing is that by giving up on God, we could lose our life and the plans He has for us.

It's been many years since my family and friends have had to endure the consequences of my addiction. My mother and father call me all the time and want to spend time with me. I am now married to a beautiful wife who trusts me completely with everything. But the most important thing is, I have a relationship with God I refuse to surrender. We should all embrace a healthy fear and understanding of what it could be like without God by our side. On Day 131, you still only have to make one of two decisions. Choose to stay with God and embrace the plans He has for you.

Prayer for the day: Heavenly Father, it seems every day I have to shuffle through a thousand different decisions and choices to be made. Help me today to realize the most important decision I have to make each and every day is to continue on this path with You. Bless me with the gift of fear, a fear that tells me to quit recovery means to lose my life and my relationship with You forever. You have brought me so far, Lord. Help me make the right decision for one more day. Amen.

◆

# Day 132: You Only Need to See Me

Do not be quick with your mouth, do not be hasty in your heart to utter anything before God. God is in heaven and you are on earth, so let your words be few.

—Ecclesiastes 5:2

Being a little kinder, a little slower to anger, a little more loving makes my life better—day by day.

—*Daily Reflections*: *Alcoholics Anonymous*

For as it is not the loudness of a preacher's voice, but the weight and holiness of his matter, and the spirit of the preacher, that moves a wise and intelligent hearer, so it is not the labor of the lips, but the travail of the heart that prevails with God.

—Trapp

Have you ever noticed everybody has something to say, and they demand to be heard? Sometimes, I believe people should record themselves when they are in the heat of the moment, and they feel like there's something they have to get off their chest. To be able to play back their words and hear the aggression, the bitterness, the conviction of being correct while they are trying to prove their point. If we could all record ourselves in the heat of the moment, there's a good chance there may not much Jesus in our behavior.

Solomon justly described the human tendency to speak without stopping and thinking before God and others. There is a tendency at times to be under so much pressure with day-to-day living we sometimes, subconsciously, want to have a justifiable reason to lash out and release that aggression. How many of us have rehearsed in our minds what we want to say to someone who has wronged us and have also rehearsed our response to their reply? This type of mindset is not only harmful to someone else but can have devastating effects on our recovery.

About 90 percent of the things you need to take care of today can be done without words. The other 10 percent should be used to praise God and to bring joy to others. So often, we fail to realize how damaging our tongues can be to others. So damaging, I can remember harmful things that were said to me when I was just a kid. Remember, today, it is your actions and the way you treat others that will have the greatest and the most positive impact on someone's life. Recovery is all about sharing the grace of God with others and making a positive lasting impact in their lives.

Prayer for the day: Heavenly Father, I pray today that I can let go of this circus tent of crazy thoughts that run through my mind. I pray today you will help me find the words that are uplifting and life-changing instead of demoralizing and crushing. Help me to be encouraging and positive in the life of others, and help me understand sometimes I only need to be seen and not heard. Amen.

◆

# Day 133: Weary and Wise

Look, I am sending you out as sheep among wolves. So be as shrewd as snakes and harmless as doves.

—Matthew 10:16

In May of 2012, a 32-carat Burmese ruby and diamond ring—that was part of the collection of Lily Safra, one of the richest women in the world—was sold at an auction. The preauction estimate for the sale was $3 to 5 million, but the final sale price ended up at $6.7 million. It is believed to be the most expensive ruby ever sold. As valuable as rubies are, the Bible tells us wisdom is far more valuable. No earthly treasure can compare to wisdom because nothing else offers the same protection, benefits, and blessings wisdom does.

Have you ever stopped to notice the things society classifies as acceptable? The world around us is changing day by day regarding how we respond to life scenarios, scenarios that draw us into its chaos and demand a verbal or physical response. It allows us to feel justified in physical violence to the point of recording it to promote it online. People deliberately become confrontational with law enforcement. School fighting and road rage incidents are direct results from the encouragement of social media.

In today's verse, Matthew is telling us to beware of such chaos in the way we as disciples are to respond. Jesus was telling His disciples they would be targets and to be wary and wise and stay clear. But if they were to find themselves trapped and cornered, they were to be as harmless as doves. This type of behavior and response is just as vital for us in recovery as well.

This is the way Jesus responded long before social media. When Jesus was falsely accused and beaten and cornered, He did not lash out and strike back with physical violence and aggression. He challenged them with love, and although it may not seem like it at the time, we now see that love wins. Remember, just because somebody says something is socially acceptable does not mean it is biblically correct. Be sagacious, and ask yourself the next time you are caught in a confrontation, "What would Jesus do?"

Prayer for the day: Heavenly Father, my behaviors and actions fall so short of being as gentle as a dove. I have come to understand and accept there are dangers around me, but what I am unable to do at the moment is to respond the way Jesus would. Help me to realize the error of my ways and to be wise by stopping and intentionally mimicking what Jesus did when He was faced with confrontation. Amen.

◆

# Day 134: All-Around Awareness

Then he came to the disciples and said, "Go ahead and sleep. Have your rest. But look—the time has come. The Son of Man is betrayed into the hands of sinners."

—Matthew 26:45

I heard about a man whose family sent him to the doctor because he constantly complained of being too sick to work. The doctor examined his patient, then told him to get dressed and meet him in his office.

When the man came into the office and sat down, he said, "Give it to me straight, doc. Don't use any complicated, fancy-sounding medical terms. My family wants the truth in plain English. What's wrong with me?"

"All right," the doctor said. "I'll make it as plain as I can. There isn't a thing wrong with you. You're just lazy."

The man sat silent for a moment, then said, "I see. Now will you give me a complicated, fancy-sounding medical term I can tell my family?"

—*Sermon Central*

One thing is guaranteed whenever you start a new journey, a journey with a new job or new friendships, and it also includes the journey of recovery. There is a guarantee the excitement and the pink cloud you were when you first arrived has probably faded away. By now, you have a specific regimen and routine you like stick to, and you have convinced yourself to be safe, you should do no more or no less. If we were to be honest, this is nothing more than an excuse not to continue working hard, which affects our awareness of what's happening in our lives.

In today's verse, we see Jesus never took away the decision to find rest and to sleep. The problem that arises for Christians is when we take our decision to rest a little too far. We are content with our current surroundings, our current achievements, and feel no need to apply the gifts God has given us in a new direction. Finding contentment in remaining stationary only means others may be suffering because of your lack of attention and assistance. Just look at the disciples' scenario in today's verse, for instance.

Today, we should remain eager to explore new areas, with the assurance God is keeping us safe. We need to uncover new talents that can be applied not only to our lives but to the lives of those who are trying to find this new way of life. Be determined today to be a disciple who is ready, willing, and able to work hard and move forward with assurance. That's the strength God and recovery give us so when the time is right, we are equipped and prepared to help those in need.

Prayer for the day: Heavenly Father, today, I began to recognize I might be simply going through the motions of the same old routine, each and every day. Help me to rise up to the challenge of being intentional and ready. Help me to do this by allowing me to try something new each and every day in order that my routine may make a difference in the life of someone else. Amen.

◆

# Day 135: He, Not I

*It is the Father living in me who is doing His work.*

*—John 14:10*

Someone once observed a wasted life is really nothing more than a collection of wasted days. As God gives us life, each one of us starts the new year with the same number of opportunities—365—that we can choose to either use and invest in eternal things or allow to drift by without taking advantage of the gift we have been given. The difference between those who succeed and those who fail is not found primarily in talent but in diligence and effort (www.ministry127.com).

One area of life I always have to deal with is understanding those who knew me at my worst may never have confidence in what I am doing today. No matter how long I have been sober and clean, some continue to think whatever I do or say is nothing more than a hustle or a con. To be honest, I sometimes have to evaluate my motives and ask myself if I'm being truly sincere and honest, or do I have ulterior reasons? I look at where I am today, compared to ten years ago, and I recognize it is something greater than I steadily at work.

One of the greatest things we can all do in this new way of life is to give credit where credit is due and realize all the success and all the blessings we are experiencing come from God working in us. We make an intentional effort to do what is right and what is necessary, but it is ultimately God's guidance and intercession that bring about our success. We come into sobriety understanding and comprehending devastation and destruction, and for a lot of us, these were only gifts. Today, let us never forget that by ourselves, we can do nothing, but by God living in us, anything and everything is possible, regardless of what others think.

Prayer for the day: Heavenly Father, I am in awe of the miraculous work You have done in my life. I pray today I may continue to remain focused and remember it is from Your guidance and Your direction I can say I am truly successful. May the blessings that have been bestowed upon me be a shining example of what it means to have God living in me. Amen.

# Day 136: Bad Blueprints

In his heart a man plans his course, but the Lord determines his steps.

—Proverbs 16:9

The passions of our life are wasted if they aren't the same passions that Jesus has.

—Source Unknown

Have you ever stopped to wonder what you would have received if you had gotten what you truly deserved? Did you deserve about a hundred DUIs for driving while impaired but somehow never received one? I have the feeling that if you are like me, you have come to realize although you have experienced a few rough roads and some devastation, God has kept you safe from having to experience what you deserve.

I say all that to say this: If God has kept you safe and out of harm's way, it must be because He has an incredible plan for you. And if He has an incredible plan already mapped out for you, which is perfect and holy and in your best interest, then it is safe to say your intentions may be restricting you from His ultimate goal, which is complete serenity and freedom from those things that bind you.

We have all heard the Serenity Prayer, and we have had a meeting after meeting on what its message means. But let me break it down so it may have a different impact on your spirit and your life and how it relates to today's verse. Here's the Serenity Prayer I use:

"God, grant me the serenity, to accept the ones I cannot change, the courage to change the one I can, and the wisdom to know that it's me."

No matter what you say or what you do, the one person who interferes with God's purpose for your life is you. When you came into recovery, was it because you wanted to learn how to better be in control of your life, or to let someone or something greater be in control of you? How's that going so far? May we always remember to be intentional to follow the path God has created for you. Any other way is simply a dead end.

Prayer for the day: Heavenly Father, so often I want to draw a blueprint for my life and present it to You for Your approval. I have so many grandiose and wonderful ideas, but they continue to fail. I pray today You will determine my steps and lead me with confidence on a path that glorifies Your name and Who You are. Continue to guide me and keep me safe, and I will continue to surrender my will and my life to You. Amen.

◆

# Day 137: Angelic Likeness

> You have made them a little lower than the angels and crowned
> them with glory and honor.
>
> —Psalm 8:5 (NIV)

Having responsibilities will do one of two things in your life: 1. You will begin to appreciate the things you have been entrusted with and maximize your potential to ensure you're serving a purpose. 2. Or you will flee from it and put your trust in the ability of others to fulfill your responsibilities. Doing the latter will ensure you're not fulfilling God's will for your life.

We are genuinely very far indeed from realizing our true potential and what we are to be responsible for. We tend to hate and hurt one another, destroy and enslave one another, indulge in all kinds of heinous crimes, and invent brutal weapons of destruction, and yet we call ourselves children of God. To understand what it means to be a child of God, you need to first embrace your position as it pertains to the hierarchy of angels and God's Kingdom. Remember, you are made in the image of God, as today's verse makes clear, and we are just slightly lower than the heavenly angels.

On Day 137 of this new recovery journey, wouldn't it be fantastic if you could begin to embrace your royal position in the Kingdom of God? Wouldn't it be wonderful if today you embrace the idea and the fact it is not your past that defines you, but it is taking responsibility for who you are in the eyes of God and claiming it openly? God gave you the Spirit to triumph and reign over all the earth, and today, you have been given the responsibility to own up and accept who you are in the eyes of God and move forward, claiming responsibility for your gifts. Don't pass off to others what God is calling you to do, what God calls us all to do, which is to be disciples to other people.

Prayer for the day: Heavenly Father, so often, I pass off my responsibility to others because I am either unsure of my abilities or I truly do not know who I am in Your sight. Lord, help me today to truly discover who I am and declare my rightful seat as a child of God. Help me to embrace my new self-worth and my new responsibilities. May I begin to understand what it means to have been crowned with glory and honor. Amen.

# Day 138: You Are Priceless

Knowing that you were not redeemed with corruptible things, like silver or gold, from your aimless conduct received by tradition from your fathers, but with the precious blood of Christ, as of a lamb without blemish and without spot.
—1 Peter 1:18–19 (NKJV)

We have all seen MasterCard's commercial "There are some things money can't buy, and for everything else, there's MasterCard." So many times, a lot of us hold on to this flaky idea our importance lies in our ability to find security from material possessions. We work very, very hard to acquire those things that give us a level of comfort, only to continue to try to reach another higher level. We never find joy and happiness for who we are and where we are, regardless of our current situation. We get bored with childhood wanting to grow up, only to find out we want to be children again. We work so hard and lose our health, making money, only to lose our money to take care of our health.

You are so much more than what you could ever dream. You are not merely what you see, skin and flesh, in the mirror. In fact, your physical body is not even you. It is nothing more than cheap material that holds all the nutrients and elements needed for your true inner self to be alive. If you took all the elements that made up your body and tried to sell them, you probably couldn't get ten dollars for them.

In today's verse, Peter tells us Jesus sees in us not merely flesh and blood, but also spirit and love. We can think and understand the same thoughts and feelings our Lord and Savior Jesus Christ had. We can share with God our thoughts and feelings and emotions, just like Jesus did. We're the only ones who can present ourselves before God and be forgiven of our sins and have the assurance of our salvation, like Jesus did. So when you stop on Day 138 and think about it, God has created you in the image of his Son, and in the eyes of God, his Son was priceless. Now, how much do you think are you worth?

Prayer for the day: Heavenly Father, I am tired of letting my past physical behaviors define who I am. Today, I embrace the understanding I am a child of God, and therefore I am priceless. I trust and believe by holding on to the thoughts and ideas that are given to me through the living Bible, I can embrace and enjoy my new identity, an identity not even MasterCard can purchase. Amen.

# Day 139: Count on It

Come to me, all who are weary in heavy-laden, and I will give you rest.

—Matthew 11:28 (NIV)

Martin Luther once said, "And though this world filled with devils that threaten to undo us, we will not fear, for God has willed His truth to triumph through us." The point Martin Luther was trying to make is, you can rest assured no matter how hard we try, there are going to be pitfalls and valleys waiting for us. At this stage of your recovery, you've probably been made aware of all the dangers, dos and don'ts, and things to watch out for by your associates. Sometimes, it can be overwhelming, and quite frankly, I myself have to push away all the naysayers and remember God is guiding me through each and every turn, without being made paranoid by everyone around me.

Unfortunately, we're still riddled with emotions of embarrassment, fear, and that never-ending feeling we may fail again. Although fear is a wonderful attribute to have in certain situations, overwhelming fear is not necessary for recovery. The devil knows if he can get you to harness this unnecessary fear and continue to worry about certain situations, he might be able to get you to rebel against the Lord.

Never forget God wants to meet you in the here and now, whether you are discouraged or on cloud 9. You can always count on the fact when you come to the Savior, you can find the assurance Matthew was talking about in today's verse. Do not be overwhelmed by all the negative Nancies of the world, who continue to disrupt your serenity and your assurance of a meaningful relationship with Christ. We didn't come this far on the road to recovery to be overwhelmed with fear. Today is not a day to be beating yourself up. Be assured God is right beside you hand in hand, and His blessings for you are never-ending. And oh, yeah, I haven't said it in a while, but the cure for addiction is just a few pages away.

Prayer for the day: Heavenly Father, there are days when I simply can't gather up the strength to smile and recognize all my blessings. Lord, when all I can see is doom and gloom, I am so grateful I can count on Your presence in my life. I pray I may always seek Your face first in all of life's scenarios, the good and bad, pain and happiness, the unassured and assurances. May I never dwell too long on my current situation without You. Amen.

# Day 140: All My Thoughts

Blessed is the one who perseveres under trial because, having stood the test, that person will receive the crown of life that the Lord has promised to those who love him.

—James 1:12 (NIV)

Pain is not good in itself. What is good in any painful experience is, for the sufferer, his submission to the will of God, and, for the spectators, the compassion aroused and the acts of mercy to which it leads.

—C. S. Lewis, *The Problem of Pain*

It's funny how all of us in recovery have so many similar qualities and characteristics. One of those characteristics I have noticed is the ability for us to ignore physical pain. For some reason, physical pain to us is not pain at all. For instance, if ever there is something we wanted to acquire or goal we want to achieve that requires physical exertion, we gladly accept and conquer it. But what I also find surprising is the complete opposite when it comes to our conscience and the spiritual pain it brings. The one common factor we have in recovery as pertains to our consciousness is when we are spiritually in pain, we can't accept it, and we do whatever it takes to be rid of it, even though it brings about physical pain. Physical pain acceptable, spiritual pain unacceptable, and needs numbing.

On Day 140 on this new journey, we have to face the reality we became spiritually debunked the first time we drank ourselves into a stupor or used a narcotic. We immediately began to feel the conscience God gives us being crushed, and from that, the shame and guilt begin to arise. At first, what we thought would be fun turns out to be a never-ending spiritual punishment. We put our physical bodies in danger by covering up our spiritual pain.

In today's verse, James tells us even the spiritual pain we feel can be overcome by standing on God's promises. How blessed we all will be when we stop masking the spiritual sickness we have and embrace God's spiritual healing. Today, you have covered a milestone if you can accept the physical pain was just a symptom of the real problem, which was spiritual bankruptcy, and only God can fill this void. Loving God with all your heart, with all your mind, with all your strength gets you through the tough times as well as assures you of eliminating not only the physical but the spiritual pain we all face, without having to become stupefied and numb. Embrace whatever pain you may be feeling by embracing God's hands.

Prayer for the day: Heavenly Father, today, I realize I may only be addressing 50 percent of the problem by neglecting to confront my spiritual pain. Taking care of my physical body is not enough, and lately, I have been using my physical strength to overcome my spiritual pain. Help me today to fill that spiritual void by resting on Your promise to be with me during this tough time. Amen.

◆

# Day 141: Paid in Full

Do nothing out of selfish ambition or vain conceit. Rather, in humility value others above yourselves.

—Philippians 2:3 (NIV)

There is the story of a little boy who wanted his mother to pay him for all the services he was rendering in the home. He left her a note that read, "For washing the dishes, you owe me a dollar. For cleaning my room, you owe me a dollar. For hanging up my clothes, you owe me a dollar. For mowing the lawn, you owe me a dollar. Mama, you owe me, pay up."

He printed a bill for her, totaling $4 and gave it to her. The mother put four dollars on the kitchen table with a note of her own.

The note simply said, "For carrying you 9 months and being sick as a dog, no charge. For staying up all night with you, night after night when you were sick, no charge. The working overtime so that I could get you those special tennis shoes, no charge. For entertaining your friends when you wanted to bring them over without notice, no charge. Signed, your mother who loves you. Total, zero."

After reading the note, the young man realized that he had lost sight of the goodness of his mother. He had turned a love relationship into a business deal. He had said to his mother what a lot of God's children say to Him: "Pay up. What's in it for me?"

—Tony Evans, *Illustrations*

I encourage every individual, whether they are in recovery or whether they are in the congregation I preach to on Sunday, to keep an inventory list of all the blessings they have received, to look back and recognize someone, somewhere had a heart like Christ to pave a pathway for you and me to find freedom for those things that could destroy us spiritually. For them to put their selfish desires aside so they may see how truly blessed they are. When we do this, we begin to realize the money someone owed you from the past, the hateful words you heard someone say about you, the job you felt was rightly yours but was denied, just isn't that important.

On Day 141 of this new journey, I challenge you to ask yourself, are the things you're currently seeking driven out of selfish ambition and vain conceit, or are you being driven by humility and a desire to put the needs of others before your own? This question should be a daily question for us all, to ensure what was freely given to us by our Lord and Savior Jesus Christ is being displayed through our behaviors to others. This is pivotal behavior thinking for both our recovery life and our spiritual life.

Prayer for the day: Heavenly Father, I can see quite clearly a lot of my actions are possibly driven by greed and selfish ambition to achieve more for myself. I can see how I am putting my wants and my desires above the needs of others, and for this, I say I am sorry. Help me today to realize my freedom and my eternal security was freely given to me when You gave Your life for me on the cross. May I begin to display a spirit of giving so others may have what was so freely given to me. Amen.

◆

# Day 142: Opinions and A— Holes

Even fools are thought wise if they keep silent, and discerning
if they hold their tongues.

—Proverbs 17:28 (NIV)

I am amazed as well as concerned at how quickly people will conform their way
of thinking and behavior based on something they heard on the news or through
idle gossip. I am worried the values we held when we were young are being erased
like words on a chalkboard because of someone's fancy talk and outlandish points
of view. Most importantly, I am concerned for those who are under the impression
it is of the utmost importance they be heard by expressing their views and their
opinions verbally, not based on biblical life experiences, but based on their current
emotions and feelings from what they witnessed on the internet or heard from a
blogger. Isn't speaking and acting out on our current beliefs and emotions what
got us where we are to begin with?

We have all heard the old saying, "Opinions are like a— holes; everybody
has one, and the majority of them stink." I say this because so often, people are
displaying their opinions without really understanding what they're saying. When
we came into recovery, we were always driven by the next hustle or some brilliant
idea we thought we had, or some crazy solution to getting clean, continuously
grasping hold of false promises and eloquent words and ideas from others, only to
find those ideas and thoughts were misleading and dishonest.

Here's a thought to chew on for a little while: What if God is asking you to be
a spiritual filter to discern what is biblically correct for your life without any verbal
response? What if God is asking you to use your gift of discernment to take what
you have heard and put it to the test biblically to see if it will pass? What if God is
asking that you not react so quickly so Jesus may act on your behalf? Hallelujah.

The most important part about today's verse is, when we speak out of turn
without truly understanding what we're saying, there's a chance we are not only
hurting ourselves but could be misguiding others as well. Make sure on Day 142,
you are putting the things you think are correct and you feel are essential to the
test, by applying scripture as your support. If what you think or feel or want to say
doesn't match up to the actions and words of Jesus Christ, then it is for sure not
worth doing or mentioning. Sometimes, the wisest person says and does nothing
at all.

Prayer for the day: Heavenly Father, I look back and often regret a lot of the things I said and did. So many times, I speak too quickly, thinking I am correct in my thoughts and actions without testing those ideas for your approval. On Day 142, I give thanks I do not think and see things the way I did on Day 1, but help me realize, Lord, I must continue to seek Your opinions and approval, each and every day. Amen.

♦

# Day 143: Fearless Fear

The fear of the LORD is a fountain of life, turning a person from the snares of death.

—Proverbs 14:27

The story is told of a nobleman who had a lovely floral garden. The gardener who tended it took great pains to make the estate a veritable paradise. One morning he went into the garden to inspect his favorite flowers. To his dismay he discovered that one of his choice beauties had been cut from its stem. Soon he saw that the most magnificent flowers from each bed were missing. Filled with anxiety and anger, he hurried to his fellow employees and demanded, "Who stole my treasures?"

One of his helpers replied, "The nobleman came into his garden this morning, picked those flowers himself, and took them into his house. I guess he wanted to enjoy their beauty." The gardener then realized that he had no reason to be concerned because it was perfectly right for his master to pick some of his own prize blossoms.

—Source Unknown

There are so many things in life we tend to get backward. For example, you have heard the old sayings, "You must have less to gain more," "You must fail before you can succeed," and "Slow and steady wins the race." Today's verse has a lot in common with these old sayings.

So often, we tend to think fear would lead to less life and not more. Simply put, that's not how it works when we have a fear of the Lord. Proper fear of the Lord is rooted in an understanding of Who God is and who we are in relation to Him. That itself is like a fountain of life flowing from reverent fear. So another saying you can add to your repertoire would be, "The abundance of life can be found in a fountain of fear."

There is an inner spiritual fear we will never understand, but we need to deliberately grasp hold to. We hold firmly to the fact our salvation and our spiritual well-being are secure as a direct response to recognizing God's holiness. The main root of our fear comes from the fact we cannot understand, nor will we ever, God's perfect and loving plan for us. We hold firmly to the idea and the understanding

God knows best, and our fear of ourselves and what we are capable of allows us to display a reverent fear for what God wants to do in our life. On Day 143, may the fountain of life that flows from your fear of the Lord release you from any turmoil or unwarranted fear you may currently be experiencing. To have a fear of the Lord frees you and gives you an abundant life, a fulfilling life called recovery.

Prayer for the day: Heavenly Father, I am bombarded daily by unnecessary fears which I can overcome if I remain fearful toward one thing in my life and that would be fear of the Lord. Help me to understand the reverent fear I need in my life in order to be completely free from all unnecessary fears. I pray I may continue to understand scripture and what it truly means my life in order that I may be a living example to others. Amen.

◆

# Day 144: Clear with Clarity

For I know the plans I have for you," declares the Lord, "plans
to prosper you and not to harm you, plans to give you hope
and a future.

—Jeremiah 29:11 (NIV)

It is probably safe to say if you have made it to Day 144 and continue to read these
devotionals every day, it's because you have experienced a change in your life
that is new and precious. You may have recently experienced what it means to be
blessed unexpectedly, or you may have been faced with an impossible scenario and
experienced God's guidance getting you through it without you using or drinking
and making it worse. We begin to have a different understanding of scripture and
how God is applying verses in the Bible into our lives.

These types of revelations go hand in hand with today's verse. If you look
at today's verse closely, you notice how so many Christians use this passage as a
prosperity verse to excite people and assure them hard times are over and they're
going to be blessed in everything they do. Today, we recognize the true meaning
behind this verse (and many other verses of scripture). Today's verse is an assurance
verse, which means we can be assured of experiencing worldly problems in our
lives, but we will have greater assurance God's plan will prevail and get us through
the tough times successfully.

It would be so beautiful if I could assure you, along with convincing myself,
the road ahead is smooth and without detours or valleys. The simple fact is this:
We made a commitment to God on Day 1 to stop using and drinking so we may be
able to face those troubles without making them worse. We did not become sober
to be excluded from our problems; we became sober to deal with them successfully.
Today's verse states God has a perfect plan for our lives that will prevail, even
during troubles, if we stay focused and remain in Him.

Take time out today and recognize those obstacles and hurdles you have
overcome in 144 days, and you will have a desire and a craving to see what
Day 145 holds for you and how God's plan for your life becomes more evident
every day. What a blessing it is to have God's clarity of what life holds for you
within scripture, without the blurred, misinterpreted views from others. Clarity
of scripture in life is a blessing in and of itself, which a lot of people never gain.

Prayer for the day: Heavenly Father, as King Solomon once prayed for wisdom, I pray today for clarity in scripture. I give thanks to You for being there for me when times were tough, and I was ready to give up. I give thanks to You for allowing me to see the bigger picture, that a life of sobriety is a life worth living. I take assurance in knowing there will be tough times ahead, but I take even greater confidence knowing Your plan will prevail in my life, regardless of the obstacles I am faced with. Amen.

◆

# Day 145: You're Qualified

Take my yoke upon you and learn from me, for I am gentle and humble in heart, and you will find rest for your souls.
—Matthew 11:29 (NIV)

A number of years ago, *Newsweek* magazine carried the story of the memorial service held for Hubert Humphrey, former vice president of the United States. Hundreds of people came from all over the world to say good-bye to their old friend and colleague. But one person who came was shunned and ignored by virtually everyone there. Nobody would look at him, much less speak to him. That person was former president Richard Nixon. Not long before, he had gone through the shame and infamy of Watergate. He was back in Washington for the first time since his resignation from the presidency.

Then a very special thing happened, perhaps the only thing that could have made a difference and broken the ice. President Jimmy Carter, who was in the White House at that time, came into the room. Before he was seated, he saw Nixon over against the wall, all by himself. He went over to him as though he were greeting a family member, stuck out his hand to the former president, and smiled broadly.

To the surprise of everyone there, the two of them embraced each other, and Carter said, "Welcome home, Mr. President. Welcome home."

Commenting on that, *Newsweek* magazine asserted, "If there was a turning point in Nixon's long ordeal in the wilderness, it was that moment and that gesture of love and compassion."

The above illustration is a fantastic example of what it means to be of comfort to others when they are in need. Today's devotion won't be long or complicated, but it will emphasize the importance of displaying love and compassion for others. On Day 145, you are more than qualified to be able to represent to others the love that was revealed and given to you.

If you can sum up what recovery and Christian living have in common, it would be love. The main ingredient that is of the most value and will guarantee an empowering life with God, as well as complete abstinence from substances, is love. First, we have to begin to love and forgive ourselves for the things we have done and be willing to display that type of love to others, every moment of our lives. This type of behavior signifies our gratitude, quantifies and proclaims our love for Christ, and secures our place among society. Look at today's verse and then ask yourself, "Am I demonstrating and living this kind of love for others?" Remember, your recovery and salvation depend on it.

Prayer for the day: Heavenly Father, as I sit here and read today's devotion, I begin to realize I am a product of love a product of forgiveness, a product of sacrifice, a product of grace. Let my actions and my life be a direct reflection to others of the love that was given to me so freely. Not only is my life depending on it, but the Christlike love I display may save the life of another in need. Amen.

---

# Day 146: No Ifs, Ands, or Buts

> But if serving the Lord seems undesirable to you, then choose for yourselves this day whom you will serve, whether the gods your ancestors served beyond the Euphrates, or the gods of the Amorites, in whose land you are living But as for me and my household we will serve the Lord.
>
> —Joshua 24:15 (NIV)

Dr. Viktor Frankl, author of the book *Man's Search for Meaning*, was imprisoned by the Nazis during World War II because he was a Jew. His wife, his children, and his parents were all killed in the Holocaust. The Gestapo made him strip. He stood there totally naked. As they cut away His wedding ring, Viktor said to himself, *You can take my wife, you can take away my children, you can strip me of my clothes and my freedom, but there is one thing no person can ever take away from me—and that is my freedom to choose how I will react to what happens to me.* Even under the most difficult of circumstances, happiness is a choice that transforms our tragedies into triumph.

If we were to stop and take a look at the actions of others, as well as ourselves, we might be shocked and amazed at how we have compromised on what we believe to be right and wrong and how we continue to make exceptions to biblical rules and principles. If anything out of the ordinary is a minute inconvenience in our lives, we want to do away with it.

So I say all that to ask this: What are you not willing to compromise? What do you hold so dear to your heart you will not conform to the ideas of others, even if it means being inconvenienced?

On Day 146, you are at a pivotal point in your new life where there are going to be times when you feel you may have to conform or identify differently to fit in and be accepted. May I say from first-hand experience, refusing to do what is right in God's eyes to find an easier, softer way in your current condition can have devastating effects. The consequences of deviation of any sort from what we know to be correct can have a spiraling downward effect, leading us back to that empty void we have been set free from.

In today's verse, when Joshua said, "But as for me and my house," it indicates that he was determined on his current course and path, no matter what anyone else felt or thought. His relationship with God was not based on any man or a particular set of rules, but the Lord alone, and he would serve God no matter what anyone else did. There are times when staying on God's course is tough, but taking the easier, softer way will lead us to fruitless results. Stay on course, and never resolve to take the road most traveled by others but, better yet, the road God has you on.

Prayer for the day: Heavenly Father, may I resolve today to have the strength and wisdom to stay on course and to never deviate from Your path. May I continue to be determined to worship You, oh, Lord, regardless of what others think or how they perceive me. I recognize today I am where I am because I refused to turn back from the path you have me on. May I keep my eyes focused on those things You would have me to see and do, and to never jump so quickly at those shiny things I think are more pleasing. Amen.

# Day 147: Can You See It?

Now faith is confidence in what we hope for and assurance about what we do not see.

—Hebrews 11:1 (NIV)

A junior high school teacher was telling her class about evolution and how the way everything in the world was formed proved that God doesn't exist. She said, "Look out the window. You can't see God, can you?" The kids shook their heads. "Look around you in this room. You can't see God, can you?" The kids shook their heads. "Then our logical conclusion is that God doesn't exist, does He?" she asked at last, certain that she had won her audience over. But one girl from the back of the classroom said, "Miss Smith, just because we can't see it doesn't mean it doesn't exist. We could do brain surgery and investigate the parts of your brain and we could do a CAT scan and see the brain patterns in your head. But we couldn't prove that you've had a single thought today. Does that mean that you haven't thought anything today? Just because you can't see it doesn't mean it doesn't exist." Seeing is believing, right? But, "just 'because you can't see it doesn't mean it doesn't exist."

—C. T. Powell, *Seeing Is Believing*

Today, I walked outside in the morning sun, and I immediately saw God. I lived to enjoy my forty-ninth birthday, and I immediately saw God. I witnessed a young boy helping a woman with her groceries, and I immediately saw God. I went to church and witnessed a life that was changed by the message of the Gospel, and I immediately saw God. I looked at my wife, who is pregnant with our son, and I immediately saw God.

I have friends who call and say I love you, and I can immediately hear God. I sit quietly in thought after lifting my prayers to heaven, and then I hear God. I read the Bible with great intensity, and I immediately hear God's voice amplified by the verses of His Word. I hear the songs of the birds, the wind in the trees, the rolling of the ocean waves, and the cry of a newborn child, and I immediately hear God.

If on Day 147 of your new life, you are having a hard time seeing or hearing God in your life, it may be because you are looking in the wrong place and listening to the wrong voice. The blessings you have received and the new life you are currently living are an amplified version of God's presence in your life. This is the type of faith today's verse is referring to.

Prayer for the day: Heavenly Father, I pray today I will allow myself the opportunity to listen intently and to look closely at the life You have given me. Today, with the sights and sounds that currently surround me, I can hear Your voice so loudly and feel Your presence all around me. Help me today to cherish the fact You are as clear as ever and as loud as the trumpets in heaven, and may I continue to declare with faith I can see You and hear You in my own personal way. Amen.

◆

# Day 148: Unpleasant Prayers

> You desire but do not have, so you kill. You covet but you
> cannot get what you want, so you quarrel and fight. You do
> not have because you do not ask God. When you ask, you do
> not receive, because you ask with wrong motives, that you may
> spend what you get on your pleasures.
>
> —James 4:2–3 (NIV)

Some years ago, Premier Khrushchev was speaking before the Supreme Soviet and was severely critical of the late Premier Stalin. While he was speaking, someone from the audience sent up a note: "What were you doing when Stalin committed all these atrocities?"

Khrushchev shouted, "Who sent up that note?" Not a person stirred. "I'll give him one minute to stand up." The seconds ticked off. Still no one moved. "All right, I'll tell you what I was doing. I was doing exactly what the writer of this note was doing: exactly nothing. I was afraid to be counted."

There's a popular phrase I used to always hear in church: "You have not because you asked not." This is very exciting when you stop and think about what the verse is saying. Literally, it says, ask and it's going to be yours. We have a tendency at times to take such verses and expect bountiful results with minimal effort. The problem with this type of mindset is, it is based on self-centered desires and wrongful motives, and in return, it produces very little fruit.

Our heavenly Father desires a relationship based on coexisting efforts on both sides. For example, how willing and able are you to give strangers all they want without them extending any of their own efforts? Would you help them? If you're like me, you would probably say, "I will match the same amount of effort you apply to help you achieve your goal." If this makes sense to you, then it probably also makes sense these are the expectations our Savior has of us. We do all we can to achieve the desires of our heart, and He will pick up the pieces we are unable to succeed in.

On Day 148, may you remember you are now in possession of gifts and talents to fulfill the desires of your heart. So often, we fail to realize God has already helped us and given us the tools necessary for us to achieve the things we seek. Be sure today you are doing everything possible to achieve those goals and those desires of your heart. The odds could be you're not succeeding, not because God isn't helping you; it may be only because you are not genuinely helping yourself with the gifts you have already been given. And oh, yeah, I haven't forgotten about sharing the passage of scripture I have come to know as the cure for all that ails us. Just keep staying focused one day at a time, and I will share it with you. You only have thirty-two days until your 180-day revelation. Hallelujah.

Prayer for the day: Heavenly Father, I pray today I remain determined to give You 100 percent of my body, mind, and soul; 100 percent of my physical efforts; 100 percent my spiritual efforts; and 100 percent of my complete life. I recognize today You have already given me so many gifts in order to achieve the desires of my heart. I pray today I may never take for granted all the gifts You have given me in the past and continue to give me today. I will display my gratitude through my efforts and hard work. Amen.

◆

# Day 149: Blessed Assurance

Trust in the Lord with all your heart and lean not on your own understanding in all your ways submit to him, and he will make your paths straight.

—Proverbs 3:5–6 (NIV)

One night, a house caught fire and a young boy was forced to flee to the roof. The father stood on the ground below with outstretched arms, calling to his son, "Jump! I'll catch you." He knew the boy had to jump to save his life.

All the boy could see, however, was flame, smoke, and blackness. As can be imagined, he was afraid to leave the roof.

His father kept yelling: "Jump! I will catch you."

But the boy protested, "Daddy, I can't see you."

The father replied, "But I can see you, and that's all that matters."

—Source Unknown

What does it take for you to have complete assurance in something or someone? When you go online to buy a product, do you make sure there's a way to return it? Before you make a reservation at a restaurant, do you check to see if it's at least 4 out of 5 stars? The truth is, we all want assurances, but another truth is, the majority of guarantees we currently have came from being willing to try something different to achieve a better result.

On Day 149 of this new journey in recovery, we must begin to ask ourselves are we truly trusting in God and intentionally taking leaps of faith? Are we challenging ourselves to conquer those things in life that are bigger than we are, acknowledging we can do all things through Christ Who strengthens us (Philippians 4:13)? Are you fearful of accepting that new job because you still feel you are not qualified for positions of authority and responsibility? Are you always so overwhelmed from past behaviors that you continue to assure yourself you can never change? Today, God is asking you to put all that to rest and find assurance in His arms. Just like in today's story, He wants you to take that leap of faith with the confidence all will be well, and your fears and reservations will be conquered.

God has brought you to where you are for a purpose and a reason. He wants nothing more than for you and Him to be hand in hand, conquering the world and meeting new challenges that seem impossible. Wouldn't it be wonderful if you took a moment to stop and realize it was God Who got you to Day 149, which in turn should give you the assurance that by taking a leap of faith in His name, He will not let you fall and will continue to carry you the rest of the way. Even if you question whether you can or cannot see God, you can be confident He sees you.

Prayer for the day: Heavenly Father, I have come to realize the only person holding me back from being completely assured is me. Today, I pray, Lord, You grant me the serenity to accept the ones I cannot change, the courage to change the one I can, and the wisdom to know that it's me. Help me to develop a heart of surrender and realize the greatest surrender I will ever have to make is to surrender my will and my life into Your hands. Amen.

◆

# Day 150: Slow to Judge

Why do you look at the speck of sawdust in your brother's eye and pay no attention to the plank in your own eye? How can you say to your brother, "Let me take the speck out of your eye," when all the time there is a plank in your own eye?

—Matthew 7:3–4 (NIV)

A minister was full of energy and enthusiasm for the Lord. One day he went to the hospital to visit one of his parishioners, who was critically ill. The minister entered the room and saw the man lying in bed with a whole host of tubes and wires attached to his body. Without any delay, the minister strode to his bedside and began to exhort him to be of good cheer. Soon the man started to wave his arms. This encouraged the minister, and so he exhorted him more and more enthusiastically. Finally, the minister ended with a rather lengthy prayer. At the final "Amen," the minister opened his eyes just in time to see the man reach for a pad of paper and a pencil. Quickly he wrote something and handed it to the minister. Then the man turned his head and died.

The minister was deeply moved to think that his visit to this man had occurred in the nick of time. Then he looked at the pad and read these words: "You are standing on my oxygen tube."

Sometimes it is easy to misread people's actions. Not all arm-waving is an expression of exuberance. Not all laughter is the laughter of happiness. Not all tears are tears of sorrow. Not all shouting is the shouting of triumph and victory. And not everyone who says, "Lord! Lord!" will enter the kingdom of God.

—Source Unknown

Living in an era of instant information, along with emails and text messages and social media platforms, can leave us confused and unsure at times of people's mindset and intentions. I have come to understand emails and text messages are the worst forms of communication. For example, when I talk to an individual face-to-face, I can judge by their expressions and body language as well as their demeanor if they are acting aggressively, kind, arrogant, or sincere. When I read a text message or an email, it is impossible to decipher people's message and what they are trying to imply. Because of this, I quickly noticed I often judge others unfairly and create unnecessary scenarios in my mind and how I'm going to attack this person in my response. This is not only unfair to the individual who sent me the message; it's definitely not Christlike behavior.

On Day 150, you don't need any more unwarranted and overly judgmental thoughts as they pertain to people around you. I have come to understand the majority of people are not out to get me, and because of the caliber of individuals I associate with today, my friends are always wanting to lift me up and not tear me down. Emails, text messages, and social media are excellent ways to engage others, to a certain degree. But we need to try not to ruin a good relationship God wants us to experience with someone by creating unfair, overly critical thoughts that are not even real. Be quick to love your brother, as you would want to be loved.

Prayer for the day: Heavenly Father, in this fast-paced world, I am prone to making fast-paced judgments against my brothers and sisters. Help me today to achieve the desire to be understanding and loving before being judgmental and vindictive. I pray I may always recognize the good in people and focus on their true intentions. Amen.

◆

# Day 151: Valuable Vulnerability

> Then Jesus went with his disciples to a place called Gethsemane,
> and he said to them, "Sit here while I go over there and pray."
> He took Peter and the two sons of Zebedee along with him, and
> he began to be sorrowful and troubled. Then he said to them,
> "My soul is overwhelmed with sorrow to the point of death. Stay
> here and keep watch with me."
>
> —Matthew 26:36–46 (NIV)

My father used to tell me if I could count my closest friends on one hand, I was truly blessed. Jesus had twelve close friends, but as it points out in today's verse, He had three truly close friends He confided in and trusted, friends He could turn to in a time of need and allow Himself to be vulnerable during one of the most challenging times in His life.

We don't allow ourselves to be vulnerable enough with each other anymore. We will go onto Facebook and tell the whole world we are feeling bad and could somebody please pray for us, and think we have the assurance all will be well. Please be aware, I appreciate people's attempt at responding on social media, but let's be honest: emojis of hands closed in prayer or somebody typing, "I will pray for you," has very little impact on my current condition.

In today's verse, even our Lord and Savior allowed Himself to be vulnerable during His time of need. He deliberately reached out to His closest friends and said, "I need you, and I am scared, and I need the help of my friends and their physical presence to see me through this." If the one Man Who was free from sin and wrongdoing made Himself completely vulnerable to the ones closest to Him, how important should it be for us to inherit this type of vulnerability in our own lives?

On Day 151, we all need to recognize the necessity of making ourselves vulnerable to others so we may overcome our current conflicts. It may begin in the workplace with someone you are close to. But it is my hope and prayer for you this type of vulnerability will be displayed with your church family, with the people you can trust the most, and as a church unit, you will receive something more than just text messages saying, "I will pray for you," with emojis attached to it. You will know what it means to let those around you help carry that burden and despair you may have by making yourself vulnerable to them. Remember, you cannot defeat the current problems you're facing alone. Make yourself vulnerable to those who love you. Together with friends and God's presence and guidance, you can overcome any obstacle you're faced with.

Prayer for the day: Heavenly Father, I have come to understand the majority of my failures are due to my inability to let others into my life. The ability to become vulnerable and accessible to others is a quality that has alluded me. Today, I pray I may allow myself to be completely open and transparent with those closest to me. I pray the ability to overcome my current situation by making myself vulnerable will allow others to react in the same manner so they may achieve success as well. Thank You, Lord, for making Yourself vulnerable. It is a quality I wish to attain. Amen.

◆

# Day 152: What the Ears Hear

Whoever has ears, let them hear.

—Matthew 11:15 (NIV)

The Chevy Nova was a relatively successful American car for many years. Encouraged by U.S. sales, Chevrolet began to market the American Nova throughout the world. Unfortunately, the Nova did not sell well in Mexico and other Latin American countries. Additional ads were ordered, marketing efforts were stepped up, but sales remained stagnant. Sales directors were baffled. The car had sold well in the American market; why wasn't it selling now? When they discovered the answer, it was rather embarrassing: In Spanish, Nova means "no go."

—*Sermon Illustrations*

Have you ever been to a meeting, regardless of what type of meeting it was, and some people always have an opinion and a suggestion about everything? They never have a question on how they can be helped but seem to know the answer on how to help everyone else. Do you think people like this are helpful or hurtful? It can be tough to tell sometimes.

People of authority are put in their current position not because they appear to know a lot by what they say, but because they displayed the ability to be teachable. It is simple to understand why this is true, and it's because people who listen more, learn more, and people who speak more, listen less. Who would you want your information from?

Jesus often informed people there was a message of importance He wanted to share and it was time to listen for those who could and would hear. So the question that has to be asked is not whether you can hear, but are you willing to listen? Today more than ever, it's imperative that we remain humble and willing to listen to what others are saying. Who knows? They may say something that changes your life.

Prayer for the day: Heavenly Father, today, I recognize the ability to listen is a gift and a talent I don't often utilize enough. Help me today to remain teachable through listening and to apply what I've learned to helping others. May the words of my mouth be of inspiration and grace, led by a teachable soul. Amen.

◆

# Day 153: Lessons from Adversity

I have told you these things, so that in me you may have peace. In this world you will have trouble. But take heart! I have overcome the world.

—John 16:33 (NIV)

Even if they try to kill you, you develop the inner conviction that there are some things so precious, some things so eternally true that they are worth dying for. And if a person has not found something to die for, that person isn't fit to live.

—Dr. Martin Luther King Jr.

The most common view of the Christian life is that being a Christian means we should be delivered from all adversity. What being a Christian truly means is being delivered into adversity, which is something completely different and somewhat uncomfortable.

If you are a child of God, then today's verse is not a surprise to you, and you understand completely about encountering adversities. But if your relationship with God is fresh and new, then it is essential to understand what your new title of being a Christian means. First, God gives us life as we begin to overcome. The difficulties of life are what builds our strength. If we were to never encounter any strain or difficulties, there would be no strength. Are you currently asking God to give you life, freedom, and joy? He cannot unless you are ready and willing to accept adversity from this life. Once you accept this adversity, you will immediately get the strength.

Begin today to overcome your fear and take the first step. From there, God will give you the nourishment needed to completely overcome your obstacles physically and mentally, even when you become exhausted. God never gives you an abundant amount of strength for the future, but just enough to take care of the problems and situations of the moment. Our temptation today is to face adversity and to be of good cheer, even during tough times, because even when your affliction seems impossible to you, it's an easy fix for God.

Prayer for the day: Heavenly Father, so often I make my troubles out to be bigger than they truly are. Help me today to take comfort in knowing my God is bigger than any problem that may arise in my life. Help me today to readily accept being a Christian means being attacked with adversity. May the problems I face today provide me the strength and the courage needed to stay on the path God has me on. Amen.

◆

# Day 154: Blocking the Community

After Jesus had finished instructing his twelve disciples, he went on from there to teach and preach in the towns of Galilee
—Matthew 11:1 (NIV)

In his classic novel, *The Robe*, Lloyd C. Douglas has a character called Marcellus, who had become enamored of Jesus. He wrote letters to his fiancé Diana in Rome. He told her about Jesus' teachings, about his miracles, then about his crucifixion, and then about his resurrection. Finally, he informed her that he had decided to become a disciple of Jesus.

In her letter of response, Diana said, "What I feared was that it might affect you. It is a beautiful story. Let it remain so. We don't have to do anything about it, do we?"
—Source Unknown

If you were to stay home after God told you to leave because you were overly concerned about your family and friends currently living there, then you would rob them of the teaching Jesus Christ would have for them. When we obey and leave all the consequences to God, the Lord then has an opportunity to go into our communities to teach, but as long as we are disobedient, we continue to block His way.

Have you ever been prone to debate with God and put what you call your perspective and your agenda into competition with His commands? If you sometimes say, "I know the Lord told me to go, but my duty is to my family and friends here," it merely means that you do not believe Jesus will do what He says.

Do you sometimes find yourself playing the part of an amateur film director, trying to direct the role of God in the lives of others? Do we become so bossy with others, implementing our thoughts and ideas upon them, that the Lord does not have room for His intercession? There are times when we must learn to keep our tongues still and our spirits alert.

On Day 154, be ready, willing, and able to move where the Lord wants you to move and to be where the Lord wants you to be. Never worry for a moment about the current location you are leaving or who you are leaving behind. Throughout the Bible, we see how the Lord commands His followers to continue to move forward, never standing still and marching forward in faith. Moving forward is just what we do in this new way of life. Hallelujah.

Prayer for the day: Heavenly Father, I pray today my grandiose ideas for my future do not get in the way of the plans You have for others. I pray I listen intently so as to know which direction You would have me go and how far You would have me to travel. May I embrace the assurance all those loved ones I leave behind will be well taken care of the presence of Your spirit. Amen.

◆

# Day 155: Cross Style Commitment

May I never boast except in the cross of our Lord Jesus Christ, through which the world has been crucified to me, and I to the world.

—Galatians 6:14 (NIV)

Someone once asked Wayne Gretzky, the great hockey player, how he managed to become the best goal-scorer in the history of the game. He simply replied, "While everyone else is chasing the puck, I go where the puck is going to be."

The Gospel of Jesus Christ will always force us to make a decision as it pertains to our will. First, I need to ask, have I truly accepted God's verdict on sin as judged by the death of Jesus on the cross? Do I even have the tiniest interest in the death of Jesus? Do we want to be identified with His death, to be fully and completely dead to all interest in sin, social conformity, and ourselves?

The one great privilege about being a disciple is, we can commit ourselves under the symbol of His cross, and that means death to all sin. When we act in confident faith in what our Lord did for us on the cross, we begin to take on a supernatural identification with His death, and this can happen immediately. And from this, you will come to know with higher knowledge that your old life was crucified with him (Romans 6:6). If you want to be sure if your will is in line with God's will, then start by measuring your level of acceptance toward the cross.

On Day 155, Paul wants us to understand in today's verse that the highest place to lose yourself and then be able to turn around and find yourself is the cross. The cross is the perfect reminder of the love that is needed to heal not only our wounds but the scars that were caused by this world. My personal scripture verse I cling to is Galatians 2:20 (NIV), which states, "I have been crucified with Christ, and I no longer live, but Christ lives in me. The life I now live in the body, I live by faith in the Son of God, who loved me and gave himself for me."

Prayer for the day: Heavenly Father, today, I give thanks for the love that was displayed on the cross. I pray I accept and understand my life begins when I become dead to my old self. I pray You will allow me to grasp the full concept of the cross and what Your sacrifice means for the world. There truly is life at the cross. Amen.

# Day 156: No Time Like the Present

Seek the LORD while he may be found; call on him while he is near. Let the wicked forsake their ways and the unrighteous their thoughts. Let them turn to the LORD, and he will have mercy on them, and to our God, for he will freely pardon.

—Isaiah 55:6–7 (NIV)

Karl Barth was lecturing to a group of students at Princeton. One student asked the German theologian, "Sir, don't you think that God has revealed himself in other religions and not only in Christianity?"

Barth's answer stunned the crowd. With a modest thunder he answered, "No, God has not revealed himself in any religion, including Christianity. He has revealed himself in his Son."

—Source Unknown

In most daily devotionals, you won't find entries that lean toward a sense of urgency and desperation. Most devotionals want us to enjoy sunshine and flowers and the blessings God has provided for us to start our day with a smile. That's not going to happen in today's devotional. Today, I want us to be sure we have turned everything over to God, and we are on course for the direction God would have us. Why, might you ask? It's simple; we are not promised tomorrow.

In today's verse, the prophet Isaiah is impressing a sense of urgency upon God's people. The importance of this verse is, Isaiah wants us to know now is the time to respond to our heavenly Father. If you were to evaluate your current situation and where you currently are as it pertains to Day 156, it is safe to say you will instinctively realize you are in the perfect position and place to incorporate a complete relationship with your heavenly Father. The reason we say "now" is the time is, our hearts are inclined to receive God's gift, which is His Son, Jesus Christ.

You see, there has never been an instance when someone turns to the Lord and finds God rejected them. The real problem is, we simply fail to return back to the Lord. We continue to tell ourselves, "I can wait until tomorrow. There are more important issues at the moment; I think I'm good with the current relationship I have with God." Billy Graham would always ask his congregation one fundamental and pertinent question: "If you were to die today, are you certain your salvation is with God?" Realize today you have never been in a better position to be 100 percent guaranteed you have surrendered your entire life into His hands.

Prayer for the day: Lord Jesus, for too long, I've kept You out of my life. I know that I am a sinner and that I cannot save myself. No longer will I close the door when I hear You knocking. By faith, I gratefully receive Your gift of salvation. I am ready to trust You as my Lord and Savior. Thank You, Lord Jesus, for coming to earth. I believe You are the Son of God who died on the cross for my sins and rose from the dead on the third day. Thank You for bearing my sins and giving me the gift of eternal life. I believe Your words are true. Come into my heart, Lord Jesus, and be my Savior. Amen.

—*The Sinner's Prayer* (by Dr. Ray Pritchard)

◆

# Day 157: Time to Trust

Can all your worries add a single moment to your life?
—Matthew 6:27

D.L. Moody once called on a leading citizen in Chicago to persuade him to accept Christ. They were seated in the man's parlor. It was winter and coal was burning in the fireplace. The man objected that he could be just as good a Christian outside the church as in it. Moody said nothing, but stepped to the fireplace, took the tongs, picked a blazing coal from the fire and set it off by itself. In silence the two watched it smolder and go out.

"I see," said the man.

—*The Interpreter's Bible*

Individual lifestyles and behaviors can build specific characteristics that are hard to break. Some of us can't stand to stay in one place for too long without the urge to move again. Some of us find it challenging to comply with rules and regulations in the workforce. I had a hard time understanding the importance of trusting others.

Jesus never put His trust in any one particular person. But with that being said, He was never suspicious or overly bitter, and He never lost hope for anyone because first and foremost, His trust was in God. He trusted completely in what God's grace and love could do for others. Ultimately, if I put my trust in human beings first, the final result will be my despair and hopelessness toward everyone. I will eventually become bitter because I insist everyone should be what no person could ever be, which is absolutely perfect and right. The only thing you can truly trust in yourself and other people is the grace of God.

In today's verse, Matthew assures us if we believe people around us will conform in a trustworthy manner, we will continue to be let down. Trusting others begins by watching God unfold His promises in your life. Once we begin to find complete trust in Him, all the old lifestyles and characteristics that continue to plague us today will start to fade away peacefully.

Prayer for the day: Heavenly Father, today, I recognize the one person I trust the least is myself. I no longer trust my decisions, my heart, my abilities, or my commitments because I have refused to trust in You. Help me today, Lord, to understand by trusting You, I can see the good in others and give them the grace and love You have given me. Today, I have decided to put my trust in You in order to gain the assurance all will be well with all those around me. Amen.

◆

# Day 158: Lavishing Love

See what great love the Father has lavished on us, that we should be called children of God! And that is what we are! The reason the world does not know us is that it did not know him.

—1 John 3:1 (NIV)

In the movie *The Mission*, one of the leading characters, a slave-trader of Brazilian Indians, is converted to a Jesuit priest. But he insists on doing penance, dragging a massive bundle through the jungle back to the Indians he used to enslave. When he climbs the cliff leading to their village, the bundle threatens to make him fall, but the Indians cut it away and it crashes to the river below the clifftop. The people he had formerly enslaved forgave him and set him free. We have the power to do that for each other.

Sin is a fundamental relationship. For the majority of us, our inner sinful nature is crying for independence from God. The entire Christian belief and faith bases its existence on the self-confident nature of sin. Sin is the one characteristic that is a guaranteed plague, which will resonate the loudest when we desire to change. How do we know if sin is still prevalent in our lives? Watch how you respond when you want to truly forgive someone who has harmed you, but something continues to pull you away from forgiveness. Sin attacks the areas God wants us to excel in, especially as it pertains to forgiveness.

To understand the ability to forgive and love others means we know God's love for us. Love is an attribute that is mimicked because of the way God has inflicted it on our own lives. Love is an attribute that is passed down from a singular source and demands our intentional expression as a way to change the lives of others. The first act that must always come from love is forgiveness. We understand this need for forgiveness because we recognize how we have all been forgiven.

Ask yourself why God is so intent on loving us. Why is it when I turn to God after I have fallen short, love is the first attribute I recognize? The reason is simply because of the power of love's contagious effect. We virtually attain an attribute of God when we intentionally put our needs aside to fulfill the needs of others. If you're having a hard time learning how to love and forgive others, it may only be because you're refusing to let God love and forgive you.

Prayer for the day: Heavenly Father, today I intentionally seek to see Your face in order that I may feel the love I so desperately need. I seek Your forgiveness in my life so I may attain the qualities necessary to love my neighbors. Help me to recognize the strength that comes from forgiveness and know those Christlike qualities are what's needed in order for the rest of the world to know You. I pray I may truly understand all the love You continue to give to me. Amen.

◆

# Day 159: Good Grief

♦ ♦ ♦

He was despised and rejected by mankind, a man of suffering, and familiar with pain. Like one from whom people hide their faces he was despised, and we held him in low esteem.

—Isaiah 53:3 (NIV)

If you go to a doctor, he diagnoses your ailment and prescribes treatment. He gives you a prescription for medication. He gives you everything you need to feel better, but you've got to work it out. In other words, you've got to go to the pharmacist, you've got to get the prescription filled, and most importantly, you've got to take the medicine in order for it to benefit you. See, God knows how to measure whether we value his salvation because if you do, you work it out. If you value it, you work it out, if you don't value it, then you don't work it out. You ignore it, you bypass it, or you marginalize it, but what you don't do is work it out.

—Tony Evans, *Illustrations*, 37

What is your best prescription against pain and sin? Have you begun to listen to those individuals around you who may be saying, "You don't need to feel your pain or acknowledge your grief"? Or the one statement I hear so often is when people say, "We are not on this new way of life to deal with pain, only to focus on happiness." If these statements are correct, then how will you ever know if you're taking the proper measures to deal with your grief and emotions if you choose to ignore them?

At the beginning of our lives, we never brought ourselves to such a point as to deal with the reality of sin. We tend to look at life through rose-colored glasses and say if we can only control our instincts and educate ourselves, we can produce a life that will slowly evolve into the life God would want us to have. As we attach ourselves to this way of thinking, we do not take into account something we have begun to experience, which is sin, and it upsets our way of thinking and all of our plans. Our past behaviors and sin have made our current way of thinking completely unpredictable, irrational, and worst of all, utterly uncontrollable.

On Day 159, we must begin to recognize and accept the fact that sin is part of life and not merely a shortcoming. Sin is utter defiance against God, and either sin or God must die in our life. The New Testament clearly states if sin rules in me, then God will surely die. Vice versa: If God rules in me, then sin will surely die. There is nothing more fundamental than that. We must accept today the feelings we are facing are the results of a life of sin, and I should accept this grief for a brief moment, so I may comprehend what a life without God feels like. Sometimes, the pain is useful for us to be grateful for the goodness of God. Hallelujah.

Prayer for the day: Heavenly Father, I accept my grief for what it truly is: a life without You. Today, I pray I may encompass the feelings I have as an indicator of when I have separated myself from Your guidance. I am grateful for the knowledge the grief and sorrow I feel can be overcome with a life filled with Your presence. Today, I choose to accept my grief, but most importantly, I have chosen to kill it by opening my heart to my loving Savior. Amen.

◆

# Day 160: Can You Feel It?

Paul, a servant of Christ Jesus, called to be an apostle and set apart for the gospel of God

—Romans 1:1 (NIV)

Jesus appeared in heaven just after his ascension and is giving a progress report on all that has happened while he was on earth.

Moses is there and he asks him, "Well Jesus, did you leave things in capable hands?"

Jesus responds, "I did. I have left behind Mary and Martha and Peter and the other disciples."

Moses said, "What if they fail?"

Jesus said, "Well, I have established the Church and filled it with the Holy Spirit and they will carry on."

And Moses said, "What if they fail?"

Came the reply, "I have no other plan."

—Source Unknown

I would not be surprised if you have stuck with this book and applied some of its principles, you may have begun to have that little tingly feeling that something is calling you to do something more significant. You see, I've come to understand my calling in ministry is not primarily to be a holy man but to be a proclaimer of the Gospel of Jesus Christ. The one all-important truth is, the Gospel of Jesus should be recognized as the abiding reality. My reality of myself is not of human goodness, or heaven, or hell, or holiness; it is the power of redemption. The need for me to understand this is so vital as it pertains to being a Christian worker today. As a believer with a calling, I have to get used to the revelation that redemption is the only reality that defines my calling and justifies my direction.

In today's verse, Paul was not overly interested in his character. Paul knew instinctively that having been called to be an apostle, he was a servant of Jesus. Paul was saved to serve. You may currently have a calling on your heart to be a disciple to others, but where Christian workers fail is when they place their desire for their holiness above their desire to know God. We do not seek a relationship with God to be more desirable in our own eyes, because if we do so, the Gospel of Jesus has not begun to touch us. God cannot deliver me on a path of redemption, while my interest is merely in my character. Paul was no longer conscious of himself, and we should no longer be conscious of who we were and our old desires.

If you have begun to recognize an inner desire to share with others what you have experienced, be sure to emphasize to everyone that you are who you are today because of the redemptive power of Christ. Let that be your reality today. With that type of understanding, the greatest desire you will begin to have is to lose your old self and to become redeemed with the new. Hallelujah.

Prayer for the day: Heavenly Father, today, I seek the wisdom to rid myself of my old way of thinking and behaviors. I declare openly You are my Lord and Savior, and from this declaration, I seek Your guidance and Your loving redemption. Thank You for all the blessings You continue to bestow upon me and for this new wonderful life. I pray for the confidence and strength to answer any calling You put on my heart to be of service to others. Amen.

◆

# Day 161: Intentional Intercession

And let us consider how we may spur one another on toward love and good deeds, not giving up meeting together, as some are in the habit of doing, but encouraging one another—and all the more as you see the Day approaching.

—Hebrews 10:24–25 (NIV)

If you're going month after month and year after year and there are no negative repercussions that ever come upon you because of your faith, then your faith has not been clearly demonstrated. You are a secret agent Christian or a spiritual CIA member. You are a covert operative because there have been no repercussions for your faith. To put it another way, if you were accused of being a Christian, would there be enough evidence to convict you or would you be found innocent of all charges.

—Tony Evans, *Illustrations*, 38

So often, there are so many things in our lives we don't want to look at, and we avoid confronting these issues by simply ignoring our personal needs and focusing on the needs of others. We would rather feel good about taking care of someone else's problems and concerns in order to feel good about who we are, without having to look at ourselves.

We shouldn't think our personal intercession on behalf of others is an immediate crisis for God to contend with. We want to be able to comfort people with God's message, but we need to leave it at that. We shouldn't tell people because we have declared their circumstance an emergency that God automatically agrees with us and views their situation in the same way.

Today, we should focus on our spiritual stubbornness. Spiritual stubbornness can be the most effective hindrance regarding God's petition on your own life, due to the fact you may be overly concerned about the lives of others rather than your own. We have to realize when we identify Jesus with our sin, it means a radical change within ourselves, not the demands of change for those people around us. Be careful of people who continuously reach out to be everyone's sponsor or spiritual guru. There's a good chance they suffer from a little spiritual stubbornness, and they may be a little spiritually inept themselves. Focus today on your current condition and how God can intercede on your behalf, for you to have a testimony that can change the life of another. And oh, yeah, that one passage of scripture I promised that can defeat all of our defects of character and social instability is still on the way. Hang in there.

Prayer for the day: Heavenly Father, today, I want to completely focus on the man who stands before me in the mirror. Intercede on my behalf, oh, Lord, and help me identify the shortcomings I continue to refuse to look at. Help me to acknowledge my shortcomings so I may be a living example for others to follow and not merely a mouthpiece demanding people follow me. Amen.

◆

# Day 162: Now I'm Alive

He led me back and forth among them, and I saw a great many
bones on the floor of the valley, bones that were very dry. He
asked me, "Son of man, can these bones live?"
I said, "Sovereign Lord, you alone know."
—Ezekiel 37:2–3 (NIV)

Tabloids are notorious for the pictures they manufacture. They
do this by creating pictures of people by matching heads with
different bodies. These magazines want to paint a picture in
order to sell magazines and papers. These pictures are often false
creations, made up in order to achieve the goal of increasing
sales. Just as a tabloid will reconfigure things to accomplish
its own purposes, the evil one is committed to changing our
picture of God, in order to sell himself.
—Tony Evans, *Illustrations,* 273

Notice if you will the past few entries in this devotional have all but left out
mentioning the problems with addiction, alcohol, sex, anxiety, self-identification,
and so on. Why, might you ask? Because on Day 162, you are not the person you
once were, and it is vital for you to associate with your new life and who God
wants you to be rather than dwell on the false images from the past Satan wants
you to hold on to.

Let me elaborate. Take today's verse, for example. After reading it, ask yourself,
"Can a sinner be turned into a saint? Can a twisted and wretched life be made
right?" There is only one appropriate answer: "Sovereign Lord, You alone know."
Don't be fooled into thinking with a little more devotional time, prayer, and Bible
reading, you might see how this could be possible. God has begun this magnificent
process in which He has breathed new life into this old and tired body and made
it new. God has declared that through our new life in Him, the only importance
our past has for us is the clear understanding of what life in the future can be like
without Him: dead and dry.

Today, do not be willing to continue reading the Word of the Bible and
assume God is working on your behalf. Do not go out and automatically think you
can take your old life and make it new all by yourself. Do you genuinely believe

God will do for you what you cannot do for yourself? Are your current personal experiences based on a beautiful realization of God's power and you are the living definition of His presence within you, not an ongoing definition of who you once were? Have you accepted the fact nothing good dwells within you apart from God? Today, you are alive, you are new, and you have exchanged all the old labels people and Satan once placed on you. The living breath of God has raised you from the valley of the dry bones and given you back your new identity in Him. Hallelujah.

Prayer for the day: Heavenly Father, today, I realize my past was the complete definition of what it means to live a life without You. Today, I take comfort in knowing You raised me from my old body and gave me a new one, which allows me to rid myself of all the old labels that used to plague me. Help me, Lord, to focus on this new journey You have me on so I may never return to the valley of the dry bones. Amen.

◆

# Day 163: Realistic Repentance

Godly sorrow brings repentance that leads to salvation and leaves no regret, but worldly sorrow brings death.

—2 Corinthians 7:10 (NIV)

Samuel Colgate, the founder of the Colgate business empire, was a devout Christian, and he told of an incident that took place in the church he attended. During an evangelistic service, an invitation was given at the close of the sermon for all those who wished to turn their lives over to Christ and be forgiven. One of the first persons to walk down the aisle and kneel at the altar was a well-known prostitute. She knelt in very real repentance, she wept, she asked God to forgive her, and meanwhile the rest of the congregation looked on approvingly at what she was doing. Then she stood and testified that she believed God had forgiven her for her past life, and she now wanted to become a member of the church. For a few moments, the silence was deafening.

Finally, Samuel Colgate arose and said, "I guess we blundered when we prayed that the Lord would save sinners. We forgot to specify what kind of sinners. We'd better ask him to forgive us for this oversight. The Holy Spirit has touched this woman and made her truly repentant, but the Lord apparently doesn't understand that she's not the type we want him to rescue. We'd better spell it out for him just which sinners we had in mind."

Immediately, a motion was made and unanimously approved that the woman be accepted into membership in the congregation.

—Source Unknown

Those of us who overcome adversity and social turmoil have what we like to call a thick outer shell. What I mean is, because of the hurdles and obstacles we've had to contend with, there is not much anybody can say or do that bothers us. We are used to being called stereotypical names and hearing degrading remarks because of our past behaviors. Because of this continual verbal lashing from others, we have become numb to someone's description of our old character defects. So if what others think about me and say about me does not bother me, then why do I feel the overwhelming need to repent and seek forgiveness? The answer is simple.

Jesus said when the Holy Spirit came, He and He alone will convict people of sin (John 16:8). You see, when the Holy Spirit stirs our conscience and brings us into the presence of our heavenly Father, it is not the relationship we have with others that bothers us, but it is our current relationship with God that leaves us feeling troubled. The wonders of our conviction of sin, holiness, and forgiveness are so intertwined, it is only made noticeable by the presence of God in our life. In other words, we are experiencing the conviction of the Holy Spirit, guiding us into God's direction, and the first step must be repentance.

The very formation of a relationship with God comes from the stirring of our inner emotions the Holy Spirit brings upon us. The sudden sharp pain from repentance is what happens when it collides with goodness. The foundation of Christianity and a relationship with God begins with repentance. True repentance must be recognized as a gift of God. If we ever fail to understand the value of repentance, we will allow ourselves once again to delve in sin. Consider it a true gift from God that we are more concerned with the approval of our heavenly Father than the judgmental viewpoints of others.

Prayer for the day: Heavenly Father, the pain and discouraging feeling I have deep inside me is the by-product of my past and the things I have done wrong. I recognize today to have a meaningful relationship with You means I must deal with my convictions through repentance. Forgive me, Lord, and read the sorrows of my heart as a true statement of repentance. I declare through prayer I need Your forgiveness to move forward in this life and the life to come when You call me home. Amen.

———————————————— ◆ ————————————————

# Day 164: Severe Stronghold

> So if the Son sets you free, you will be free indeed.
>
> —John 8:36 (NIV)

A top 10 summary of biblical candidates in case you wonder if you're qualified:

1. Adam: good man but has wife trouble. 2. Noah: former pastorate of 120 years with no converts, problem with the bottle, and a wayward son morals problem. 3. Abraham: scandal ridden, offered wife to another man, child abuse. 4. Joseph: dreamer, prison record. 5. Moses: poor communicator, stutters, unanswered murder charge. 6. David: affair with neighbor's wife, hired a hit man to kill husband. 7. Solomon: husband of more than one wife, in fact parsonage too small. 8. Elijah: prone to depression and nervous breakdowns. 9. Elisha: reported to have live with a single widow at former church 10. Hosea: our congregation could not handle his wife's occupation.

—*Sermon Illustrations*

One of the worst positions to be in is to accept things are not going to get better on your behalf, and you are prone to repeat whatever stronghold has a grip on you. You are hanging pictures on your mental jail cell walls, and you are settling in to get comfortable. You have declared your stronghold is greater than you and the promise of a magical cure is not going to happen for you. In biblical terms, the word *stronghold* means addiction.

Let's be realistic for one second. There is no Bible verse, prayer, preacher, or twelve-step solution that is going to save you when you have accepted complete doom rather than fully accepting the Son of God. You may say, "I accepted God fully on Sunday." My question to you is, who did you accept on Monday? Did you return to that old way of thinking, which convinces you your freedom lies within yourself rather than in the hands of God?

God pays no attention to our inability to have faith in ourselves. A lack of confidence in ourselves is a typical part of our sinful nature. God's plan can run straight through our natural life. We must see to it we are willing to aid and assist God rather than completely give up on Him. We must be ready to display ourselves as partners and work alongside Him. What a glorious revelation to know the Son has set us free indeed.

Prayer for the day: Heavenly Father, I have become so tired of giving up on myself. My trust in You is so limited, and I have become surrounded by my doomsday scenarios for my life. Today, I commit myself to work alongside You to fulfill the purpose You have for my life, which is freedom from my strongholds. Continue to guide me, oh, Lord, and develop my sense of awareness of You in my life. Today, I refuse to give up on You as well as myself. Amen.

◆

# Day 165: Frivolous Fretting

Refrain from anger and turn from wrath; do not fret—it leads only to evil.

—Psalm 37:8 (NIV)

A man said, "My wife and I promise that we would never go to bed angry. We haven't slept together in seven years."

—Tony Evans, *Illustrations*, 16

Right about now, there is a good chance you're trying to tackle a new adventure or accept a new calling, the experience of a new job, the calling of a relationship amongst a group of new friends and family or church, the desire to want to take that leap of faith and test your new skills without the cumbersome lifestyles of the past. If this statement is right for you today, then you will need peace of mind more than ever. Why, might you ask? Because your reality is about to smack you in the face and be at the forefront of your life.

For life to work properly, we have to be able to find peace and harmony during heartache and disappointment. The four elements go hand in hand. There is no perfect life of peace and harmony that doesn't have a certain level of disturbance in its mix. When you're trying to find that ideal job, don't worry; there are going to be some nos before you finally get that yes. When you're trying to find that right group of friends who can encourage you and keep you grounded and inspire you, don't worry; some of them are going to let you down and turn on you. Just when you're ready to perform at your best, life on life's terms is waiting for us all.

When these life cycles occur, don't fret, but better yet, welcome these obstacles into your life. To do the opposite would coincide with today's verse and lead to evil. Fretting means getting ourselves out of joint, both mentally and spiritually. It is inevitable when we begin to worry, the end result is always sin. When we become overly worried, it leads to the wicked desire of wanting to have our own way, thus forcing a separation between God and us. Our Lord and Savior never worried because He came to earth not to accomplish His own will, but to achieve the will of the Father. Shouldn't that be our will today? Once we begin to focus on what God wants, we are much less likely to fret, become angry, or even sin.

Prayer for the day: Heavenly Father, I have begun to notice my worries and my fretting take up a majority of my time, time that could be better spent seeking Your will and not my own. Help me to accept my obstacles as a blessing and a learning tool so I may be strengthened to achieve those goals You have for me. Thy will be done on earth as it is in heaven (Matthew 6:10). Amen.

◆

# Day 166: Real Wisdom

◆ ◆ ◆

If any of you lacks wisdom, you should ask God, who gives
generously to all without finding fault, and it will be given to you.

—James 1:5 (NIV)

Duck hunters use decoys. Today, these decoys have gotten
pretty fancy. The decoys quack like ducks, move like ducks,
look like ducks, and act like ducks. In fact, the ducks think
that they are ducks and the real ducks end up being dead ducks
because they can't tell what's real. For the Christian, there are
many moving decoys out there and their job is to extricate us
from the intimate experience of our faith. We must look beyond
what a person says or how they perform to determine their
authenticity. We must evaluate and test the spirits. We must be
on guard for decoys moving all around us, acting like the real
thing, in order to deceive.

—Tony Evans, *Illustrations*, 74

Today's illustration focuses a lot on other people being fake or phony. It tells us to
be aware of the people around us so we might not be fooled by what they say or
do. But I think what is most important is, we remember to look in the mirror to
be assured we are not fake or phony ourselves.

You may have begun to notice that on Day 1 of this journey, you were relying
heavily on the support and guidance of others. But now on Day 166, asking for
help is beneath your character because it may be a sign to others you're not the
great recovery guru you want everybody else to think you are. Remember, asking
for support and guidance regardless of where you are in your journey is the wisest
thing you could ever do. How do we know this? Even Jesus Himself asked for help
from others in His darkest hours: "Then He said to them, 'My soul is consumed
with sorrow to the point of death. Stay here and keep watch with Me'" (Matthew
26:38).

Jesus would have been a real phony if He had not allowed Himself to display
His human characteristic of fear. Jesus emptied Himself of His deity to take on
human characteristics we all possess and then needed the help of real and true
friends at His lowest point. If our Lord and Savior demonstrates His true character
by reaching out to others for help, then this should be an indicator of how we

should respond when things get tough. If you hurt, let others know you hurt. If you're sad, lonely, lost, confused, ready to return to that old lifestyle that used to beat you down, tell somebody. Most importantly, remember to recognize Jesus and pray He brings those people into your life who allow you to empty yourself unto them, for you to be filled and renewed. Welcome to the day you have obtained real wisdom by being transparent and vulnerable to others.

Prayer for the day: Heavenly Father, today, I continue to make choices based on how I want others to view me. I leave certain areas of my life open to destruction because I refuse to be vulnerable and ask for help. I pray I always remember the wisest of men reach out for guidance from others to obtain a sense of peace and security in their life. Lord, I pray you would direct true friends and true believers into my life and intercede so I may continue to succeed with You. Amen.

# Day 167: Certainly Certain

Dear friends, now we are children of God, and what we will be has not yet been made known. But we know that when Christ appears, we shall be like him, for we shall see him as he is.

—1 John 3:2 (NIV)

Whenever you are on a 3 Lane Hwy. you are going to have to choose which lane you want to be in even though there may be lanes to your right and to your left. Once you are sure about your decision, you are expected to stay in that lane and not swerve into other lanes, because if you start to move left and right then you are nothing more than an accident waiting to happen. There is a certain time and an appropriate way to change lanes. God's word gives you the correct lane to travel in. That Lane is based on the written word and affirmed by the work of the Holy Spirit in terms of specific application. Stay in your lane and do everything God tells you to do and He will make your way prosperous.

—Tony Evans, *Illustrations*, 21

We all want to have the certainty we are moving in the right direction. Our natural instinct is to be perfect and precise, as we are always trying to determine what will happen next in our lives. If we are left with a feeling of uncertainty, then we assume we are doing a bad thing. We think we have to reach some predetermined goal for success, but in reality, that is not the nature of the spiritual life. The nature of our spiritual life is to be certain when we are uncertain. It sounds a little strange, doesn't it?

Certainty signifies nothing more than a commonsense life. Uncertainty is to be connected to your spiritual life, which is a beautiful thing. To be confident in our heavenly Father forces us to be uncertain in our behaviors, our thoughts, with the certainty we are unsure of what tomorrow may bring. We are not always sure of what our next step should be, but we are confident of God and His sovereign plan.

In today's verse, John signifies there is always a level of uncertainty, even though we are children of God. Eventually, God will make known those things we are uncertain of, and we will become confident of Who He truly is. Do not be discouraged because you are unsure of what God is doing, but be encouraged because you are sure God is doing great things for you.

Prayer for the day: Heavenly Father, today, I take comfort in knowing even though I often feel unsure and uncertain about my current direction, I am certain You are in charge and leading me in a wonderful direction. I pray today I remain humble enough to accept the uncertainty I feel as the next indication of where I'm at spiritually. Today, I take certainty in knowing my uncertain feelings are not an indication of how much You love me, but confirmation on how much more I need You. Amen.

---

# Day 168: Wishing or Waiting?

◆ ◆ ◆

Each of you should use whatever gift you have received to serve others, as faithful stewards of God's grace in its various forms.
—1 Peter 4:10 (NIV)

If you can start the day without caffeine ... If you can always be cheerful, ignoring aches and pains ... If you can resist complaining and boring people with your troubles ... If you can eat the same food every day and be grateful for it ... If you can understand when your loved ones are too busy to give you any time ... If you can take criticism and blame without resentment ... If you can resist treating a rich friend better than a poor friend ... If you can face the world without lies and deceit ... If you can overlook it when those you love take it out on you when, through no fault of yours, something goes wrong ... If you can conquer tension without medical help ... If you can say honestly that deep in your heart you have no prejudice against creed, color, religion or politics ... Then, my friend, you are almost as good as your dog.
—*Preachers Sourcebook Illustrations*, 463

There are going to be times when we can't understand why we can't do what we want to do, when we want to do it. When God appears to be making us wait and seems to be unresponsive to our needs, don't be foolish and fill that time with monotonous and unproductive tasks. We should simply wait.

This critical time of waiting may be what is needed to teach us the meaning of sanctification and how to be completely separate from sin and become a little more holy. One of the things we always seem to want to do is to run before God gives us His directions. If you have the slightest doubt about what you are preparing for, then God is most certainly not doing the guiding, and when you are in doubt of God's guidance, then you should wait.

In today's verse, Peter asks that we use our gifts to serve others, but rarely do we find people who have determined that waiting patiently is truly a gift. When it feels as if God is no longer roaming through the aisles of our hearts and spirit, we immediately want to set a course to seek gratification by our own doing. We are compelled to try any and every harebrained idea to keep us busy, when all God wants us to do is sit still and wait on Him. Our natural devotion, in the beginning, may have been enough to attract us to Jesus, to make us feel His irresistible love, but that natural devotion will never make us true disciples. Our devotion and life to God is fulfilled when we wait on His guidance, not our natural desire to want to do good. To be truly good means that on Day 168, we wait for His guidance and then act accordingly.

Prayer for the day: Heavenly Father, I continue to convince myself that the faster I go, the more tasks I complete, the happier You are. I recognize today all the activities and jobs of the world continue to leave me with a void because none of them were directed by You. Help me today, Lord, to wait on Your direction and seek a path that brings me fulfillment. Help me to realize and accept one of the most important gifts I could ever obtain is the gift of waiting patiently for divine guidance. Amen.

◆

# Day 169: Pressure to Perform

No one who wants to become a public figure acts in secret. Since you are doing these things, show yourself to the world.

—John 7:4 (NIV)

Speedy Morris, a basketball coach for La Salle University, was shaving when his wife called out to tell him he was wanted on the phone by Sports Illustrated. Speedy Morris was so excited by the prospect of national recognition that he nicked himself with his razor and ran, with a mixture of blood and lather on his face and fell down the steps. But when he got to the phone the voice on the other line said: "For just seventy-five cents an issue you can get a one-year trial subscription."

—*Preachers Sourcebook of Creative Sermon Illustrations, 222*

The countdown is on. You are just about ten days from that pivotal six-month mark. Do you have a job prospect yet? Better yet, do you have several jobs lined up but don't know which one to take? You might have several safe residencies to move into, but you're not sure which is the best for your situation. Well, guess what? If you are feeling overwhelming pressure, then there might be a chance God has not shown you His complete plan for you just yet.

We want so desperately to have everything lined up and perfect, and why shouldn't we? We have gone to all the classes, listened to all the lectures, went to countless church services as well as twelve-step meetings, and obeyed all the rules. We may have even gone on Facebook and Instagram and posted beautiful pictures of ourselves and made wonderful comments about how we are doing. But inside, there's so much pressure.

Jesus knew there would be a time and a place when people would know who He indeed was. The great thing is, Jesus never forced Who He was on anybody. You either love Jesus, or you love the world. If you love the world, then there is a good chance you are feeling the pressures to conform to it to be accepted. You want others to visually witness you have everything in order and you are doing well. If you love Jesus, you already know He loves you for who you are and not some great performance.

When we are entirely in tune with where Christ wants us, there is never the pressure to appear perfect before the public. The time will come, and it could be as soon as tomorrow, that a complete plan will be put before you, eliminating any unnecessary pressure to conform to worldly views. On Day 169, you have already been performing correctly.

Prayer for the day: Heavenly Father, I have either subconsciously or consciously submitted myself to unnecessary pressures. I have pressured myself to fit into this worldly mold that will only accept me if I accept it. Today, Lord, I pray I perform in a manner that reassures You I am under no pressure from You. I know in Your perfect time, all the pieces of my life will come together perfectly. Amen.

◆

# Day 170: Top Ten

♦ ♦ ♦

I can do all this through him who gives me strength.
                              —Philippians 4:13 (NIV)

Suppose you have a sponge and a pitcher of Pepsi-Cola. If
you dip your sponge into Pepsi and squeeze it, what's going
to come out? 7-Up? No, when you squeeze a sponge soaked in
Pepsi, Pepsi is going to gush out of it. If you saturate your mind
with questionable movies, videos, magazines, novels, music, and
entertainments, do you think that holiness and happiness and
godliness will flow out?
                    —*Preachers Sourcebook of Sermon Illustrations*, 560


There are only ten days to go before we reach the 180-day mark. With that being
said, sometimes it is important to see what our minds are focused on and determine
if we feel good about our strength and abilities in moving forward. So, here's a
simple assignment. It's easy to make a list of those things bringing you joy, but
today, make a list of the top ten things that are heavy on your mind and bring
you the most concern and frustration. It can be anything from relationships with
family, church, job outlook, money, transportation, serenity, peace of mind, and
so on; you get the point. Write down these ten items, and when you're finished,
go back and read today's verse all over again. I think then you will understand the
meaning of Philippians 4:13.


1.

2.

3.

4.

5.

6.

7.

8.

9.

10.

Prayer for the day: Heavenly Father, as I come across the last ten days of my initial journey, I call on You for strength. My Lord, I pray You will strengthen my body, my mind, and my soul. I pray for the filling of Your Spirit in me and You will grant me the assurance of Your presence. I come to You for wisdom to choose the course that allows me to grow and have an understanding. I come to You for serenity, oh, Lord for my heart and my spirit. Bless me with the spirit of peace as I continue to feel Your love unfolding within me. Your strength allows me to do all things. Amen.

◆

# Day 171: What's Your Vision?

> Do not conform to the pattern of this world, but be transformed
> by the renewing of your mind. Then you will be able to test and
> approve what God's will is—his good, pleasing and perfect will.
> —Romans 12:2 (NIV)

In the autobiography of Martin Luther King Jr., Dr. King
tells of growing up in Atlanta, Georgia: *I remember another
experience I used to have in Atlanta. I went to high school on the
other side of town—to the Booker T. Washington high school. I had
to get the bus in what was known as the fourth Ward and ride over
to the west side. In those days, rigid patterns of segregation existed
on the buses, so that Negroes had to sit in the backs of buses. Whites
were seated in the front, and often if whites didn't get on the buses,
those seats were still reserved for whites only, so Negroes had to stand
over empty seats. I would end up having to go to the back of the bus
with my body, but every time I got on the bus, I left my mind up on
the front seat. And I said to myself, "One of these days, I'm going to
put my body up there where my mind is."* And he did. Our bodies
always end up where our minds are.
—*Preachers Sourcebook of Creative Sermon Illustrations*, 555

We all love visualizing where we are going to be tomorrow, a month from now,
or even a year from now. Even today, I continue to envision the next phase of
my life after God has helped me complete my most recent goals. Having a visual
understanding of where you want to go is a critical element in relaying your
message to God and asking Him to help you get there. But what if I told you that to
get you there, God is going to have to make some changes and some shifts in your
environment, which you might not approve of because you do not understand its
importance. In other words, you visualized where you want to go and asked God
to get you there, but you may be shocked at the changes He is making around you
to accomplish your wish. When this happens, do not revert and conform back to
the patterns of this world, but be transformed by the renewing of your mind, as
it states in today's verse.

On Day 171, part of your journey is beginning to recognize God works in
mysterious ways for the betterment of your life. He is maneuvering people and

friends in and out of your life. He is changing your demographics and moving you around geographically. He has you in the midst of what seems to be chaos for the pieces of the puzzle to begin to fit so you may clearly see His glorious plan for you. At first, it never makes sense what God is doing. I have found this is often the case. But the most significant thing I have found is, when I witness God's crazy transformations in my life, I go with it. I do not transform back into the patterns of this world. I do not invoke my will upon the will of God. I simply accept this is God's way of guaranteeing I receive the desires of my heart abundantly and to the fullest.

As Martin Luther King Jr. stated in today's illustration, visualize your success and where you want to be a year from now. Recognize there are some obstacles currently in the way, and your goals and your dreams will have to be given to God so He may remove those barriers. Allow your heavenly Father to shift the pieces of your life around so your desires may be fulfilled. If Martin Luther King Jr. were alive today, he would see how God granted him the life he once visualized.

Prayer for the day: Heavenly Father, I feel the overwhelming need to conform to what the world wants me to do so I may achieve the visual goals I have in my mind. Help me today, Lord, to accept the fact that change takes time, and it takes an understanding that being uncomfortable doesn't mean You're not going to bring me comfort. I thank You, Lord, for shifting the pieces of my life around so they fit perfectly into your plan and grant me the life I continue to visualize today. Amen.

———————————————— ◆ ————————————————

# Day 172: K I S S

♦ ♦ ♦

But you, dear friends, carefully build yourselves up in this most
holy faith by praying in the Holy Spirit, staying right at the
center of God's love, keeping your arms open and outstretched,
ready for the mercy of our Master, Jesus Christ. This is the
unending life, the real life!

—Jude 1:20–21 (The Message)

Companies sometimes have staff audits. A staff audit is designed
to analyze who is where, and whether they are producing at the
level they ought to be producing for the position that they
occupy. The point is to make sure that the right people are in
the right place, doing the right things in the right way. One of
the questions on the floor during an audit is "Does the staff
members job and productivity contribute to the goals of the
company?" This is the same question God wants answered.
How does the life of every Christian contribute to his kingdom?

—Tony Evans, *Illustrations*, 54

If you are like me, you probably have this overbearing impulsive mindset that has
convinced you, you must be on the move at all times, or else you're failing. If this is
you, then do not adhere to your impulsive thoughts or desires. There was nothing
impulsive or thoughtless in the actions of our Lord but only a gentle, calm strength
in which He never got into a panic. Most of us develop a Christian relationship
along the lines of our desires and not along the lines of God's nature.

Our impulsiveness is nothing more than a trait that is derived from our
natural-born life, and we, just as our Lord does, should always ignore it because it
hinders our development as disciples. Impulsive behaviors are okay for children,
but they are devastating for men and women because they are nothing more than
spoiled brats. Impulsiveness should be an intuition thought derived and subjected
to spiritual discipline.

In today's verse, Jude asks us to carefully build ourselves up in this new and
holy faith. It is not demanding we do exceptional things for God because, let's face
it, the reason we try so hard to do extraordinary things is so we feel good about
ourselves, not because we want God to feel good about us. On Day 172, let's be
exceptional in the ordinary things of life and present ourselves holy in our ordinary

streets, among ordinary people. Trust me; this is not something that is learned easily in six months. Continue this day to strive to be good at those things that are simple and right in the eyes of God. The acronym "KISS" is often used in the rooms of recovery and is perfect for today's devotional. It means, "Keep It Simple, Stupid." And oh, yeah, the biblical verse I promised you to defeat and break your chains is still on the way. Hang in there.

Prayer for the day: Heavenly Father, every day, it seems I ride on the coattails of impulsiveness. I constantly act before I think, forcing me to have to react when my actions are wrong. Help me today to render myself free of the impulsive desires to want to take control and be the captain of my ship. I pray I keep things as simple as possible for You to make possible the greatest thing in my life: spiritual freedom. Amen.

◆

# Day 173: It's Only Stuff

Why should I fear when evil days come, when wicked deceivers surround me—those who trust in their wealth and boast of their great riches?

—Psalm 49:5–6 (NIV)

Wisdom is a prize only available to people willing to work to find it. Many kids have the memory of prizes in a cereal box. The prize would always be at the bottom. Many a child would go digging around in the box but to be told by their mother to take their hands out. There was this understood rule among parents that children cannot just reach in and pull out the prize but had to eat their way to the prize. The prize could not be enjoyed without eating the cereal first. The prize would only be available to the child who did the job of eating first. The prize at the bottom of the cereal box would not be easily attainable.

—Tony Evans, *Illustrations*, 340

How resourceful and wise are you at this moment? Have you come to accept the fact your overall success is going to depend on your hard work and not the handouts of others? Or are you someone who can only find assurance from material items? In other words, do you find yourself wrapping your mind around acquiring stuff to feel successful?

We all tend to base our security and happiness on the number of things we have or how large our savings account is. But be assured of this: If on Day 173, your heart still finds joy and peace from the material items you acquire, then you are in a perilous scenario because that means your heart is in the wrong place. You have just declared you trust the security of this world rather than the assurance of your heavenly Father.

Do not let yourself fall into the trap of feeling like your success is based on the amount of stuff you have acquired before you start your new life. from the day you were born until the day our heavenly Father calls you home, He always supplies you with what you truly need. If even the birds in the sky have a nest to live in and food to eat, how much more do you think your heavenly Father loves you? Here is a verse to remember and a source to rely on:

Look at the birds of the air; they do not sow or reap or store away in barns, and yet your heavenly Father feeds them. Are you not much more valuable than they? Can anyone of you by worrying add a single hour to your life?

—Matthew 6:26–27 (NIV)

Prayer for the day: Heavenly Father, today, I keep my prayers short and to the point, without demanding material things to find my happiness. Today, I pray for Your continued guidance in my life, as I see it was and still is You, and not my stuff, that has brought me from the depths of my despair. Thank You, Lord, for Your continued guidance. Amen.

◆

# Day 174: What's His Return?

Follow God's example, therefore, as dearly loved children and walk in the way of love, just as Christ loved us and gave himself up for us as a fragrant offering and sacrifice to God.

—Ephesians 5:1–2 (NIV)

As the offering tray past, a little girl took the tray, put it on the floor, and stood up in the offering plate. The usher said, "Honey, why are you doing that?" And she said, "Because they taught me in Sunday school that my whole body was to be offered to the Savior." This little girl got the point that she was the one who belonged in the tray, and that God does not want donations.

—Tony Evans, *Illustrations*, 40

Who would've ever thought the reality of redemption would play out as it has in your life? Think about this for a second. We came into recovery wanting food, and we were fed. We longed and yearned for fellowship and friends, and we were given a brotherhood and a family. We longed for the day the reality of who we are today will not be determined by who we were in the past. We sought after someone greater than ourselves to fill our empty void, even though we had nothing to offer and no way to pay for it, and Jesus made us whole. In other words, you've been redeemed.

As you think about the last paragraph, recognize it as an investment of love in your life, an investment made on your behalf because of your decision to walk alongside Christ. But let me ask you this: What kind of return is Jesus getting on His investment in you? As you read today's verse, are you following God's example as loved children?

While walking in love, Christ made the ultimate investment in you, which was His life on the cross. Does His return on His investment in you look like the sacrifice of your time and your efforts to help someone in need? Does His investment in you look like you're making choices based on biblical principles and not the motivation of greed? Does His investment in you look like a desire to remain hand in hand with Him, regardless of your current circumstance? Does His investment in you look like the ability to say no when your addiction wants you to say yes?

Redemption is such a wonderful by-product of a Christ-centered life, but I pray we may never take it for granted. May we always remember that what was so freely given to us can be readily taken away at a moment's notice because of the choices we make. Continue to work diligently to ensure that God is getting the full return on His entire investment in you. Jesus is not demanding you give your life; He wants you to invest your heart.

Prayer for the day: Heavenly Father, as I continue to think about how far You have brought me, I am in awe of my new life. A new life that was freely given to me because of Your love. I pray I continue to take into account the ultimate investment You made in me Your life. I pray my life may be a shining example of the gratitude I continue to have and my actions display a happy return for Your investment in me. Amen.

◆

# Day 175: Wake Up

God's way is perfect. All the LORD's promises prove true. He is a shield for all who look to him for protection.

—Psalm 18:30

Archbishop Jeffrey Frances Fisher once said, "The ever-living Christ is here to bless you. The nearer you keep Him, the nearer you will be to one another."

Everybody has heard the old saying you can lead a horse to water, but you can't make him drink, and if you try to make him drink, he will only kick the devil out of you. On Day 175, it is my hope and prayer this devotional book resonates the same familiar adage over and over each and every day you read it. The message is this: Without the guidance of our heavenly Father and our daily desire to be closer to Him, a lot of us may fail in this journey.

In the garden of Gethsemane, our heavenly Father displayed a sense of urgency and needing to be close to someone, therefore asking the disciples to be with Him during His time of trouble. The disciples failed Jesus by going to sleep, and when they realized what they had done, they felt despair. This can happen to us. Jesus is pleading with us to continue to be with Him every day in recovery, but if we fall asleep and leave Him behind, the outcome can, and will, leave us lost and wandering in despair.

There is not a single verse in the Bible nor is there a magic sermon or whimsical answer that can cure you of your current stronghold and addiction if you are not intentional and committed to this relationship with Christ. You've been led to the Word of God; you've been given information and tools to make a sound judgment on what to do. The only thing left is to be sure you accept God's perfect way, believe His proven promises, and rely on Him every day as a shield for your protection against those things that would lead you away. Continue to stay awake so Jesus is never left behind.

Prayer for the day: Heavenly Father, help me today to truly realize the severity of walking alone. As I get closer and closer to each new day, I want to leave with the understanding that not a single day can go by where I am not in tune with You. Thank You, Lord, for leading me to the living waters and giving me the drink of life. I no longer want to be forced into acceptance of Who You are. Today, I have the assurance from Psalm 18:30 that You are all I need. Amen.

# Day 176: Learning to Lead

Remember your leaders, who spoke the word of God to you.
Consider the outcome of their way of life and imitate their faith.

—Hebrews 13:7 (NIV)

When we lay down our lives in humility and forgiveness for
someone else, we are following Jesus' lead.

—Dan Brokke

What is your opinion of leadership? Are you the type of person who easily follows instructions, or are you the type of person who would rather give instructions? Are you an individual who attracts people to you? Do they rely on you for guidance? Maybe you're the type of person who is not sure what it takes to lead effectively and responsibly. Either way, we are required to lead in some form or fashion.

Think for a moment of the individuals who are just entering recovery, and it is Day 1 for them. What will you do if they come to you for help? How are you going to help them? What's the first thing you want them to see in you? Will you choose to be a leader to them, or will you pass off the responsibility to someone else? To easily answer those questions, think back to what was done for you on Day 1 when someone was there to be a leader for you.

First, we must remember, we chose to follow godly people who were rested comfortably in the body of Christ. True leaders show a level of faithfulness to the Word of God by first, conducting themselves appropriately. Second, we often recognize leaders because we see them and not always because we hear them. It is their act of kindness, or it is a humble gesture that forces us to nominate them as leaders.

If you are still confused about the characteristics and qualities of a leader, then the best example I can give you is what Jesus did. Jesus recognized we were in need and lost, and He came down from his throne, emptied Himself of His deity, and took on the role of a humble servant. He met us with grace and with love and with forgiveness. He told us to only do the will of the Father and to love one another. It was because of those qualities and characteristics that we were, and still are, attracted to Him as a leader. This is what continues to make great leaders today. Display these Christlike qualities first, and others will follow.

Prayer for the day: Heavenly Father, I pray I accept my role as a leader humbly and peacefully. I pray the love and grace that was given to me is readily evident in my life. Help me today to lead people in a direction guided by Your Word and mimicking the actions of Jesus Christ. I pray I never take for granted the responsibility given to me on Day 176. Amen.

◆

# Day 177: Go to Work

Then Jesus came to them and said, "All authority in heaven and on earth has been given to me. Therefore go and make disciples of all nations, baptizing them in the name of the Father and of the Son and of the Holy Spirit, and teaching them to obey everything I have commanded you. And surely I am with you always, to the very end of the age."

—Matthew 28:18–20 (NIV)

What would you say about a fireman who saw your house burning down and said, "It'll burn itself out in a little while"? What would you say about a policeman who saw juveniles vandalizing your property and simply said, `"Well, you know, boys will be boys"? What would you say about a doctor who, when telling you that you had cancer, simply said, "Take two aspirin and rest"? You would probably say they are not taking their job seriously. And I would not be taken my job seriously if I did not tell people about the place called hell.

—Tony Evans, *Illustrations*, 93

Priorities are pivotal to know who we are and what we are called to do. For example, you may currently be focused on trying to find a job, but you're not sure what you're good at or where to even look. Frustrating, isn't it? The reason may be because your priorities are in the wrong place. While you are spinning your wheels, going around in circles, people around you are lost and need direction. You're not supposed to be looking for the job you want. You're supposed to be doing the task Jesus has commissioned you to do by His authority from heaven.

In today's verse, the key to the disciples' work was the authority of Jesus, and so it is for you. Sometimes, we are under the impression God is there to assist us in our endeavors. But Jesus places Himself as a sovereign leader over His disciples, which includes all of us, and thereby directs us to our most important job: passing the freedom that was so freely given to us onto others.

The first job at the top of our list of priorities is teaching and preaching and testifying our living experiences, past and present, to those in need. The Great Commission in Matthew 28 is not a suggestion but a direct command that implies what our first order of business should be. In other words, on Day 177, you have been commissioned (commanded by Jesus) to go and not merely make converts but to make disciples. Once you recognize this is your current job and the position you have been given, based on your heart's desire and willingness to continue following Christ, all of your priorities will fall into place. Isn't it great to know what your number one job is? Now under the authority of Jesus Christ, go and make disciples of others.

Prayer for the day: Heavenly Father, I accept the challenge in my current position, which You have given me under Your authority. You first asked me to live a life that is pleasing to You, and from that life, You have asked me to assist others in doing the same. Today, I pray for the assurance I am qualified for this position, and I accept it as my top priority. Thank You, Lord, for the direction You have given me and the life I currently enjoy. Amen.

◆

# Day 178: Just a Walk with Thee

God is our refuge and strength, an ever-present help in trouble.
—Psalm 46:1 (NIV)

"What *refuge* is there for a person who is oppressed with the knowledge that there are a thousand new books he ought to read, while life is only long enough for him to attempt to read a hundred?" God will never ask me to do more than I am able to do.

—Source Unknown

The reason some of us stay so overwhelmed and full of grief is we are currently living as poor examples of someone who recognizes Christ is the Almighty. We have begun to attain a few Christian attributes and experiences, but we might not have genuinely surrendered and abandoned our old behaviors to Jesus Christ. Whenever there are difficult situations, are you taking comfort or struggling?

Today, you must take comfort in knowing you have spent the last 177 days getting ready to succeed at Day 1 all over again. That's right. To live successfully, we must first be trained on how to live. God has been molding and preparing you for the day you leave from behind your current walls of safety, into a new world and a fresh start. The surface of your success has barely been scratched. Are you ready to live?

This type of reality is so real, but then again, so is today's verse. Please do not be discouraged by the chaos the world has in store for you. Be strengthened by the fact when that world feels like it is caving in around you, God is there to keep you standing. God did not bring you through 178 days of new growth and peace to drop you into confusion and chaos as soon as you journey out on your own. Today's verse guarantees us regardless of how many days of recovery we have, there is going to be trouble as well as spiritual peace. Learning how to live in both arenas is the key to a fruitful walk with God. Take comfort in knowing what you are facing will never be more than you can handle. Our heavenly Father assures us of that, and He also assures us our days of success will significantly outweigh any days of turmoil.

Prayer for the day: Heavenly Father, today, I recognize as I get closer to the end of my 180 days, my journey has only begun. You have prepared me for the time when

I will stand outside the comforts of my current confines and be forced to make godly decisions in a different realm. Thank You for the grace You have bestowed upon me and getting me to this point in my life, where I am entirely assured You are my refuge and strength when I begin to feel defeated. Walk with me, Lord, every day. Amen.

◆

# Day 179: You Must Remember

Remind the people to be subject to rulers and authorities, to be obedient, to be ready to do whatever is good, to slander no one, to be peaceable and considerate, and always to be gentle toward everyone.

—Titus 3:1–2

One of the greatest tragedies in the twentieth century was the sinking of the Titanic. This large ship hit an iceberg, and many people died as a result. There is another tragedy with the Titanic. Most of the lifeboats that held people saved from death were only half-filled. They were unwilling to turn back and share in their salvation.

—Tony Evans, *Illustrations*

An inevitable fact for all of us is, the further along we make it in recovery, the greater the chance we may forget how bad our lives were and from where we came. Do you vividly remember how you once lived to survive? Can you humbly recall the dark and dank emotions that used to haunt you, to no avail? Is the compassion you currently have for others real because you can remember so vividly what it was like to start anew?

When we begin to take this message of recovery to others, we have to remind ourselves, first and foremost, where we came from, remember once we, too, were foolish and disobedient. We were misled and became slaves to so many desires and wicked pleasures. But by the grace of God, our Lord and Savior saved us, not because of the good things we had done but because of His mercy.

Finally, remember what it took to get you to Day 179. Remember to share with others you had to listen and obey authority, become obedient, and be ready to do whatever was right and good. Remember to share with the new beginner you had to become peaceable and considerate, and you always had to be gentle toward everyone, to do good deeds with honorable and humble intentions. That is what is meant when we read today's verse, Titus 3:1–2. When we remember and recall the pain and disgust that riddled our soul and our flesh when we first came to recovery, it becomes even easier to continue to do those things in direct line with Kingdom living. We must never forget what we once were and how God has transformed us into who we are now. Last but not least, congratulations;

tomorrow on Day 180, you will complete this first phase of the rest of your life by remembering never to forget.

Prayer for the day: Heavenly Father, I pray I never forget the devastation from which I came. May I continue to remember those things that caused me to seek You first. Help me to remind others how far Your grace and Your mercy have brought me. May I never forget to display the same love to others that was given to me. Thank You, Lord. Amen.

◆

# Day 180: The Answer You've Been Waiting For

> When an impure spirit comes out of a person, it goes through arid places seeking rest and does not find it. Then it says, "I will return to the house I left." When it arrives, it finds the house unoccupied, swept clean and put in order. Then it goes and takes with it seven other spirits more wicked than itself, and they go in and live there. And the final condition of that person is worse than the first. That is how it will be with this wicked generation.
>
> —Matthew 12:43–45 (NIV)

> The frustrated Christian life occurs when we try to live for God instead of allowing Christ to live through us. If you try to live for God, you will fail. You might have limited success toward religion, but you will not discover the depth of what God has designed for you
>
> —Eddie Snipes

Now we begin. Now we begin to incorporate each detail of our journey into a new life and relationship with just us and our Savior, a relationship guarded by what we say, by what we think, and by what we do. But we must remember, we cannot defend all these areas alone. It can only be accomplished when our bodies, hearts, and souls have demanded the presence and the accompaniment of the Holy Spirit to reign and rule our entire being. How do we know this to be true? Better yet, how do we accept this as the pivotal key for a successful and complete recovery? The answer lies in today's verse.

Today's verse gives a clear indication of what it means when we declare we are addicted or, better yet, we have a stronghold that possesses us. Through many years of pain and turmoil, we cried out in desperation to God for His intercession in our lives, to remove the stronghold that had us physically and spiritually bound in chains, a stronghold that completely possessed and encompassed our hearts and souls.

From this prayer of desperation, God answered you in the form of grace. Grace is His gift, which is allowing you to dwell in a safe environment for your heart and soul to be swept clean of your strongholds and addictions. On Day 1, your soul was simply an empty vessel, a dry sponge, a blank canvas, awaiting the arrival of the component that would make you complete. On Day 180, you need the certainty you have filled this void mentioned in verse 44.

The danger for relapse begins when we only acknowledge we have removed those elements that possessed us and left our souls without a divine tenant or occupant. There is no one guarding our spirit, and inevitably, the strongholds that used to have possession of us return and bring along seven friends (verse 45). Ask anyone in recovery who has experienced relapse, and they will say, "It was if I had never stopped using or drinking, and incredibly, it was ten times worse." Today's verse reinforces the fact that although your house may currently be clean, your stronghold is stirring about, waiting to reenter and take up occupancy once again within you. So what's the answer?

First, we must remember that our spiritual and moral desire to be closer to God is not enough. The desire to be like Christ is not the same as being Christlike. The desire to make disciples is not the same as being a living disciple. The success of our recovery, as well as a fruitful life, begins when we intentionally decide to allow Christ to fill the void that was left when our addictions and strongholds were released from within us, to enable the presence of Christ within you the opportunity to manipulate your spiritual conscience, for you to be able to make Christlike choices, to have a clear, definitive answer as to what is right and what is wrong. When our spiritual void has been filled with the presence of Christ, we have the gift to make perfect choices derived from a divine presence within us. You no longer make choices that were conjured up by your mortal mind, leaving you lost and corrupt.

If you are already sure of what your life without Christ was like based on your past experiences, then common sense should tell you the opposite would have to be the cure. The cure is a life with Christ, made possible by your intentional acceptance of His presence into your spiritual void. Hallelujah.

You have made it to the perfect place where God can now take over the rest of your journey. I pray you continue to intentionally stay on your path through your direct connection with your Savior. May the words from today's verse (and those from every other day) sink deep within you and into your new life. Now go and make disciples of others. Amen.

Prayer for the day: Heavenly Father, today, I choose to fill the void that was left by my past with the presence of Your Son, Jesus. I pray by this new incorporation, I am allowed the opportunity to make perfect Christlike decisions. I realize some days will be tough, and I recognize other days will be such a blessing, but regardless of my current scenario, I will intentionally walk and live in the presence of my Lord and Savior, Jesus Christ. Thank You, Lord, for being the cure for my life and filling the void that would have eventually led me on a path of destruction had I left it empty. I pray these things because today, I believe. Amen and amen.

◆

Printed in the United States
by Baker & Taylor Publisher Services

Printed in the United States
by Baker & Taylor Publisher Services